Other Books and Series by Jeff Bowen

Cherokee Intermarried White 1906 Volume I thru *X*

Applications for Enrollment of Creek Newborn Act of 1905 Volumes I thru *XIV*

Applications for Enrollment of Choctaw Newborn Act of 1905 Volumes I thru *XX*

Choctaw By Blood Enrollment Cards 1898-1914 Volumes I thru *XX*

Oglala Sioux Indians Pine Ridge Reservation 1932 Census Book I
Oglala Sioux Indians Pine Ridge Reservation Birth and Death Rolls 1924-1932 Book II

Census of the Sioux and Cheyenne Indians of Pine Ridge Agency 1896 - 1897 Book I
Census of the Sioux and Cheyenne Indians of Pine Ridge Agency 1898 - 1899 Book II

Northern Cheyenne Tongue River, Montana 1904 - 1932 Census 1904-1916 Volume I

Northern Cheyenne Tongue River, Montana 1904 - 1932 Census 1917-1926 Volume II

Identified Mississippi Choctaw Enrollment Cards 1902-1909 Volumes I, II & III

Sac & Fox - Shawnee Estates 1885-1910 (Under Sac & Fox Agency) Volumes I-VIII
Sac & Fox - Shawnee Estates 1920-1924 (Under The Sac & Fox Agency, Oklahoma) & Wills 1889-1924 Volume IX

Visit our website at **www.nativestudy.com** to learn more about these and other books and series by Jeff Bowen

Portrait of Tecumseh from Lossing's
The Pictorial Field-Book of the War of 1812
is a pencil sketch drawn by Pierre Le Dru,
a young French trader at Vincennes, circa 1808.

Other Books and Series by Jeff Bowen

Compilation of History of the Cherokee Indians and Early History of the Cherokees by Emmet Starr with Combined Full Name Index (Hardbound & Softbound)

1901-1907 Native American Census Seneca, Eastern Shawnee, Miami, Modoc, Ottawa, Peoria, Quapaw, and Wyandotte Indians (Under Seneca School, Indian Territory)

1932 Census of The Standing Rock Sioux Reservation with Births And Deaths 1924-1932

Census of The Blackfeet, Montana, 1897- 1901 Expanded Edition

Eastern Cherokee by Blood, 1906-1910, Volumes I thru XIII

Choctaw of Mississippi Indian Census 1929-1932 with Births and Deaths 1924-1931 Volume I
Choctaw of Mississippi Indian Census 1933, 1934 & 1937, Supplemental Rolls to 1934 & 1935 with Births and Deaths 1932-1938, and Marriages 1936-1938 Volume II

Eastern Cherokee Census Cherokee, North Carolina 1930-1939 Census 1930-1931 with Births And Deaths 1924-1931 Taken By Agent L. W. Page Volume I
Eastern Cherokee Census Cherokee, North Carolina 1930-1939 Census 1932-1933 with Births And Deaths 1930-1932 Taken By Agent R. L. Spalsbury Volume II
Eastern Cherokee Census Cherokee, North Carolina 1930-1939 Census 1934-1937 with Births and Deaths 1925-1938 and Marriages 1936 & 1938 Taken by Agents R. L. Spalsbury And Harold W. Foght Volume III

Seminole of Florida Indian Census, 1930-1940 with Birth and Death Records, 1930-1938

Texas Cherokees 1820-1839 A Document For Litigation 1921

Starr Roll 1894 (Cherokee Payment Rolls) Districts: Canadian, Cooweescoowee, and Delaware Volume One
Starr Roll 1894 (Cherokee Payment Rolls) Districts: Flint, Going Snake, and Illinois Volume Two
Starr Roll 1894 (Cherokee Payment Rolls) Districts: Saline, Sequoyah, and Tahlequah; Including Orphan Roll Volume Three

Cherokee Intruder Cases Dockets of Hearings 1901-1909 Volumes I & II

Indian Wills, 1911-1921 Records of the Bureau of Indian Affairs Books One thru *Seven*

Other Books and Series by Jeff Bowen

Native American Wills & Probate Records 1911-1921

Turtle Mountain Reservation Chippewa Indians 1932 Census with Births & Deaths, 1924-1932

Chickasaw By Blood Enrollment Cards 1898-1914 Volume I thru *V*

Cherokee Descendants East An Index to the Guion Miller Applications Volume I
Cherokee Descendants West An Index to the Guion Miller Applications Volume II (A-M)
Cherokee Descendants West An Index to the Guion Miller Applications Volume III (N-Z)

Applications for Enrollment of Seminole Newborn Freedmen, Act of 1905

Eastern Cherokee Census, Cherokee, North Carolina, 1915-1922, Taken by Agent James E. Henderson   Volume I (1915-1916)
Volume II (1917-1918)
Volume III (1919-1920)
Volume IV (1921-1922)

Complete Delaware Roll of 1898

Eastern Cherokee Census, Cherokee, North Carolina, 1923-1929, Taken by Agent James E. Henderson   Volume I (1923-1924)
Volume II (1925-1926)
Volume III (1927-1929)

Applications for Enrollment of Seminole Newborn Act of 1905 Volumes I & II

North Carolina Eastern Cherokee Indian Census 1898-1899, 1904, 1906, 1909-1912, 1914   Revised and Expanded Edition

1932 Hopi and Navajo Native American Census with Birth & Death Rolls (1925-1931) Volume 1 - Hopi
1932 Hopi and Navajo Native American Census with Birth & Death Rolls (1930-1932) Volume 2 - Navajo

Western Navajo Reservation Navajo, Hopi and Paiute 1933 Census with Birth & Death Rolls 1925-1933

Cherokee Citizenship Commission Dockets 1880-1884 and 1887-1889
Volumes I thru *V*

Applications for Enrollment of Chickasaw Newborn Act of 1905
Volumes I thru *VII*

SAC & FOX - SHAWNEE DEATHS, CEMETERY, BIRTHS, & MARRIAGE CARDS
(UNDER THE SAC & FOX AGENCY, OKLAHOMA)
1853 - 1933

VOLUME X

TRANSCRIBED BY
JEFF BOWEN

NATIVE STUDY
Gallipolis, Ohio
USA

Copyright © 2022
by Jeff Bowen

ALL RIGHTS RESERVED
No part of this publication can be reproduced
in any form or manner whatsoever
without previous written permission from the
Copyright holder or Publisher.

Originally published:
Santa Maria, California
2019

Reprinted by:

Native Study LLC
Gallipolis, OH
www.nativestudy.com

Library of Congress Control Number: 2022900261

ISBN: 978-1-64968-139-3

Made in the United States of America.

This series is dedicated to
Tanner Tackett
the Constant Gardner
and Friend
and
In memory of
Raina Mae Fulks.

Ab·sen·tee

noun: **absentee**; plural noun: **absentees**
> 1. a person who is expected or required to be present at a place or event but is not.

(According to Webster)

Shawnee

noun, plural Shaw-nees, (especially collectively) Shaw-nee.
> 1. a member of an Algonquian-speaking tribe formerly in the east-central U.S., now in Oklahoma.

(According to Dictionary.com)

Shawnee Teaching

"Tagi nsi walr mvci-lutvwi mr-pvyaci-grlahkv, xvga mytv inv gi mvci-lutvwv, gi mvci-ludr-geiv. Walv uwas-panvsi inv, wa-ciganv-hi gi gol-utvwv u kvgesakv-namv manwi-lanvwawewa yasi golutv-mvni geyrgi.

"Tagi bemi-lutvwi walr segalami mr-pvyaci-grlahkv, xvga mvtv inv gi bemi-lutvwv, gi bemi-ludr-geiv gelv. Wakv vhqalami inv, xvga nahfrpi Moneto ut vhqalamrli nili yasi vhqalamahgi gelv!"

Translation:

"Do not kill or injure your neighbor, for it is not him that you injure, you injure yourself. But do good to him, therefore add to his days of happiness as you add to your own.

"Do not wrong or hate your neighbor, for it is not him that you wrong, you wrong yourself. But love him, for Moneto loves him also as He loves you!"

Thomas Wildcat Alford
circa 1936

Special Note

You will notice throughout these volumes the author has attempted to duplicate from the original documents places on the page that were destroyed due to water damage. Whole sections of a page could be missing or torn into multiple pieces. In order to duplicate the damage you will find various shapes with a white format to try to represent the damage and the loss of the ability to completely transcribe many of the pages.

TABLE OF CONTENTS

Introduction	ix
DEATHS	3
CEMETERY	89
VITAL STATISTICS	121
BIRTHS	127
MARRIAGE CARDS	181
INDEX	305

INTRODUCTION

The history of the Shawnee is fascinating. Naturally the most famous Shawnee known would be Tecumseh, born circa. 1768, after four other siblings before him. His father was Puckeshinwa, a Shawnee war chief from Ohio. Puckeshinwa crossed the Ohio close to what is now Gallipolis with his fourteen year son Chiksika by his side. As they followed the lead of Chief Cornstalk during the fall of 1774. Tecumseh's famous father was mortally wounded during the fight they would soon encounter. The Shawnees were unexpectedly discovered by a couple of early morning turkey hunters from the settlement called Point Pleasant. These hunters ran as fast as possible back to where the Ohio and Kanawha Rivers meet and sounded the alarm that the Shawnees were coming, the fight lasted most of the day but not without loss to both sides. The Shawnees were badly outnumbered. Pucheshinwa was carried back across the Ohio or as the Shawnees called it the *Spaylaywitheepi*, with the intention to take him back to his village. He must have known his time was short as he laid there telling Chiksika to make sure he devoted his time not only to Tecumseh's but also his younger brothers training in becoming warriors. Pucheshinwa succumbed to his wounds shortly after that request and was secretly buried deep in the forest that day. Chiksika saw his father mortally wounded while defending their home. He had a reverence for his father as a great warrior. He wanted to follow his father's path and not die an average death. In his heart, it had to be on the battlefield as a warrior. Tecumseh followed his brother's every step and planned to die defending his land as his father and brother had. There was no surrendering or giving in to the Americans.

There are several descriptions out there of Tecumseh from his contemporaries, but David Edmunds found one during his research that seems to be the most commanding of any found. "Captain John B. Glegg, Brock's aide-de-camp, who was present at the meetings between Brock and Tecumseh, recorded one of the most vivid descriptions of the Shawnee. According to Glegg, in August 1812 Tecumseh still was in the prime of his life, giving the impression of a man ten years younger. Tecumseh's appearance was very prepossessing; his figure light and finely proportioned; his age I imagined to be about five and thirty [he actually was forty four]; in height, five feet nine or ten inches; his complexion, light copper; countenance, oval, with bright hazle eyes, beaming cheerfulness, energy, and decision. Three small silver crowns, or coronets were suspended from the lower cartilage of his aquiline nose; and a large silver medallion of George the Third, which I believe his ancestor had received from Lord Dorchester, when governor-general of Canada, was attached to a mixed coloured wampum string, and hung around his neck. His dress consisted of a plain, neat uniform, tanned deer-skin jacket, with long trousers of the same material, the seams of both being covered with neatly cut fringe; and he had on his feet leather moccasins, much ornamented with work made from the dyed quills of the porcupine."[1]

There were approximately 39 years that passed between Tecumseh's and his father's deaths.

It is hard to believe that the Shawnee's history being as extensive as it was during the early stages of the United States that their descendants' records were so closely guarded under the care of a vegetable bind in an leaky attic. Not only the Shawnee's but also the Sac & Fox, the Pottawatomie and the Kickapoo. There are also many other tribal affiliates to be found in this series, not to mention someone like Jim Thorpe and his family members of the Sac and Fox tribe. Not only was he a gold metal Olympian and multiple sport competitor, but at the time one of America's favorite sons. Thank goodness someone was finally conscious of the situation. The description in the next paragraph explains the neglect of these important documents as given by the Oklahoma Historical Societies Microfilm Catalog.

"In 1933 a survey of Indian tribal records in Oklahoma revealed that the files of the Shawnee and the old Sac and Fox agencies had been sadly neglected, and the lack of space for storing them properly had resulted in much loss. Charles Eggers, Superintendent of the Shawnee Agency, reported that most of the non-current records of his agency were boxed in a storehouse. The papers of the old Sac and Fox Agency were in the loft of a warehouse which was also used for storing vegetables. The roof of the building leaked and the papers were in danger of destruction from moisture. Following the passage of the Congressional Act of March 27, 1934 (H.R. 5631 Public No. 133) which placed the tribal records in the custody of the Oklahoma Historical Society."

As described above the history of the Shawnee people isn't an ordinary history but an extraordinary time in all of our ancestors' lives. Reading Allen W. Eckert's extensive studies taken from what is known as the Draper Papers, a historical record meticulously documented beginning circa 1830. Though Draper covered an approximate time between the 1740's to the 1810's, his collection covered documents and transcriptions concerning Boone, Kenton, Rogers Clark and Joseph Brant, not to mention a considerable amount of Shawnee history from the entirety of the Ohio and Mississippi Valley's. Other authors such as Colin G. Calloway and R. David Edmunds provide an in depth study of the Shawnee people as well as Tecumseh and his life leaving no rock unturned in their research.

As you read different references you find diverse opinions on Tecumseh's mother as to what tribe she came from. Eckert through Draper's work says, "This was

---

[1] Tecumseh, R. David Edmunds Pg. 162-163, Para. 3-4

when Pucksinwah, then twenty-six, led the war party against the Cherokees that had resulted in the capture of Methotasa."[2] Indicating Tecumseh's mother might have been Cherokee. Yet, R. David Edmunds writes, "In 1768, while the Iroquois were selling Shawnee lands at the Treaty of Fort Stanwix, a Creek woman married to a Shawnee man gave birth to a son at Old Piqua, a Shawnee village on the Mad River in Western Ohio. The woman had a difficult labor before giving birth in the small lodge especially constructed for that purpose, some distance from the family's wigwam. The mother, Methoataske (Turtle Laying Its Eggs), had grown up among the Creek villages in Alabama and had met her husband when some of the Shawnee sought refuge among the Creeks during the 1750s. The father Puckeshinwa, remained with his wife's people until about 1760, when the family left Alabama and migrated to Ohio."[3]

You also will find different opinions on how they dressed back then or wore their hair. In Edmunds' book *Tecumseh*, his brother the Prophet Tenskwatawa states, "Warriors should again shave their heads and wear the scalp locks worn by their ancestors." And yet in Thomas Wildcat Alford's *Civilization*, he says, "We boys wore our hair short, very much as the girls of today wear their hair bobbed. This is the way Shawnee men always have worn their hair. Never did they braid it, as some other tribes do."

Alford's book *Civilization* out of the many resources read was likely one of the most informative and enjoyable references in the study. Thomas Wildcat Alford was born in 1860 and belonged to the Absentee Shawnee tribe. He states that he was a descendant of Tecumseh. He spoke about when his family slept under the stars each night and that he never had an English name until his father had him go to school at a Quaker mission. Mr. Alford also talks about two things with real clarity. Alford educates us about clans in the sixth chapter, expounding upon the active history of the Shawnees and the different responsibilities of each as well as divisions among the clans that created tribal changes. These dissensions were nothing new. Anyone that has read extensively about the Shawnee will realize that Alford understood his people and their history. When he wrote about tribal clashes or divisions during the early days, he managed to translate on paper their strength and character. He showed for generations they literally believed they were given an ability to make themselves self-reliant when it came to survival. They traveled far and wide following their own path while installing their own way of life that made them powerful adversaries whether it be against the British, the French or the Americans moving west. Other tribes found them to be awful enemies or potent allies. Then he compares their tribal government

---

[2] A Sorrow in Our Heart, Allen W. Eckert Pg. 22, Para. 3

[3] Tecumseh, R. David Edmunds, Pg. 17 Para. 1

and the clan leaders to being quite similar to the U.S. Presidency and the different government entities. Alford also brings up business committees for the tribe.

He starts with a concise description of the clans, "Originally there were five clans composing the Shawnee tribe, including the two principle clans, Tha-we-gi-la and Cha-lah-kaw-tha, from one of which came the national or principal chief. The remaining three, the Pec-ku-we, the Kis-pu-go, and the May-ku-jay, each had its own chief who was subordinate to the principal chief in national matters, but independent in matters pertaining to the duties of his clan. Each clan had a certain duty to perform for the whole tribe. For instance the Pec-ku-we clan, or its chief, had charge of the maintenance of order and looked after the celebration of things pertaining to religion or faith; the Kis-pu-go clan had charge of matters pertaining to war and the preparation and training of warriors; the May-ku-jay clan had charge of things relating to health and medicine and food for the whole tribe. But the two powerful clans, the Tha-we-gi-la and the Cha-lah-kaw-tha, had charge of political affairs and all matters that affected the tribe as a whole. Indeed, the tribal government may be likened to the government of the United States, in which each state (clan), with it governor (chief), is sovereign in local matters, but subordinate to the president of the United States (principal chief) in national matters. The difference is that the president of the United States must be elected, and may be changed with each election, while the principal chief came to his office by heritage and held it for life, or during good behavior.

At the time of which I write the Shawnee tribe had been divided for many years, and only the Tha-we-gi-la, the Pec-ku-we, and the Kis-pu-go clans were represented in the Absentee Shawnee band. These three clans always had been closely related, while the Cha-lah-kaw-tha and the May-ku-jay had always stood together, and were represented in the group that I have mentioned as living in Kansas at the time of the Civil War."[4]

As referenced earlier Thomas Wildcat Alford brought up their present Indian agent, Thomas, on September 13, 1893, wanting him to present a list of prominent men in their tribe to hold positions on a business committee. This presented a whole new world for the tribe with new pressures through white change so to speak. The government was instilling in their world the destruction of their heritage in tribal customs and culture all to control Indian land through allotment. When he was being told to help form this committee, he was actually being told, what we are doing is we are wiping out your way of life forever. The Congress of the United States was presenting the abolition of all tribal governments so the land could be manipulated through the Curtis Act of 1898. They said, we are splitting the land up. They were allotting so many acres to each tribal member. How much they got depended on

---

[4] Civilization, Alford; Pg. 44, Para. 1-2

whether they planned to farm or raise cattle. If they were building herds they were given double the land for grazing. Alford said, "It was on the thirteenth day of September, 1893 that Agent Thomas informed the Shawnees that he had been directed by the Commissioner of Indian Affairs to submit for approval the names of seven of the most prominent men of the tribe who would constitute a Business Committee to supersede the chiefs and councilors of the old tribal government. The Business Committee was to represent the Absentee Shawnees as a tribe in all dealings with the United States and to act in an advisory capacity to the individual members of the tribe. They were to certify to the identity of grantors of sales of land and to act for the tribe in other matters.[5]

During the study it was noticed that the Curtis Act being enacted on June 28, 1898 and Alford's mentioning its initiation during 1893 became a point of interest or at least premature. It was found that Congress had actually started working in this area of seizure approximately five years prior to the agent's notification, "In 1893 Congress began a special allotment process for the Five Tribes, enacting a number of laws that affect the governmental powers of the tribes. Some of these laws, like the 1889 and 1890 Acts, extended certain Arkansas laws over Indian Territory and expanded federal court jurisdiction; they are relevant today only insofar as they may indirectly affect tribal judicial powers."[6]

Their mention of these laws only being relevant today, though actually not spoken, plead plausible deniability while coinciding with the Indian Reorganization Act of 1934. The government was on a mission. Land and control. The allotment had to take place. They were wanting statehood. They were wanting the Native people to be under one umbrella with everyone else. Tribes were nations. Just like a foreign nation, they were their own government. Originally our constitution was modeled after the Iroquois model, had to start somewhere? So what we did was split up the land among the people that already owned it. Then we took what was left, approximately 90 million acres and sold it at a profit. Who got the money? Only the politicians at the time know? But years after taking the chiefs and councils away there was likely mass chaos like a town hall today. So the government likely was wanting out of the tribal control business. At least enough that they could just control it without being in the bullseye so to speak. Congress and the state had already achieved its goals. So this act was written with the statement that it was a model to make all think we do this for you. "The IRA was intended to provide a mechanism for the tribe as a governmental unit to interact with and adapt to a modern society, rather than to force the assimilation of individual Indians.

---

[5] Civilization, Alford; Pg. 161, Para. 2
[6] Federal Indian Law, Cohen; Pg. 781, Para. 3

The IRA was also an attempt to improve the economic situation of Indians. The Act was intended to stop the alienation of tribal land needed to support Indians, and to provide for acquisition of additional acreage for tribes. Tribes were encouraged to organize along the lines of modern business corporations; a system of financial credit was included to reach this economic objective."[7] Interestingly enough Cohen and Alford both mention this same organizational technique, only one as law and another as a tribal member.

It is disconcerting just in reading a reference from Senator Charles Curtis as he mentioned in his biography that by the time Congress finished rewriting the bill he had submitted he hardly recognized it. "Officially titled the "Act for the Protection of the People of Indian Territory", the Act is named for Charles Curtis, congressman from Kansas and its author. He was of mixed Native American and European descent: on his mother's side -Kansa, Osage, Potawatomi, and French; and on his father's - three ethnic lines of British Isles ancestry. Curtis was raised in part on the Kaw Reservation of his maternal grandparents, but also lived with his paternal grandparents and attended Topeka High School. He read law, became an attorney, and later was elected to the United States House of Representatives and Senate. He served as Vice-President under Herbert Hoover. In the usual fashion, by the time the bill HR 8581 had gone through five revisions in committees in both the House of Representatives and the Senate, there was little left of Curtis' original draft. In his hand-written autobiography, Curtis noted having been unhappy with the final version of the Curtis Act. He believed that the Five Civilized Tribes needed to make changes. He thought that the way ahead for Native Americans was through education and use of both their and the majority cultures, but he also had hoped to give more support to Native American transitions."[8]

The records within this series concern The Absentee Shawnee as well as many other people with different tribal affiliations. Also within these pages are closely related tribes that were under the same agency (The Sac & Fox Agency, Oklahoma) for many years like the Sac & Fox, the Pottawatomie and the Kickapoo. There are likely state recognized Shawnee tribes in the United States, but, "The Absentee Shawnee Tribe of Indians of Oklahoma (or Absentee Shawnee) is one of three federally recognized tribes of Shawnee people. Historically residing in the Eastern United States, the original Shawnee lived in the areas that are now Ohio, Indiana, Illinois, Kentucky, Tennessee, Pennsylvania, and other neighboring states. It is documented that they occupied and traveled through lands from Canada to Florida, from the Mississippi River to the eastern continental coast. In contemporary times, the Absentee Shawnee Tribe headquarters in Shawnee, Oklahoma; its tribal jurisdiction

---

[7] Federal Indian Law, Cohen; Pg. 147 Para. 1-2
[8] Curtis Act of 1898, Wikipedia

area includes land properties in Oklahoma in both Cleveland County and Pottawatomie County." [Today,] "There are approximately 3,050 enrolled Absentee Shawnee tribal members, 2,315 of whom live in Oklahoma. Tribal membership follows blood quantum criteria, with applicants requiring a minimum of one eighth (1/8) documented Absentee-Shawnee blood to be placed on its membership rolls, as set forth by the tribal constitution. Though it is not a formal division, there is a social separation within its current tribal membership between the traditionalist Big Jim Band, which kept cultural traditions and ceremonies and has its primary populace in the Little Axe, Norman area, and the assimilationist White Turkey Band, which adopted European ways of the European majority, with many families based in the Shawnee area. Regardless of historical viewpoints, the bands cooperate for the future of the tribe."[9]

When this study was first pursued an old Xerox copy of a catalog that sat on the shelf for twenty five years was the first place searched for a viable source. It was titled, "Catalog of Microfilm Holdings in the Archives & Manuscripts Div. Oklahoma Historical Society 1976-1989". As mentioned in the description from this catalog's Introduction for the Sac and Fox Indian Agencies, it states, "In 1901 the Sac and Fox Agency was divided. The Sac and Fox Agency itself remained at the old site near Stroud with jurisdiction over the Sac and Fox and the Iowa. The Shawnee, Potawatomi and Kickapoo Agency (sometimes simply called the Shawnee Agency) was established about two miles south of Shawnee, Oklahoma. The agencies continued their separate existence until 1919 when they were merged becoming the Shawnee Agency.

Of course today in 2018, everything is digital and on the computer. You have to be thankful for having an old catalog and books on a shelf. There is nothing like the feel of holding a book in your hand. You can pick it up when you want and let your eyes travel to anywhere or any time in history. It has solid print that nobody can manipulate or change. It's just yours to wrap yourself up in without any glowing distractions as Native Americans call them, "Talking Leaves".

Jeff Bowen
Gallipolis, Ohio
NativeStudy.com

---

[9] Absentee-Shawnee Tribe of Indians Wikipedia

Sac and Fox-Shawnee – <u>DEATHS</u>
Undated and 1853 – 1924

Sac & Fox – Shawnee
1853-1933   Volume X

Col
Please to insert in your circular for bids "Hair Ribbon per yd.
as it is used in all casses[sic] for burial purposes, for tying on
their leggings & doing up the Hair x
W. B. Watts

		The United States		
1853			To Josiah Smart	Dr
Feby 18	To Burial Suit for Kiah-wah (a man			
	consisting of the following articles to wit			
	one 3 pt Wht Blanket	2.75		
	1 3/4 yds Scarlet cloth	2.18 3/4		
	2 yds calico	.30		
	1 pap. paint	.15	5.38 3/4	
March 9	To Burial Suite for No-tah-hah (a man same as above		5.38 3/4	
" 16	" do do for Thah-wah-mus-wah " " "		5.38 3/4	
Apr 14	" do do " No-shah-kum (a man same as above		5.38 3/4	
" 15	" do do " Cu-co-ah (a man same as above		5.38 3/4	
" 30	" do do " Ky-ah-twi-tue (a man same as above		5.38 3/4	
May 1	" do do " Kah ke kah (a man same as above		5.38 3/4	
" 31	" do do " Maw-me-com-a-shie (a man " "		5.38 3/4	
Feby 18	Burial suit for Ke-shah-che-quah (a woman- cons-			
	isting of the following articles (To wit			
	one 2 1/2 pt Wht. Blanket	2.25		
	1 3/4 yd Blue cloth	2.18 3/4		
	3/4 Scarlet Cloth	2.18 3/4		
	3 yds Calico	.50		
	2 yds ferreting	.12		
	1 pap. paint	.15	5.86 1/4	
Mar 11	To burial suit for Ba-she-quah (a woman same as above		5.86 1/4	
" 15	" do " for Waw-pre-nan-a-sock " "		5.86 1/4	
" 16	" do " Ke-shah-ko-quah (a woman " "		5.86 1/4	
" 26	" do for Kum a quah (a woman) same as above		5.86 1/4	
" 28	" do for Top pro ise (a woman) same as above		5.86 1/4	
" 30	" do for Nah-nah-tos-quah (a woman) "		5.86 1/4	
Apr 8	" do for Ah-no-suh-aske (a woman same "		5.86 1/4	
" 12	" do for Quos que ton a e quah (a woman) "		5.86 1/4	
" 20	" do for Chah-ka-ah-quah (a woman) same as above		5.86 1/4	
" 30	" do for Pe-we-ne (a woman) same as above		5.86 1/4	
May 4	" do for Pe-i-chu-kah (a woman) " "		5.86 1/4	
	Amt carried forwd,		113.48	

****

1853	Amt. Brot. forwd:		113.48
May 12	To Burial suit for Pu twon (a woman) same as above		5.86 1/4

Sac & Fox – Shawnee
1853-1933   Volume X

" 16	" do " for Ateh wah nah so " " "		5.86 1/4
June 2	" do for Ah puh u puh ah kah (a woman) "		5.86 1/4
" 2	" do " Huch e waw kasee (a woman "		5.85 1/4
March 11	To Burial suit for Cup a he co consisting of the following articles (a girl) 1 1/2 pt Wht Blkt	1.60	
	1 1/2 yds blue cloth	1.89 1/4	
	1/2 yds Scarlet cloth	.62 1/4	
	3 yds Calico	.36	
	2. ferreting	.24	
	1 pap. paint	.15	4.59
16	To Burial Suite for Maw-ke-se-quah (a girl consisting of the following articles one 2 1/2 pt Wht Blkt	2.50	
	1 1/2 yds Blue cloth	1.87 1/4	
	3/4 " Scarlet cloth	.83 3/4	
	3 " calico	.30	
	2 yd ferreting	.04	
	1 pap. paint	.15	5.30 1/4
Apr 20	To do for Kiah kah krise (a girl) same as above		5.30 1/4
" 7	To do for Maw-sine-a-sah, a son (a boy) consisting of the following articled (towit) 2 pt wht blkt	2.00	
	1 1/4 yds Scarlet cloth	1.56 1/4	
	3 " Calico	.30	
	1 pap paint	.15	4.01 1/4
May 2	To do for My mu ku (a boy) same as above		4.01 1/4
Apr 8	To do for Hy-ah-pit (child consisting of the following articles 1 point Wht Blkt	1.25	
	3/4 yds Scarlet cloth	.83 3/4	
	2 yds Calico	.20	
	1 pap paint	.15	2.53 3/4
" 22	To do for Moler a child Same as above		2.53 3/4
" 20	To do for Maw-pek a child consisting of the following articles one 1/2 pt Wht Blkt	1.60	
	1 yd Scarlet cloth	1.25	
	2 yds Calico	.20	
	1 pap. paint	.15	3.20
	Amt carried forwd		168.43 1/2

****

1853	Amt Brot. forwd,	168.43 1/2
May 24	To Burial Suite for Boy Pu-she-she-nuns bond same as above	3.20
" 27	" do do Pus-co same as above	3.20
June 2	" do " Black Soldiers son same as above	3.20
" "	" do " Black Soldiers son Som[sic] as above	3.20
Apr 20	To Burial Suite for Pis-ku-nah-nun son consisting of the following articles one 1 1/2 pt Wht Blkt 1.60	
	1 yd Scarlet cloth 1.25	
	3 yd calico .36	

Sac & Fox – Shawnee
1853-1933 Volume X

	1 pap paint	.15	3.30
May 4	To burial Suite for an nah she nas thah (a boy) consisting of the following articles (To wit)		
	one 2 pt Wht Blkt	2.00	
	1 3/4 yds Scarlet cloth	2.18 3/4	
	3 yds calico	.30	
	1 pap. paint	.15	4.63 3/4
" 20	To do do for Mah-was-cums-quah (a girl) same as above		4.63 3/4
June 4	To Burial Suit for Sah-nah-quet consisting of the following articles (to wit) 1 2 1/2 pt Wht Blkt	2.25	
	1 1/2 yds Scarlet cloth	1.56 1/4	
	3 yds calico	.30	
	1 pap paint	.15	4.26 1/4
June 14	To Burial Suite for Har-shi-oh consisting of the following articles (to wit) 1 2pt Wht Blkt	2.00	
	1 1/4 yds blue cloth	1.56 1/4	
	3/4 Scarlet cloth	.93 3/4	
	2 yds calico	.20	
	2 " ferreting	.14	
	1 pap paint	.15	4.81
June 20	To Burial Suite for Hog consisting of the following articles to wit one 1/4 pt White Blanket	1.60	
	1 1/4 yds Scarlet cloth	1.66 1/4	
	2 yds Calico	.25	
" 21	1 pap. paint	.15	3.51 1/4
" 20	To do for Kateh-e-mam-ah sys boy same as above		3.51 1/4
	amounting to		$209.98 3/4

Rec^d Sac & Fox Agency June 30th 1853 of B A James

Indian Agent Two hundred & nine Dollars and ninety
Eight & 3/4 cents in full of the above account
(Signed triplicate)   Josiah Smart

I certify on honor that the above account is correct
and that I have actually this 30th day of June 1853
paid the amount thereof
                                          B A James
                                          Indian Agent

Voucher No 12

Josiah Smart
$209.98 3/4

Abstract No 2
2° qr 1853

Sac & Fox – Shawnee
1853-1933   Volume X

30 June
Retained

                                                          Sept 30, 1853
            The United States
1853   To Josiah Smart   Dr
July 1st   To burial suite for Ne-tew-wah consisting
            of the following articles (to wit) $ cts
            1 2 1/2 white point Blanket $2.25
            3/4 yds scarlet cloth .93 3/4 3 yds calico .30 cts   1.23 1/4
            1 3/4 yds blue cloth $2.18 3/4 2 yd ferreting 4cts 2.22 1/4
            1 paper paint   .15   5.86 1/2
" 22   To do for Wah-ko-nah-qua   same as above   5.86 1/2
August 6   To do do Caw-ah-ke   same as above   5.86 1/2
"   8   To do do O-ke-mah-quah   same as above   5.86 1/2
"   11   To do do Ush-e-tah   same as above   5.86 1/2
Sept 21   To do do Sah-kah-co-ne-quah   same as above   5.86 1/2
" 21   To do do Nah-much-e-sac   same as above   5.86 1/2
August 6   To burial suite for Nah-pah-co-mac consisting of
"   "   the following articles (towit)
"   "   To 1 3 point white blanket 2.75 1 3/4 yds scarlet cloth 2.98 1/4
                                                           $4.93 1/4
"   "   " 3 yds calico .30   1 paper paint .15   .45   5.38 3/4
"   21   To do for Kat-Kah-sah se   same as above   5.38 3/4
"   "   To do do Me-am-e-sah   same as above   5.38 3/4
"   22   To do do Pah-o-sah   same as above   5.38 3/4
Sept 10   To do do Shaw-wah-kah   same as above   5.38 3/4
" 15   To do do Nah-co-sah   same as above   5.38 3/4
" 22   To do do Wah-shaw-com-e-quah   same as above   5.38 3/4
" 29   To do do I-ah-pum-a-sah   same as above   5.38 3/4
August 18   To burial suite for Mesh-she-ah-a-quah consisting
            of the following articles towit
               1 2 point white blanket $2.00
               1 1/4 yds blue cloth   1.56 1/4
               3/4 yds scarlet cloth   .93 3/4
               3 yds calico .30 paper paint. 15   .45
               2 yds ferreting   . 4   4.99
"   "   To do do for Wall-co-so-quah   same as above   4.99
Septr 2   To do do for Ah-que-so-tah   same as above   4.99
                                     Amt carried over $99.12 1/2

                          ****

1853   Amt brot apr $99.12 1/2
August 25   To burial suite for Bap-tiste, consisting
            of the following articles (Towit)
            1 1/2 pt white blanket $1.60 1 1/2 yd blue cloth $1.56 1/4 3.16 1/4

Sac & Fox – Shawnee
1853-1933   Volume X

	1/2 yd scarlet cloth .62 1/2 2 yds calico .20	.82 1/2	
	1 paper paint .15 2 yds ferreting 4	.19	4.17 3/4
" 31	To do do for Wah-a-to-kah same as above		4.17 3/4
Septr 3	To burial suite for Mac-qua-es consisting of		
	the following articles (Towit)		
	1 2 1/2 point white blanket $2.25 paper paint 15 $2.40		
	1 1/2 yds scarlet cloth $1.87 1/2 3yds calico 30	2.17 1/2	4.57 1/2
August 30	To do do for Sah-ou-tah same as above		4.57 1/2
Sept 16	To do do " Ke-wah-se same as above		4.57 1/2
" 30	To do " for Mah-ta-cah same as above		4.57 1/2
			$125.78

Rec^d Sac & Fox Agency September 30th 1853 of
B.A. James Indian Agent One hundred and Twenty
five Dollars and Seventy eight cents in full of
the above account.
(Signed triplicate)   Josiah Smart

I certify on honor that the above account is
correct and just and that I have actually this the
30 day of September 1853 paid the amount thereof.

                                    B.A. James
                                    Indian Agent

****

Voucher No 8

Josiah Smart

$125.78

Abstract B.

3° qr 1853

30th Septr

Retained.

	The United States		
		To Josiah Smart	Dr
1853			$ cts
Octr 1	To burial suite for Pap-e-am-e-sqah		
	consisting of the following articles (to wit)		
	2 1/2 pt white blanket	$2.25	

Sac & Fox – Shawnee
1853-1933   Volume X

	1 3/4 yd blue cloth	2.18 3/4	
	3/4 yd scarlet cloth	" .93 1/4	
	3 yd calico 10 cts per yd	" .30	
	2 yd ferreting 4 1 paper paint 15	" .19	5.86 1/2
2	To do do for Me-kes-sah same as above		5.86 1/2
30	To do " for Paw-ne-ah-quah same as above		5.86 1/2
Nov. 16	To do for Sketch-ah-we same as above		5.86 1/2
" 28	To do for Nah-kah-pe same as above		5.86 1/2
Decr 7	To do for Cah-tah-quah same as above		5.86 1/2
" 9	To do for Ah-sah-e-quah same as above		5.86 1/2
" 12	To do for Ah-put-ah-pe same as above		5.86 1/2
1854			
Jany 14	To do for Ke wah e sah same as above		5.86 1/2
" 17	To do for Nah no ah-ke hot same as above		5.86 1/2
1853			
Octr 7	To burial suite for Wah-pah-co-nue consisting of the following articles (Towit)		
	1 3 pt white blanket	2.75	
	1 3/4 yd scarlet cloth	2.18 3/4	
	3 yd calico 30 paper paint .15	.45	5.38 3/4
" 8	To do for Ah-nah-me same as above		5.38 3/4
" 24	To do for So so kah as ko same as above		5.38 3/4
Nov 5	To do for Katch um me same as above		5.38 3/4
" 26	To do for Cho wah same as above		5.38 3/4
" 27	To do for Kah kah ke same as above		5.38 3/4
Octr 10	To burial suite for Cat tah whah consisting of of[sic] the following articles (Towit)		
	1 pt white blanket	1.25	
	1 yd blue cloth	1.25	
	1/2 yd scarlet cloth	" 62 1/2	
	2 yd calico 20 paper paint 15	" 35	
	2 yd ferreting 4	4	3.51 1/2
	Amt. carried over		$94.49

****

	To amt brot forward		94.49
Octr 11	To do for So-quah co pe same as above		3.51 1/2
Octr 8	To burial suite for Co to ke mac consisting of the following articles (Towit)		
	1 1/2 pt white blanket	1.60	
	1 1/4 yd blue cloth	1.56 1/4	
	1/2 yd scarlet	.62 1/2	
	2 yd calico 20 paper paint 15	35	
	2 yd ferreting	4	4.17 3/4
" 24	To do for Pol-O-quah same as above		4.17 3/4
" 26	To do for Nah-no-me-co-se same as above		4.17 3/4
" 29	To do for Cah to cah same as above		4.17 3/4

Sac & Fox – Shawnee
1853-1933   Volume X

Nov 5	To do for Nah sha tah same as above			4.17 3/4
Nov 24	To burial suite for Ah as ke consisting of the following articles (Towit)			
	1 pt white blanket	1.25		
	1 yd scarlet cloth	1.25		
	2 yd calico 20 paper paint 15	.35		2.85
" 25	To do for Pe y ae same as above			2.85
" "	To do for Kah wah same as above			2.85
" 27	To do for Caw cah same as above			2.85
" 30	To do for Ah quaw me same as above			2.85
Decr 20	To do for Sah ah sam me same as above			2.85
				$135.99 1/4

Rec^d Sac & Fox Agency Febry 17th 1854 of B A James Indian Agent One hundred and thirty five Dollars and ninety nine and a fourth cents in full of the above account
(Signed triplicate)   Josiah Smart

I certify on honor that the above account is correct and just and that I have actually this 17th day of Febuary[sic] 1854 paid the amount thereof

B A James
Indian Agent

****

Voucher No 1

Josiah Smart

$135.99 1/4

Abstract B

1st qr 1854

Febry 17th

Retained

The United States
                  To Kingie & Whistler   D^r

1854
July 1st To burial suite for Wah cah ke sheak consisting of the following articles (Towit) (a man)
        1 3 point white blanket $3.50

Sac & Fox – Shawnee
1853-1933   Volume X

	1 3/4 yd scarlet cloth $1.60 per yd	2.80	
	3 yd calico 37^{cts} 1 paper paint 20^{cts}	.57	$6.87
August 3rd	To do do for Sah Kau quah same as above		6.87
" 5th	To do " " Kah non win a kah same as above		6.87
" 10th	To do " " Muc cau same as above		6.87
" 20th	To do " Pe sah co min e quah same as above		6.87
" 25th	To do " Mat tah quah same as above		6.87
" 30th	To do " Wah sah pete same as above		6.87
Septr 6th	To do " Mas ko ah nah same as above		6.87
" 10	To do " No tuck ke a quah same as above		6.87
July 2nd	To burial suite for Quas que consisting		
	of the following article towit (a woman)		
	1 2 1/2 point white blanket	$2.75	
	1 1/4 yd blue cloth	2.80	
	3/4 yd scarlet cloth $1.20 3 yd calico	1.57	
	2 yd ferreting 12^{cts} 1 paper paint 20	.32	7.44
" 5th	To do do for So sin a quah same as above		7.44
" 10th	To do do for Ah sap e quah same as above		7.44
" 15th	To do do for Nah hah pe same as above		7.44
" 20th	To do do for Pan nah ah kah same as above		7.44
August 11th	To do do for Ne she tah same as above		7.44
Septr 3rd	To do do for Ke shah pe same as above		7.44
" 24th	To do do for She ke nah same as above		7.44
July 18th	To burial suite for Nan e so que consisting		
	of the following articles (to wit)		
	1 2 1/2 point white blanket	$2.75	
	1 1/2 yd scarlet cloth $1.60 per yd	2.40	
	3 yd calico 37. 1 paper paint 20	" 57	5.72
	Amt carried over.		$127.07

****

	To amt brot forward		$127.07
July 24th	To do do for Wah nah me same as above		5.72
August 22nd	To do do for Paw ka take same as above		5.72
Septr 3rd	To do do for Wah pon o sack same as above		5.72
" 21st	To do do for Se po ah son same as above		5.72
July 1st	To burial suite for Ke she mac consisting of		
	the following articles, towit		
	1 2 point white blanket	$2.00	
	1 yd scarlet cloth	1.60	
	2 yd calico 24^{cts} 1 paper paint 20	44	4.04
" 18	To do do for Ke [??] ah pe tuc same as above		4.04
August 28	To do do for An no coq it same as above		4.04
Septr 3	To do do for Sah cah lon e quah same as above		4.04
" 22nd	To do do for Wah pah nat quah same as above		4.04
			$170.15

Sac & Fox – Shawnee
1853-1933   Volume X

Rec^d Sac & Fox Agency September 30th 1854 of B.A. James
Indian Agent One hundred and seventy Dollars & fifteen cents in
full of the above account
(Signed triplicate)   <u>Kingie & Whistler</u>

I certify on honor that the above account is correct and just and
and that I have actually this the 30th day of September 1854 paid the
amount thereof
                                                      B.A. James
                                                      Indian Agent
                    ****

Voucher No 3

Kingie & Whistler

$170.15

Abstract B

3rd qr 1854

Septr 30th

Retained

Articles of agreement made and entered into this 9th day of May 1855. Between the Sac & Fox tribe of Indians in the Sac & Fox Agency of the first part and M. S. Randol a Merchant of said Nation of the second part; Witnesseth, That whereas M. S. Randol was the burial bidder for furnishing merchandize[sic] for burying the Dead of the Sac & Fox tribe of Indians for one year from the date hereof. Now in consideration of the premises above mentioned, the party of the second part binds himself to furnish the following articles of Goods at the following prices, for the purpose of burying the dead of said tribe of Indians, viz

Three point white Blanket for Three dollars & seventy five cents.
Two & half point white blanket ~~for~~ for Two dollars & seventy five cents.
Two point white blanket for Two dollars
One point white blanket for One dollar fifty cents
Scarlet & Blue cloth at One dollar & sixty cents per yard
Ferreting at six cents per yard

Sac & Fox – Shawnee
1853-1933   Volume X

Calico at Twelve cents per yard, and to furnish all of the above articles of the best quality and to deliver the same in good order to the Indians of said tribe on the presentation of an order by them for said goods signed by their Agent and in no other way.

And the said B.A. James as Indian Agent for the Sac & Fox Agency doth hereby binds the said tribe of Indians to pay unto M. S. Randol for the Goods he may furnish under this contract; Quarterly, half yearly or as the pmt may be on hand which can be applied to said purpose.

In testimony whereof said parties have hereunto subscribed their names the day and date above written.
(Signed triplicate)

                                                   B.A. James
                                                   Indian Agent
                                                   M.S. Randol

---

Sac & Fox Agency

Burial Contract

of

M. S. Randol

9th May 1855.

                                                                           9th May

Retained.

The United States
                                To M. S. Randol D^r

1854			
July 17th	To burial suite for Wah pah kepe consisting of the following articles towit. (a man)		
	1 3 point white clanked	$3.75	
	1 3/4 yds scarlet cloth $1.60 per yd	2.80	
	3 yd calico 12^{cts} per yard	.36	$6.91
" 20th	To do for Wap pe same as above		6.91
" 25th	To do for Scah pe co kah same as above		6.91
" 30th	To do for Wah pep a quah same as above		6.91
August 1st	To do for Kish lue co kuk same as above		6.91
" 5th	To do for Me chin e mas same as above		6.91
" 10th	To do for Wah pon e sat same as above		6.91

Sac & Fox – Shawnee
1853-1933   Volume X

" 15th	To do for Pe ah mas ke	same as above		6.91
" 30th	To do for We sheh ka	same as above		6.91
Septr 2nd	To do for We pah tah	same as above		6.91
" 15th	To do for Mah se ke ne quah	same as above		6.91
" 20th	To do for Kep pe hone	same as above		6.91

July 15   To burial suite for We she wah consisting
           of the following articles Towit (a woman)
           1 2 1/2 point white blanket $2.75
           1 3/4 yd blue cloth $1.60 per yd   2.80
           3/4 yd scarlet cloth $1.60 per yd   1.20
           3 yd calico 30cts 2 yds ferreting 12cts   .28   7.23

August 23rd	To do for Mus kuk e ah kah	same as above	7.23
" 30	To do for Ke man tah	same as above	7.23
Septr 14	To do for Na ah ke	same as above	7.23
July 3rd	To do for Ah sah som	same as above	7.23

" 6   To burial suite for Ke sah co consisting
           of the following articles Towit   (child)
           1 1 point white blanket $1.50
           1 1/2 yd blue cloth $1.60 per yd   2.40
           2 yd calico 24cts 1 yd ferreting 6cts   " 30   4.20

" 13   To do for Sah po cat   same as above   4.20
                                      Amt carried over $127.47

****

                                                             $127.47
           Amt brot forward.
July 18th To do for Pe am e co   same as above   4.20
" 25   To do for Me co ah   same as above   4.20
August 1st To do for Mah he tah   same as above   4.20
" 3   To do for Co pah co   same as above   4.20
" 10   To do for Wah sae a cah   same as above   4.20
" 20   To do for Wah co se   same as above   4.20
Septr 1st To do for Me tah co se   same as above   4.20
" 4   To do for Ka Kah cho   same as above   4.20
" 7   To do for Se pe ah son   same as above   4.20
" 10   To do for So no quah   same as above   4.20
" 15   To do for Wah co se co   same as above   4.20
" 20   To do for Ke o sah kuk   same as above   4.20
" "   To do for Kah non e quah same as above   4.20
" 30   To do for Ah som e see   same as above   4.20
" "   To do for Pam e see   same as above   4.20

Recd Sac & Fox Agency September 30 1855 of B A James Indian Agent One hundred and Ninety dollars and forty seven cents in full of the above account.
(Signed triplicate)   MS Randol

Sac & Fox – Shawnee
1853-1933   Volume X

I certify on honor that the above account is correct and just and that I have actually this the 30th day of September 1855, paid the amount thereof.

B A James
Indian Agent

****

Voucher No 5

M S Randol

$190.47

Abstract B

3° qr 1855

Septr 30th

Retained

The United States
                            To M. S. Randol   Dr

1856
Febry 6th   To burial suite for Pam e kah (a woman)
                consisting of the following articles (Towit)
                1 2 1/2 point white Blanket $2.75
                1 3/4 yd Blue cloth $1.60 per yd   2.80
                3/4 yd scarlet cloth $1.60 per yd   1.20
                3 yd calico 36cts   2 yd ferreting 12cts   48   7.23
" 17th   To do for Wah wah ke   Same as above   7.23
March 1st   To do for Pe-ke-quah   Same as above   7.23
" 8th   To do for O-co so quah   Same as above   7.23
" 15th   To do for Puc e nah   Same as above   7.23
" 20   To do for Chah co sah   Same as above   7.23
" 28   To do for Wo shah co   Same as above   7.23
April 1st   To do for Quah cu pit   Same as above   7.23
" "   To do for Pah pe quah   Same as above   7.23
" 8th   To do for Mack kah co mah   Same as above   7.23
" 10th   To do for Pe she quah   Same as above   7.23
" 11   To do for Mah me ac   Same as above   7.23
                To burial suite for Ket tah te se   (a man)
                consisting of the following article (Towit)

Sac & Fox – Shawnee
1853-1933   Volume X

Febry 12th	1 3 point white blanket	$3.75	
	1 3/4 yd scarlet cloth $1.60 per yd	2.80	
	3 yd calico	.36	6.91
March 10th	To do for Wah pe woe same as above		6.91
" 12th	To do for Kan nah so same as above		6.91
April 6th	To do for Nes son e wah same as above		6.91
" 10	To do for Mes e quah cah same as above		6.91
" 12	To do for Mes e kah same as above		6.91
Febry 1st	To burial suite for Quah e mah consisting		
	of the following article (to wit) children		
	1 1 point white blanket	$1.50	
	1 1/4 yd blue cloth $1.60 per yd	2.00	
	1/2 yd scarlet cloth " " "	.80	
	2 yd calico 24^{cts} 1 yd ferreting 6^{cts}	.30	4.60
	Amt carried over.		$132.82

****

	Amt brot forward		$132.82
Febry 18th	To do for Mac ke se tah same as above		4.60
" 27	To do for Pat tus kas ke same as above		4.60
March 1st	To do for Osh e tah same as above		4.60
" 3rd	To do for Ke tah same as above		4.60
" 7	To do for Sac Ket te pah same as above		4.60
" "	To do for Te she pah same as above		4.60
" 13	To do for Wah sah co nah same as above		4.60
" 20	To do for Mak e see same as above		4.60
" 25	To do for Ne co sah mac same as above		4.60
April 3rd	To do for Cah tue e nac same as above		4.60
			$178.82

Rec^d Sac & Fox Agency April 18th 1856 of B A James Indian Agent One hundred and Seventy Eight Dollars and Eighty two cents in full of the above account.
(Signed triplicate)   MS Randol

    I certify on honor that the above account is correct and just and that I have actually this the 18th day of April 1856 paid the amount thereof.
B A James
Indian Agent

****

Voucher No 1

MS Randol

$178.82

Sac & Fox – Shawnee
1853-1933   Volume X

Abstract B

2° qr 1856

18th April

Retained

Department of the Interior
Office Indian Affairs
January 31st, 1857.

Sir
    I have to acknowledge the receipt of your letter of the 24th ultimo, containing applications relative to the three suspended vouchers in your accounts.

Yours Respectfully,
Your [illegible] Servant

Geo W Manypenny
Commissioner

B.A. James, Esqr.
   Indian Agent,
     Sac & Fox Agency,   Kansas Territory.

****

Jany 31st 1857

Acknowledging by letter in
regard to suspended voucher
Burial clothes

Omaha, Neb

Oct. 1st 1898

Capt W.A. Mercer

SUBJECT.

Sac & Fox – Shawnee
1853-1933   Volume X

Hate that Nah tah wah Nah mah
a Sac & Fox Indian deed at Exposition

****

We, the Chiefs and members of the Sac and Fox of the Mississippi Council of Oklahoma, in Council Assembled do resolve that in view of the fact the Allwise and Supreme Creator has suddenly removed one of our member, by name Henry Miller, from our midst and he being away from home and his family in destitute circumstances, that we desire to provide for him a suitable and civilized burial and that we respectfully request the Honorable Commissioner of Indian Affairs to pay from the $5000 set apart for the support of the National Government, the sum of $20 with which to pay for a coffin:

		Witnesses
Chief McKosato	Hisxmark	W.R. Gulick
Moses Keokuk	Hisxmark	Mary Antoine
Edgar Mack	Hisxmark	
David Wakolle	Hisxmark	
William Shaw	Hisxmark	
Ulyses S. Grant	Hisxmark	
Edward Mathews	Hisxmark	
Jack Bear	Hisxmark	

Dated at Sac and Fox Agency, Okla.
October 30th, 1900.

I, William Hurr, official Interpreter at Sac and Fox Agency, Okla. certify that I was present when the above resolution was passed by the Sac and Fox Council, that I witnessed their signatures to the resolution and am satisfied that they understood the same and it was their true wish and intent.

..William Hurr........
Official Interpreter.

Dated Sac and Fox Agency, Okla.
October 30th, 1900.

Sac & Fox – Shawnee
1853-1933 Volume X

UNITED STATES INDIAN SERVICE,

CERTIFICATE OF INSPECTION.

Sac & Fox Agency Ok

December 28th, 1900

I HEREBY CERTIFY that I have carefully inspected, for the Indian Department, The Coffin described in attached invoice

~~weighing~~

and found the same to be made of good material, well finished suitable for the requirements. and ~~of quality fully equal to the sample on which~~

was delivered on the ~~contract dated~~ ~~; was awarded~~. The same ~~has this~~ 13th day of November , 1 900, ~~been properly marked by the contractor, and stamped by me, and delivered~~ to The Sac & Fox Council

for transportation to the burial of Henry Miller

and I also certify that I have signed this certificate in duplicate.

William R Gulick
Inspector of Supplies.

****

Sac & Fox – Shawnee
1853-1933 Volume X

VOUCHER FOR OPEN MARKET PURCHASES.

THE UNITED STATES,
       To   E. L. Conklin   , Dr.

DATE OF PURCHASE. 1900		DOLLARS	CENTS
Oct. 30	To one Coffin (for Henry Miller, Sac & Fox Indian)	20	00

Received at   Sac and Fox Agency, Okla   December 28, 1900   ~~189~~
of   Lee Patrick,   U. S. Indian Agent,
Twenty ($20.00) and 00/100   Dollars,
in full of the above account.

    W.R. Gulick   E L Conklin

  I CERTIFY, on honor, that the above account is correct and just; that the articles therein named were required for immediate use   for Henry Miller, Sac and Fox Indian
that there is no contract for the delivery thereof; that authority for the purchase is shown by letter from the Commissioner of Indian Affairs dated   Dec. 6, 1900, ~~189~~, a copy of which is hereto attached; that the articles were purchased at   Sac and Fox Agency, Okla   of the person named in the original invoice of purchase annexed hereto, and delivered to me at   Sac and Fox Agency, Okla   on the 30th day of   October, 1900 , 189..., and that the same appear on my Return of Property for the   2nd   quarter, 1901
  I FURTHER CERTIFY that the prices charged therefor are reasonable, and the lowest for which they could be obtained, and that I have actually, this   28th day of   December   1900 ~~189~~, paid the amount thereof, viz: Twenty ($20.00) and 00/100   dollars, and have taken the claimant's receipt therefor in triplicate.

                Lee Patrick
Dated at Sac & Fox Agency, Okla. Dec. 28, 1900   *U.S. Indian Agent.*

           ****

Sac & Fox – Shawnee
1853-1933 Volume X

CASH.

Voucher No. 28

OPEN-MARKET PURCHASE

2nd Quarter, 189__.

E. L. Conklin

$20.00

		1900
Paid	Dec 28 th	~~189~~

Check No. 2177

Asst. Treas. U. S. St Louis
Mo

State whether paid in cash or by check; if by check, give number and date of the check and the name of the bank or institution upon which it is drawn.

Any disbursing or other officer of the United States or other person who shall knowingly present, or cause to be presented, any voucher, account, or claim to any officer of the United States for approval or payment, or for the purpose of securing a credit in any account with the United States, relating to any matter pertaining to the Indian Service, which shall contain any material misrepresentation of fact in regard to the amount due or paid, the name or character of the article furnished or received, or of the service rendered, or to the date of purchase, delivery, or performance of service, or in any other particular, shall not be entitled to payment or credit for any part of said voucher, account, or claim; and if any such credit shall be given or received, or payment made, the United States may recharge the same to the officer or person receiving the credit or payment and recover the amount from either or both, in the same manner as other debts due the United States are collected; PROVIDED, That where an account contains more than one voucher the foregoing shall apply only to such vouchers as contain the misrepresentation; AND PROVIDED FURTHER, That the officers and persons by and between whom the business is transacted shall be presumed to know the facts in relation to the matter set forth in the voucher, account, or claim; AND PROVIDED FURTHER, That the foregoing shall be in addition to the penalties now prescribed by law, and in no way to affect proceedings under existing law for like offenses. That, where practicable, this section shall be printed on the blank forms of vouchers provided for general use. (Act March 1, 1883 § 8, 22 Stat. 451; Act July 4, 1884, § 8; Cir. 113 Ind. O.)

Sac & Fox – Shawnee
1853-1933   Volume X

Sac and Fox Agency, Okla.,
...Dec. 28th.... 1900.

..I.... certify that ...I... have delivered to Lee Patrick, U. S. Indian Agent, at ......Sac & Fox Agency, Ok............................. the following described goods: ....1 Coffin for Henry Miller.. on the ..10th... day of ..Nov...1900.

Witnesses:

....W.R. Gulick..............   ...E.L. Conklin.........

****

                                                                  1900
            SAC AND FOX AGENCY, OKLAHOMA, Nov 13 ~~1899~~
M Lee Patrick U.S. Ind Agt.
   Sac and Fox Agency Okla

                        To ~~J.B. CHARLES, U.S.I. Trade~~r, Dr.
                           E. L. Conklin
                        GENERAL MERCHANDISE.

To Coffin for Henry Miller	20	00

Sac & Fox – Shawnee
1853-1933   Volume X

Finance,
56630,57858,1900
57859,56631,1900
56919,58627, 1900
Authy. 68309
2 Inclosures

DEPARTMENT OF THE INTERIOR,

OFFICE OF INDIAN AFFAIRS,

WASHINGTON, December 6, 1900

The U. S. Indian Agent,
 Sac & Fox Agency, Oklahoma.

Sir:

~~WWWWWWWWWWWWWWWWWWWWWWWWWWWWWWWWWWW~~

 You are further advised that authority has been granted for the settlement of an indebtedness amounting to $25.00, incurred by the U. S. Indian Agent, Sac & Fox Agency, Oklahoma, during the current quarter, as follows:

  Lee Patrick, Indian Agent, for traveling expenses on official
   business, inspecting Indian leases and loading of
   Government freight, $5.00

  E. L. Conklin, open market purchase of one coffin for burial
   of a deceased Sac & Fox Indian,   20.00
                        —————
                        $25.00

all as requested and for the reasons fully set forth in your letters of the 13th ultimo, and evidenced by the two vouchers herewith returned for payment and file with your quarterly accounts.

       Very respectfully,

       A. C. Tonner,
W.A.S.(C.)   Assistant Commissioner

Sac & Fox – Shawnee
1853-1933 Volume X

Department of the Interior.

INDIAN SCHOOL SERVICE.

Carlisle, Pa., Dec. 11, 1900.

Mr. Lee Patrick,
   U.S. Indian Agent,
     Sac & Fox Agency, Okla.

Sir :-

    It becomes necessary to report the death of Fannie Gibson, a Shawnee pupil of this school from your agency. Her uncle, John Gibson, was notified of her sickness and death, which occurred Dec. 5th of tuberculosis.

                Very respectfully,
                    RH Pratt
                Major 10th Cavalry, Supt.

(P)

DEPARTMENT OF THE INTERIOR
UNITED STATES INDIAN SERVICE

SAC AND FOX AGENCY, IOWA.
Toledo, Jan. 30, 1901.

Maj. Lee Patrick,
   U.S. Indian Agent
     Sac & Fox Agency, Okla.

Sir:

    An Indian enrolled at your Agency, Wo-Ska-Nau, by name, died at the Winnebago Agency, Neb. on Jan. 28, 1901, and was brought to this Agency to-day for burial. He with some Winnebago Indians, who are enrolled at this Agency, were visiting at the said Winnebago Agency, where he took sick and died. I do not know any of the particulars in the case.

Very respectfully,

Wm G Malin

U.S. Indian Agent.

DEPARTMENT OF THE INTERIOR
UNITED STATES INDIAN SERVICE

Nadeau, Kansas,

August 11th, 1904.

W. C. Kohlenberg,
Supt. & Spl. Disb. Agent.

Sac & Fox Agency, Okl.

Dear Sir:-

In reply to your letter of the 1st. inst. I have to inform you that Ella Dupins, or Johnson is still living. David Johnson died some time in 1894, and Artur[sic] the son of David and Ella Johnson died very soon after the father, I think Supt. Edwards at the Kickapoo School can give you the dates of the death of these persons.

Very respectfully,

C.L. Williams,

Supt. & C.

by __J. A. Scott__
Leasing Clerk.

****

Sac & Fox – Shawnee
1853-1933   Volume X

STATEMENT OF ACCOUNT		
Cushing, Okla., June 25 190 5		
Mr Kohlenberg		
IN ACCOUNT WITH **FUSON & BRENNAN,**		
DEALERS IN		
FINE FURNITURE,		
UNDERTAKING A SPECIALTY.		
2	Coffins $20.	40^{00}
2	[Illegible] $5^{00}	10^{00}
	Total amount	$50^{\underline{00}}$
	Hauling	300

****

W. H. FUSON   MARTIN BRENNAN

FUSON & BRENNAN,
Dealers In
FINE FURNITURE, CARPETS, LINOLEUMS, ETC.

CUSHING, OKLA. June ^{27} 190 5

Mr W C Kohlenberg

Sac & Fox – Shawnee
1853-1933   Volume X

Dear Sir you will find enclose statement of funeral goods for Grace Mason & Indian man that were killed at village night before last which [illegible...] as soon as convenient &

Oblige

Fuson & Brennan

DEPARTMENT OF THE INTERIOR
UNITED STATES INDIAN SERVICE

Sac and Fox School, Iowa.

Toledo, January 22, 1906.

W. C. Kohlenberg,
   Supt. & Spl. Disb. Agent.
   Sac and Fox Agency, Okla.

Sir:-

   Replying to your favor of the 2nd. instant, relative to the date of the death of Wah-pah-ne-se, the husband of Pone-wya-tah, I will say, that after making inquiries of the head men of the tribe, I have at last arrived at an approximate date of the said death of the said Wah-pah-ne-se. According to the best information obtainable, this death took place about 16 years ago. Ma-ke-so-pe-at, Pone-wya-tah's youngest child was born a very short time after the death of his father, Wah-pah-ne-se, and his age at this time according to the pay rolls, is 16 years. I have not examined the records of the office, which are not in good condition, but will do so, when I have a little leisure and if exact data can be obtained, will so inform you.

Very respectfully,

Wm G Malin
Supt. & Spl. Disb. Agent.

****

DEPARTMENT OF THE INTERIOR
UNITED STATES INDIAN SERVICE

Sac and Fox School, Iowa.

Toledo, May 22, 1906.

Sac & Fox – Shawnee
1853-1933 Volume X

Hon. W. C. Kohlenberg,
    Supt. & S. D. A.
        Sac and Fox Agency, Okla.

Sir:-

    Replying to your favor of the 14th, instant, relative to the Sha-que-quot matter, will say, that I called the Business Committee of this tribe together yesterday, and laid this matter before them. After some deliberation, they all agreed to one fact, "That Wah-pah-ne-se, died in the fall before his youngest son, Ma-ke-so-pe-at, was born, and that the said youngest son was born in the spring following his father's death." With this information at hand, I began a search of the old records of this officer, (which are very imperfect, except for the past 15 years), but I found enough to prove the truthfulness of the statement of the said business committee. These records show conclusively, that the said Ma-ke-so-pe-at, was born April 1st, 1888,[sic] The same Pay Roll that records the birth of this child, shows that Wah-pah-ne-se was dead at the date of the Annuity payment, which was made, January 6, 1888, hence, as Wah-pah-ne-see's death is noted on this Pay Roll, it follows that he died during the year preceeding[sic] this payment, or in 1887. This record is deficient, only in the fact, that it does not give the exact date of his, (Wah-pah-ne-se's) death. This record places the year of his death, beyond cavil, as had he died during the year 1886, his name would not appear in the 1886 pay roll, and it is conclusive evidence that he died after the Annuity Payment of 1867 was made.

    It is the custom here, and I presume, elsewhere, to make one payment of annuity after after[sic] the death of any annuitant, to the friends or heirs of the deceased, and as it appears that this post mortem payment was made after the annuity payment of 1887, it follows that he died during the said year of 1887, or very early in the year 1888, as this payment was made January 6, as stated above. I hope this will forever set this matter at rest. I am very glad to be able to aid you in this matter and have ~~this~~ ~~matter~~ it definitely settled.

    In regard to the heirs of the John McKuk estate, will say, that Nellie Davenport left neither father nor mother, no husband nor children, no sister, and but one brother, Seba, who is here sole, and only heir.

Sac & Fox – Shawnee
1853-1933   Volume X

If I can be of use to you in any matter of business relative to the Indians, do no fail to command my services.

Very respectfully,
Wm G Malin
Supt. & Spl. Disb. Agent.

Ora Shaquequot died _____ leaving as her sole and only heir at law her niece & nephew Pa phia na, Ne pan se qua

---

M. W. MERRITT & CO.
DEALERS IN
GROCERIES FURNITURE AND UNDERTAKING

RECEIVED
JUN 29 1906
SAC & FOX AGENCY,
OKLAHOMA

Prague, O. T. June 26th 190 6

Mr Colenburg[sic]
   Sac & Fox Agency, Okla.

Dear Sir:

   Mr. J. Appletree purchased a casket here for Margaret Bigwalker for $30.00
   Please look this up for us.
        And Oblige
           M W Merritt V [?].

We have an account against Frank Carter for 17\underline{50}$ for balance of coffin gotten by Joe Northfork, gotten Feb 6 = 06.

[The letter below typed as given]

Otoe Agency Okla
Jan 9/1906

W.C. Kohlenberg
   Sac & Fox Agency
      Okla

RECEIVED
JAN 10 1907[sic]
SAC & FOX AGENCY,
OKLAHOMA.

Sac & Fox – Shawnee
1853-1933 Volume X

Sir

Mr Kohlenberg I just got your letter answering mine yesterday so I will now answer you again about my sister Mary Roubedeaux yes she died 20th day of Dec. and boy Rufus was born 20th of Nov. I will be very glad if you set out a good plan for them childrens I have one of them in my care and mother and sister has the care of the other two. The boy Rufus is in care of Charley Tohees wife. Well I was glad to hear you wont pay him Faw Faw any of the childs money no more good for the child hope you do the same with my nieces and nephew as their fathers dont belong to our band of Indians
well Mr Kohlenberg dont forget my girl to next pay roll you make, Ozettie. This is all hope you help me out with them childrens of Mary Roubedeaux write let me know what could be done are if you going to let the father draw for them

Ozettie Kihega
Born
Aug 21 1906

From yours Respfully
Julia Kihega

Department of Justice.

Office of the United States Attorney.
District of Oklahoma.
Guthrie.

RECEIVED
FEB 4 1907
SAC & FOX AGENCY,
OKLAHOMA.

February 1, 1907.

W. C. Kohlenberg, Esq.,

Supt. & Spl. Disb. Agent.

Sac & Fox Agency, Oklahoma.

Dear Sir:-

Your letter of January 29th, relating to the death of Gertrude Givens Brown, received. I shall send, to the County attorney of Pottawatomie County, a list of witnesses furnished, and ask him to have them subpoenaed for the next grand jury. I will be at Tecumseh in person, and wish you could arrange to be there at the same time. I will ascertain the date on which the grand jury meets and advise you.

Very respectfully,

John Pambogo
U.S. Attorney.

M.   OFFICE OF SUPREME MEDICAL DIRECTORS   ROCK ISLAND, ILL. June 14, 1907.

Health Officer,
    Sac & Fox Agency, Okla.

Dear Sir:

    Under date of June 1st, we addressed you a communicatiom[sic] in reference to the application of one, Pellano Rosengrant, asking that you kindly give us the exact cause of death as shown by your records of his father, Thomas Rosengrant, who died at the Sac & Fox Agency, Oct. 22, 1900, after an illness of three weeks. To date we have received no reply. Will you kindly let us hear from you and greatly oblige,

Yours fraternally,

E.L. Kerns
F A Smith
B.E. Jones

SUPREME MEDICAL DIRECTORS.

    No health officer located at this place. Unable to state time or cause of death or party mentioned in the foregoing.

Sac & Fox – Shawnee
1853-1933 Volume X

RECEIVED
JUL 25 1907
SAC & FOX AGENCY,
OKLAHOMA.

Shawnee, OT.
July 22, -'07

Mr. W.C. Kohlenberg
   Sac & Fox Agency
     Oklahoma.

Mr. K.
    I have just a little time to write a short letter to you this evening. I want to let you know that I cant be up to the school if Jack Bear is getting bad he has been very sick. Today we had to get Dr. Harryman to come down from Shawnee and he will be over tomorrow with another Dr. He tried three kinds of medicines but they did'nt[sic] do him good.
    ~~Please let me know~~
          Will close
            From Bertha

[On opposite side of page]

        Pattequa

       To WC.

J. S. McCormick   I. W. Patton

McCORMICK & PATTON,
Dealers In
FURNITURE,   STOVES,   IMPLEMENTS.
BUILDERS AND GENERAL HARDWARE.
UNDERTAKING A SPECIALTY.

            Redrock, Oklahoma. July 24   190 7

Kollenburg Supt

   Dear Sir
      Maggie Burguss[sic] died yesterday evening and been trying to get Phone through to you or telegraph you regarding casket for her and cannot get either So sent out a $35^{\underline{00}}$ Dollar casket – Can you protect us on this Deal

            Yours Truly
            McCormick & Patton

STATEMENT

Aug 19th 190 7

*M*r Frank Smith

Sac & Fox Indian

To L. P. Coffey Dr

TERMS

To Black Cloth Casket for Wife	$35 00
Received Payment in Full for the above Account L.P. Coffey Per Ira Little	
Recpt Many Thanks	

****

REFER IN REPLY TO THE FOLLOWING:
Land
71457-1907
225

Subject:
Authority to
approve check.

DEPARTMENT OF THE INTERIOR
OFFICE OF INDIAN AFFAIRS
WASHINGTON

RECEIVED
SEP 2 1907
SAC & FOX AGENCY,
OKLAHOMA.

August 29, 1907

Sac & Fox – Shawnee
1853-1933   Volume X

The Superintendent in Charge,
    Sac and Fox Agency, Oklahoma.

Sir:

    In compliance with your request of August 20, 1907, you are hereby authorized to approve the check of Frank Smith for $35.00, to enable him to pay for a casket purchased for the proper burial of the remains of his wife. This check is to be drawn on his inherited Indian land funds of which he has $445.77 on deposit in the First National Bank, of Chandler, Oklahoma.

                    Very respectfully,
                      F.E. Leupp
TBW:LM   Commissioner.

****

STROUD, OKLA. 12/4 **190 7**

W. C. Colnburg[sic]   RECEIVED
                    DEC 5 1907
                    SAC & FOX AGENCY,
IN ACCOUNT WITH **S. E. JONDAHL** OKLAHOMA.

FURNITURE HARDWARE QUEENSWARE STOVES
MUSICAL INSTRUMENTS AND SEWING MACHINES

To bal on Casket for	
Frank Davis	20 $\frac{00}{}$

Sac & Fox – Shawnee
1853-1933 Volume X

STROUD, OKLAHOMA April 2 190 8

W. C. Kollenberg[sic]

Sac and Fox Agency

IN ACCOUNT WITH **S E JONDAHL**

FURNITURE HARDWARE QUEENSWARE STOVES
MUSICAL INSTRUMENTS AND SEWING MACHINES
A FULL LINE OF UNDERTAKING GOODS

Dec	31	To casket for Addie Padequa	Paid	4/6/08 35.00
Feb	21	To coffin for Austin Grant Baby		10.00
				45.00

DEPARTMENT OF THE INTERIOR
UNITED STATES INDIAN SERVICE

Office of Indian Affairs
Received
Feb. 2, 1909.
P-8907.

Subject:
Request for Authority to
Settle Indebtedness.

1 incl.

The Commissioner of Indian Affairs,
Washington, D. C.
Sir:

Sac & Fox – Shawnee
1853-1933 Volume X

I respectfully request the authority be granted for the settlement of an indebtedness amounting to $4.50 incurred by me in the second quarter, 1909, as represented by the voucher inclosed. I have sufficien[sic] funds on for payment from the appropriation:

"Indian Schools, Support, 1909",

Voucher No. 8, $4.50
Irregular labor; for digging the grave of Josie

Harrison, a school pupil, as follows:
WM. Reynolds, one day, 1.50
Isaac Hunter, " " 1.50
Grant Quigg, " " 1.50

Very respectfully,
(Signed), W. C. Kohlenberg,
MLD/ 1 encl. Supt. & Spl. Disb. Agt.

Office of Indian Affairs,
Washington, Feb. 2, 1909.
Returned approved:-
(Signed), R. G. Valentine,
Acting Commissioner.
WAP- SES- JAC- HD- 1 incl.

MIDLAND VALLEY RAILROAD COMPANY **RECEIVED**
OPERATING DEPARTMENT APR 6 1909
SAC & FOX AGENCY,
JNO. H. HARRIS OKLAHOMA.
GENERAL SUPERINTENDENT

MUSKOGEE, OKLA. April 4, 1909.

Hon. W. C. Kohlenberg,
Supt. & Special Disbursing Agent,
Sac & Fox Agency Okla.

My dear sir:--

Sac & Fox – Shawnee
1853-1933   Volume X

I presume you have noted in the press dispatches the reported death of my brother Dr. Wm Jones in the Philippine Islands. I have received no authentic reports except a telegram from Dr. Geo. A. Dorsey of the Fields Columbian Museum, Chicago, which read, "Doctor Jones death confirmed by War Department, have written you." I have not received the letter mentioned but presume this is authentic.

It is the expressed wish of my father that the remains be transported to the United States for interment, and I have asked Dr. Dorsey if it is the intention of the Fields Museum to do so, and I thought perhaps if you deem it proper, to secure the co-operation of the Indian Department to transfer his remains and to get details of his murder, we would highly appreciate your assistance in our behalf.

        Believe me, your friend,
          Levi W. Jones

****

MIDLAND VALLEY RAILROAD COMPANY
OPERATING DEPARTMENT

JNO. H. HARRIS
GENERAL SUPERINTENDENT

RECEIVED
APR 15 1909
SAC & FOX AGENCY,
OKLAHOMA.

MUSKOGEE, OKLA. April 13, 1909.

Hon. W. C. Kohlenberg,
   Supt. & Special Disbursing Agent,
      Sac & Fox Agency Okla.

Dear sir:--

    I acknowledge receipt of your kind letter of the 6th inst and appreciate very highly your many kind expressions of sympathy and the high esteem ion which my brother Dr William Jones was held: I also thank you got your interest in taking this matter up with the Department with a view of securing co-operation in having his remains transported to the United States for interment, and since writing you, we are informed by the War Department that under the rules and regulations governing in the Philippine Islands, application would have to be made by my father for his removal and this cannot be done until after 18 months from date of burial; this seems to be the prevailing situation. I have no doubt this will be carried out.

We are also informed by Dr. Dorsey of the Fields Columbian Museum in Chicago that he has sent a man to Manila to take charge of Willie's papers, trunks and other belongings, and I presume, to make report and look into his murder. Yet, after talking with parties who have spent some years on the Islands, one could hardly be surprised at his murder; as I have talked with a Midland Valley employe[sic] here who was an officer in the regular army in the Islands for over five years, and he says, that any one who goes among these wild people alone, as Willie did, simply puts himself up as a target to be killed.

We all regret his untimely end very much,

Sincerely yours,

Levi W. Jones

****

[The next four letters typed as given]

Prague Okla
April 3, 1909

RECEIVED
APR 5 1909
SAC & FOX AGENCY,
OKLAHOMA.

Mr Kohlenburg[sic]
Friend & Bro
I got Telgram from my son Frank & one from Levi Report my son William Jones been killd in Phillippine also I see in Papers wel my Frind this Hard ~~one~~ on me old man as I am
yours Fratnity
H C Jones

****

Sac & Fox – Shawnee
1853-1933   Volume X

Prague Okla
April 6th PM

RECEIVED
APR 5 1909
SAC & FOX AGENCY,
OKLAHOMA.

Dear Friend & Bro
I got letter from Miss Andrews of Hampton Va, & cliping William died same day He was wounded with Balaed & Speared Oh this is Terrble news Report Reced from Jon Smith of ~~Manille~~ Phillipine his Leueant scaped wounded too He was killed 50 miles south Eschagne He was killed March 28th same day will his Birthday

Wel Poor boy Just to think well all his hard work is Ended He is no more

Fratenity yours
H C Jones

****

Prague Okla
May 17th 10

RECEIVED
MAY 18 1909
SAC & FOX AGENCY,
OKLAHOMA.

Brother Kohlenberg
I Reced your letter with cliping give more information My Poor son Wills death

Yours Fraterily
H C Jones

****

RECEIVED
AUG 30 1909
SAC & FOX AGENCY,
OKLAHOMA.

Aug 27 1909

W.C. Kohlenburg
Friend & Brother   its to slow I got Poor Williams things first Mr Skiff director of Museum was not gone to let me see any thing till I give him some sharp words He thin Phone to their Attey & Mr Heck advice Mr Skiff let us go over what late Dr Jones left when we came to see it its old Trunk & a few cloths & a few Books some Papers I should been glad to meet Prof Dorsey its his direction way Mr Skiff act But after He under stand matter He treat us good, Mr Wells is help me of Prague

Sac & Fox – Shawnee
1853-1933   Volume X

[The letter below typed as given]

J. H. LENEHAN, GENL. AGENT   C. R. STREET, ASST. GENL. AGENT   D. OSTRANDER, GENL. ADJUSTER

RECEIVED
[illegible] 1909

Phenix Insurance Company

OF BROOKLYN, N.Y.

SAC & FOX AGENCY,
OKLAHOMA.

A. G. WILLIAMS, SOLICITOR
PERKINS, OKLA.

WESTERN AND SOUTHERN DEPARTMENT, CHICAGO

_____May 28_____ 190 9

Mr Kohlenberg

        Dear Sir

Bessie Roubidoux   Died May 10 – 1909 and i suppose thire will be another Division in the Estate of Mary and i will come down someday Soon

                      Robert Roubidoux

[The letter below typed as given]

                    Chattanooga Okla
                    June 8, 1909

Mr. Thackery
        Kind Sir

I will write you afew lines to let you know the little Twins Nellie & Stella Ford got here all Safe we meet them to Chattanooga but they got here 3 days to late to see their Grand Mother she was buried the day before they come. we was all afful disspointed for them not coming sooner for their Grand Ma was afful aneous to see them the day before she died she ask me if we got a letter for her from you stateing you had sent the twins but we are glad to have them come they have to aunt and one uncle here the Twins Grand Mother is my Mother I am their Aunt
I will close from Mrs Salena
                Kane

Chattanooga Okla
R R No1   Box 100.

Sac & Fox – Shawnee
1853-1933 Volume X

SEE LETTER

No.	181	Date	6/21/09
From	La Clair Adelaide		
	Chattanooga, Okla		
In Drawer	Indian Folder	Ford, Nellie	F.Po. 2
In re	Visit of Nellie & Stella Ford		

****

SEE LETTER

No.	67	Date	6/15/09
From	Adelaide La Clair		
	Chattanooga Okla		
In Drawer	Indian Folder	Ford, Nellie	Folder No. 1
In re	Nellie & Stella Ford	Vacation	

DEPARTMENT OF THE INTERIOR

UNITED STATES INDIAN SERVICE

RECEIVED
JAN 31 1910
SAC & FOX AGENCY,
OKLAHOMA.

Sac and Fox Agency, Okla.,

Jan. 5, 1910.

Mrs. Annie Longshore,

Sparks, Okla.

Dear friend:

    Will you kindly advise me as to the date of death of your child and also tell me which one it was. It has been reported that there was a death in your family but we have no record as to which of the children it was and this is necessary. It may be a mistake and that it was one of your sisters[sic] children, and I would thank you to give me the information under the inclosed envelope which requires no postage.

    Thanking you in advance, I am,

Very respectfully,

W.C. Kohlenberg

WCK Supt. & Spl. Disb. Agent.

[The letter below typed as given]

Perkins Okla 3/18/10
Mr. Kohlenberg-
Dear sir I thought I would write a few lines to you and tell you that Jake Dole lost his little Boy- Joseph Dole, he dide 18 of March. and I Been down in Bed over two week I had the New Monea fever. I am getting Better now I can get around in the house I think I will Be all right ina few days I understand that there is a check for my wife. She cant go untill I get Beter thou she can com an sign it.- This is al oblige me
    Joe Springer

H. C. Jones

Prague Okla. March 2 1910

W.C. Kohleburg
  Supt Sp & Dis Agent
Friend & Brother
    Thrsa Wood is no more She died 7 A m yesterday will Buri her 11 this morning
        Yours Truly
        HC Jones

Sac & Fox – Shawnee
1853-1933   Volume X

THE WESTERN UNION TELEGRAPH COMPANY.
----------INCORPORATED----------
24,000 OFFICES IN AMERICA.   CABLE SERVICE TO ALL THE WORLD.

This Company TRANSMITS and DELIVERS messages only on conditions limiting its liability, which have been assented to by the sender of the following message. Errors can be guarded against only by repeating a message back to the sending station for comparison, and the Company will not hold itself liable for errors or delays in transmission or delivery of **Unrepeated Messages**, beyond the amount of tolls paid thereon, nor in any case where the claim is not presented in writing within sixty days after the message is filed with the Company for transmission.
This is an UNREPEATED MESSAGE, and is delivered by request of the sender, under the conditions named above.
ROBERT C. CLOWRY, President and General Manager.

NUMBER	SENT BY	REC'D BY	CHECK
km	X	ca	[illegible]

RECEIVED at 1^{25} pm   19

Dated   Canton SD 5/12

To   M[sic] C Kohlenberg   Supt Sac & Fox Agency

                               Stroud Ok

    Silas Hawk Just Died will

    burry[sic] here Saturday

                               Hammer Supt

[The following four letters typed as given]

                          Hulbert Okla
                          Aug 4, 1910

Dear Sir:-
    Mr. Frank A Thackery
I thought I would drop a few lines this morning in regard to some matter you would hafter to look after. If it is so. We have heard that our Sister Ella Wassom is dead we heard she died about three weeks ago:
I think she on the roll as Ella Cochram. White Wassom is her husband name
        Please find out if you can
          Yours respectfully
           Charles Chisholm
           Wm Chisholm

                    ****

Sac & Fox – Shawnee
1853-1933   Volume X

[Copy of other side of letter on page 42]

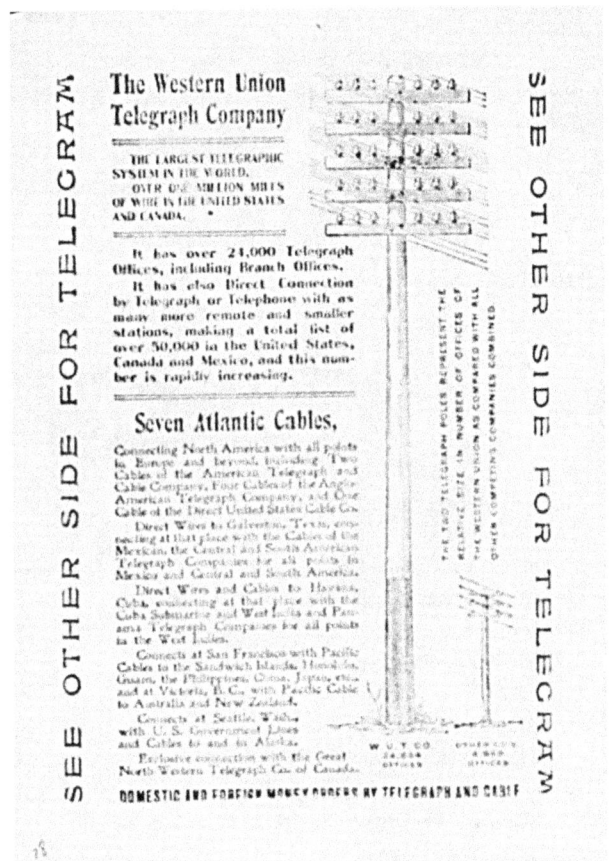

****

Sac & Fox – Shawnee
1853-1933   Volume X

                                  Hulbert Okla
                                  Aug13, 1910

Dear Sir:-
     Mr. Frank A Thackery
Received your letter [illegible] her post Office is Dale Okla please let us know rightaway

                       Yours respectfull
                            Chas and Wm Chisholm
  Ans soon

Mrs Ella Cochran, now Wasson
                    Is she dead?

                  ****

                      Chattanooga Okla
                      Oct. 5. 1910.

Mr Frank A Thackery
    Kind Sir
In reply to your letter Oct 3, I will state that Mr John Moses LaClair never was marrid. Died 1891 age 24 years
Mrs Zoia Dichine
   Died 1882 age 28 years   Left 3 children

Mrs Louisa Roselius
   Died 1901 age 28 years   Left one child.

Mr Oscar LaClair Died 1902 age 22 years Left 2 Children

Mrs Una May Ford Died 1904 age 21 years left 2 children

   I will send names of Heirs living
Mr Oliver La Clair

Mr Charles Monroe LaClair
Mrs Mary Edwards
Mrs Salina Kane
and I know that all heirs are will to sell Land as soon as possible Pleas answere as soon and let me know what has been done I pt Hairs names and ages the way I understood

Sac & Fox – Shawnee
1853-1933   Volume X

> Respectfully
> Mrs Salina Kane
> RFD No 1 Box 33   Chattanooga Okla

****

> Chattanooga Ok
> Oct 22, 1910

Mr Frank A Thackery

Dear Sir I receved your letter asking addres of Mrs. Oscar LaClair   She is Married again her addres is

> Mrs Ira Phillips
> Normon
> (RFD 6)   Okla

the Children are both living and with her their address is the same I dont know her age as for my part I dont want to lesse this allotment I want to sell it as soon a possible

> Res
> Mrs Salena Kane

[The letter below typed as given]

RECEIVED
OCT 28 1910
SAC & FOX AGENCY,
OKLAHOMA.

> Cushing Ok
> Oct 25, 1910

Mr. Kohlenberg
> Dear Agent

I guess you have heard of my Terrible Loss. Julia Brown, my wife Died Oct 20-at 5-3 ad was buried at Avory Cemetry on the 21- she left me a Girl Baby born Oct 19 – I named hur after hur mother she was such a Dear Girl to me.. I have the other children with me. were keeping home by our selves..

> Yours Truly
> G. T. Brown

Sac & Fox – Shawnee
1853-1933 Volume X

The German American Trust Co.
Denver, Colorado

RECEIVED NOV 16 1910
SAC & FOX AGENCY,
OKLAHOMA.

Nov- 12<u>th</u> 1910

W. C. Kohlenberg
   Sac & Fox – Okla.
Dear Sir:-
   I've been expecting a letter from you for some time – with the possible information that you had heard from the Department.
   How about it?
   The news of the death of my sister.
   [Illegible] me – something awful – poor girl – hard work and a b<u>ig</u> family – finished her too soon- One just must ad<u>just</u> ourself to these things although it is hard. When I think of the others who have gone in our family.
   The weather is simply id<u>eal</u>. the Sun is really too warm – at mid-day- for comfort - at this season. Trusting you are well, and will let me hear from you soon. I am
                Most truly –
                Fannie Banister

2651 Vine St
   Denver, Colo.

Sac & Fox – Shawnee
1853-1933   Volume X

Funeral Notice

JOSEPH ANTHONY LANGER
Son of A. J. and CLARA LANGER

Born at Humphrey, Neb., on Jan. 18, 1904; came to Oklahoma, with parents, in 1905; died in Davenport at 9 p. m., Dec. 4, 1910. Lingered in late illness three weeks.

SERVICES
Funeral Services will be held at the family residence in Davenport, Okla., Wednesday, Dec. 7, 1910, at 2 p. m. Father Trienekens officiating

Burial will be at the Davenport Cemetery

[NOTE: The following had written "Deaths in my territory" but no name was given. The paper was badly damaged and some writing was difficult to read.]

Martha Mack	died	Aug 15 – 1911
She pah tho quah		July 23 – 1910
baby girl of She pah tho quah		July 16 – 1911
Stella Blue coat		Oct 7 – 1911
[bab]y girl of Frank Spybuck		Oct 2 – 1911
[Illegible] com e pit		Oct 11 -1911
[An]geline Whipple		Nov – 1911
[Illegible] che pease		Jan 20 – 1912
[Illegible] of cha po che pease		Jan - 1912
[Illegible] twins		Feb. 13 – 1911

Sac & Fox – Shawnee
1853-1933 Volume X

[W]hite Brown   Jan 18 – 1911
[Illegible] lde   Mar 17 – 1912
[Illegible]   Oct – 1911
[Remaining paper with names and dates completely gone]

Topeka, Kansas.
March 13, 1911.

Supt. F. A. Thackery,
    Shawnee, Okla.

Dear Sir:

Has my lease been approved of? The reason I am anxious to know is my mother Mrs. Louisa Hartman, who wrote to you recently, is dead. She died March 1, 1911 & I would like to get the money in order to help pay the funeral expenses & then bills which we have to meet.
Hoping to hear from you soon I am,
                Yours respectfully,
                    Lizzie Hartman
                    506 Lawrence St.
                    Topeka,
                    Ks.

[The letter below typed as given]

Stark Okla
Aug 23 – 1911

Hon W.C. Kohlenberg
    Dear Sot
I was asked to inform the Indian Office of the correct Date of my childs Herbert Longshore Death the correct Date is April 22 – 1911
                Very Resp

                Annie Longshore

Sac & Fox – Shawnee
1853-1933   Volume X

STATEMENT OF ACCOUNT

STROUD, OKLA. Aug. 23/'11. 191

W. C. Kohlenberg

Sac and Fox, Okla.

RECEIVED
AUG 24 1911

In Account With   SAC & FOX AGENCY, OKLAHOMA.

S. E. JONDAHL

FURNITURE AND UNDER-TAKING

DAY PHONE NO. 8
NIGHT, NO. 7

To Casket.	Carl Ward,	25.00
" "	Amos Blacks wife.	40.00
		$65.00

Please send me check for the above if you can. as we have some large bills to pay the 25th. and collections are poor.

Respectfully,
F. N. Jondahl.

Sac & Fox – Shawnee
1853-1933 Volume X

DEPARTMENT OF THE INTERIOR
UNITED STATES INDIAN SERVICE

RECEIVED SEP 23 1911 SAC & FOX AGENCY, OKLAHOMA.

Kickapoo Training School.

Horton, Kans. 9-20-11.

Supt. W. C. Kolhenburg[sic],
    Sac & Fox Agcy.,
        Stroud, Okla.

Dear Sir:-

    I have to report that Victor Neal, ne[sic] your people is dead. After his money was transfered[sic] to this office by you I gave Victor a check for $25.00 to fit him out in new clothes. He took the train at Horton, Kansas September 14th, after cashing his check, and went to St. Joseph, Mo., where he filled up on bad whiskey and lay around drunk Friday and Saturday the 15th and 16th. About 9 P.M. Saturday the 16th, he was run over by switch engine on the Burlington R.Ry., track which cut off one are and one leg. He was moved to the St. Joseph Hospital where he died Sunday morning the 17th of September about 5 o'clock.

    I was called up by telephone Sunday evening by the undertaker, who had the body, informing me of the Indian's death and asked what should be done with the body. The Indian's idenity[sic] was not know any further than that he came from Horton and had been in the costody[sic] of the police on several previous occasions. He gave his name as "Neil Reichter". I went over to St. Joseph to try and identify the body which I found to be that of Victor Neal. After confering[sic] with W. C. Margrave, a Sac and Fox Indian, I had the body of Victor enbalmed[sic] and buried in Mt. Auburn Cemetery, at St. Joseph Mo., which took place Friday Tuesday[sic] September 19th. The body can easily be moved if Victor's people want it moved.

    I will send you a copy of the coroner's verdict after the case has been disposed of. The coroner's jury meets in St. Joseph September

22nd. I will be present and will inform you of any other facts concerning Victor's death that may be brought out at the hearing.

Very respectfully,
Edwin Minor
Supt. & Spl. Disb. Agt.

EM-JLS.

DEPARTMENT OF THE INTERIOR

UNITED STATES INDIAN SERVICE

Seneca School, Quapaw Agency,
Wyandotte, Oklahoma.
December 5, 1911.

Supt. J. A. Buntin,
   Shawnee Indian Agency,
      Shawnee, Oklahoma.

Sir:

    I am writing you in regard to the Joseph Sacto, who I understand was allotted in the Pottawatomie Reservation, under your superintendency.

    At the time of his death he was married to a Quapaw Indian woman of this superintendency, whom he left surviving him, together with a daughter, Marie Sacto, now about 7 years of age. Mrs. Sacto reports to me that she was informed by her husband that he had an allotment of 80 acres with the Pottawatomies of Shawnee Indian Agency. She further informed me that she had never received any benefits from this land since her husband's death.

    The said Joe Sacto was killed by railroad train January 12, 1907, near Quapaw, Oklahoma, located within this Agency.

    Any information you can give me, will be gladly appreciated, as I am anxious to assist this woman in obtaining her rights.

Very respectfully,
Ira C. Deaver
Superintendent.

Sac & Fox – Shawnee
1853-1933 Volume X

DEPARTMENT OF THE INTERIOR
UNITED STATES INDIAN SERVICE

RECEIVED
DEC 14 1911
SAC & FOX AGENCY,
OKLAHOMA.

SHAWNEE INDIAN AGENCY,

Shawnee, Oklahoma
December 11, 1911.

Supt. W. C. Kohlenberg,
    Sac and Fox Indian Agency,
        R. R. #2, Stroud, Oklahoma.

Dear Sir:

    I have your letter of December 2, 1911, making inquiry relative to the age, date of death, names of children, their ages and if dead, date of death, of Bill Smith (Kaw-kaw-tos), a deceased Kickapoo Indian under this agency, and in reply you are advised that the majority of the Indians here are not well informed as to the date of death of Bill Smith but state that Ke-the-quah, his mother, will know who now resides under your agency.

    Bill Smith died near the Sac and Fox Agency about ten years ago, at the age of twenty years. He is said to have never been married nor had he any children by any woman.

    If there is anything further we can do call on us,

        Very respectfully,

        J.A. Buntin
RS   Superintendent.

DEATHS

[Key:] No., Name., Age., Sex., Date. Name of Living Relative., Relation., Tribe.

243, Samuel Johnson, 63, M., 2-2-1911, Emily Johnson, Wife, Sac & Fox.
244, Benjamin Hallowell, 58, M., 2-7-1911, Lizzie Hallowell, ", Iowa.
((245, Carl Ward, 16, M., 12-31-1910, Cora Ward, Mother, Sac & Fox.))
246, Mary Black, 34, F., 2-24-1911 , Amos Black, Husband,   "

Sac & Fox – Shawnee
1853-1933 Volume X

247, Clifford E. Labelle, 2, M., 3-2-1911, Linda Labelle, Mother, "
248, Bion Sullivan, 6, M., 4-19-1911, Maggie Parkinson Harris, Gr-Mother, "
249, Guy Garfield Henley[sic], 7d, M., 1-4-1911, Minnie Rider Hensley, Mother, "
250, Charley Howard Small, 20, M., 5-24-1911, Jac Small Lincoln, Half brother, Iowa.
P.S. Carl Ward died 12-31-1911 but no[sic] knowing if this was noted in your last report I give his death here.

V.P.M.

Perkins Okla Feb 17 1912

Mr. W.C. Kohlenberg   Sir

Mr. Joe Ambler Died 8 day of Feb. and we want and got Mr. Tom Fowey to stand good for the coffin at Perkins it cost $35^{\underline{00}}$ thirty five Dol and Joe Ambler widow want it paid out of his lease money and Mr. Tom Fowey want me to write to you about it so you can let Mr Towey know how you can do that

This is all from

Joe Springer

RECEIVED
FEB 19 1912
SAC & FOX AGENCY,
OKLAHOMA.

DEPARTMENT OF THE INTERIOR

UNITED STATES INDIAN SERVICE

Kaw Training School,

Washunga, Okla., April 2, 1912.

J.A. Buntin, Supt.,
    Shawnee Indian Agency,
        Shawnee, Oklahoma.

Dear Sir:

In reply to your letter of March 29, 1912, permit me to report that Mary Pappan died about 3 years ago, leaving a husband, Joseph Pappan, and the following named issue:-Isaac Pappan, Sophia Pappan, Steve Pappan and Ruby Pappan.

Very respectfully,

[Name Illegible]
Supt. & Spl. Disb. Agent.

Sac & Fox – Shawnee
1853-1933 Volume X

[The letter below typed as given]

    Shawnee Okla
    June 10 1912
    Mr. Buntin
We thought we would ask your advice in the case of Angline Whiple of Tah- ing can of her a have been taking care of her from Sep 13 up to her death is 9 day of Dec a cook for her an wash her for she was up and down most of her time
she send for me at Sacred Heart said she was sick an no boby to take care of her when i got there she was sick in Bed
that was in the year of 1910 about Sep 13 the same year she was sick most of the time
in May she taking sick an kept getting worse all the time we board her from May untill she died she taking the Bed in Sept 1911 about the twenty 20 day of Sept an stayed in Bed on tell she died 9th day of Dec
        Joel [Illegible]
Letter left by Mrs Steve [Illegible]

    Norman, Okla.
    July 26, 1912.
Mr. J.A. Buntin,
    Shawnee, Okla.

Dear sir:-
    I let you know that my father died yesterday morning at 8.15 a.m. July 25, 1912. and you don't know how I feel over my father Mr. Snake Man, here today I have no father now and I am going to ask you if I can stay or I will go back to my work sometime with my wife's work, and I am not feeling well any how just over death of my father I guess or feeling crying some time I tell you Mr. Buntin my father his a best man down here among these Indians
Thompson Alford knows my father well please let him know death of my father. I have been here at my father's place ever since I left at office and my wife she's over to her mothers six miles east from my father's place please meet my request Mr. Buntin. to stay little longer on account of my father's death just mother living now. my wife was to go home three weeks the day she left at school, and I

Sac & Fox – Shawnee
1853-1933   Volume X

like to stay that long too on account of my father's death   my mother she like for me to stay that and she told me to tell you to send her check 25^{\underline{00}}$ Mary Coffee Pot and Lizzie Coffee Pot 25^{\underline{00}}$ their address is
         Norman, Okla
         c/o Albert Snake
         R.F.D. 7
please let me hear from you friend in regard to staying little longer
        Very Respt.
        Jno. E. Snake
        Norman, Okla
        c/o Frank Spybuck
        R.F.D. #6.

[Copy of original Death Certificate]

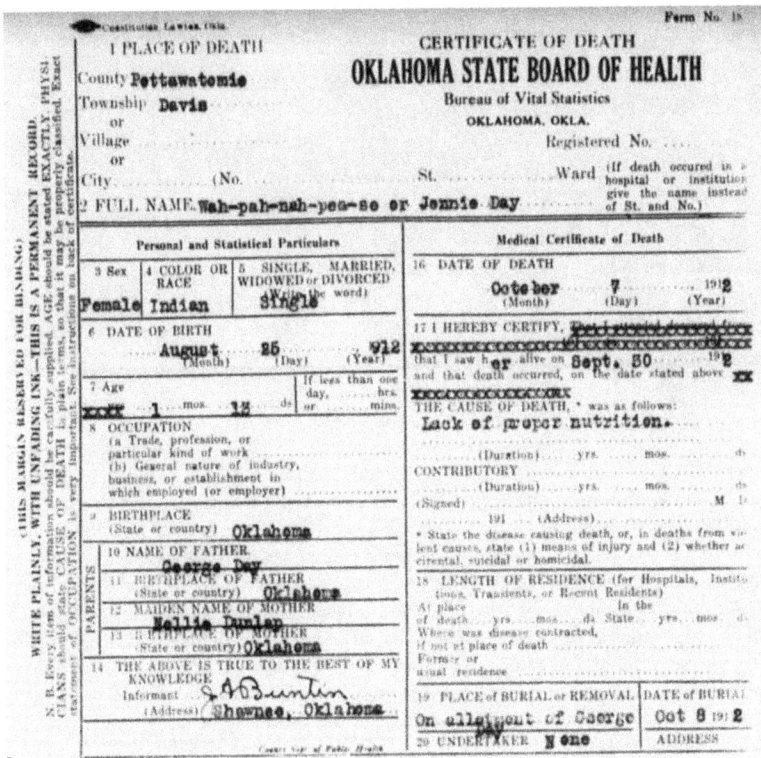

Sac & Fox – Shawnee
1853-1933   Volume X

****

[Transcription of Death Certificate on page 55]

CERTIFICATE OF DEATH
OKLAHOMA STATE BOARD OF HEALTH
Bureau of Vital Statistics
Oklahoma, Okla.

PLACE OF DEATH:
    Pottawatomie County
    Davis Township
FULL NAME: Wah-pah-nah-pea-se or Jennie Day
    Female – Indian – Single
DATE OF BIRTH: August 25, 1912
AGE: 1 mo 13 da
BIRTHPLACE: Oklahoma
NAME OF FATHER: George Day
BIRTHPLACE OF FATHER: Oklahoma
MAIDEN NAME OF MOTHER: Nellie Dunlap
BIRTHPLACE OF MOTHER: Oklahoma

INFORMANT: J.A. Buntin Shawnee, Oklahoma

DATE OF DEATH: October 7, 1912
CAUSE OF DEATH: Lack of proper nutrition
PLACE OF BURIAL or REMOVAL: On allotment of George Day
DATE OF BURIAL: Oct. 8, 1912

SENATE BILL NO. 188

Section 2. The State Commissioner of Health shall have power to make and enforce any and all needful rules and regulations for the prevention and cure and to prevent the spread of any contagious, infectious or malarial diseases among persons. Tto[sic] establish quarantine and isolate any persons affected with contagious and infectious diseases. To remove or cause to be removed any dead, decaying or putrid body, or any decayed, putrid or other substance that may endanger the health of persons or domestic animals, to condemn or cause to be destroyed any impure or diseased article of food that may be offered for sale. To superintend the several boards of health in the counties, cities, villages, towns and townships. To establish rules and regulations for the keeping and reporting of all vital statistics, births, deaths, marriages and divorces, as prescribed by this Act.

    Section 24.   It shall be the duty of all physicians practicing in each county in this state to within thirty days report to the County Superintendent of Public Health all

Sac & Fox – Shawnee
1853-1933 Volume X

births and deaths, and the disease with which said person died and the age and sex, which said report shall be verified by affidavit of the said physician, and for each and every such report shall receive as compensation therefore the sum of ten cents, to be paid from the contingent fund of such county. It shall be the duty of the Clerk of the District Court to report to the State Board of Health the record of all divorces had in said court upon the close of the term of which said divorce was granted. The said County Superintendent of Public Health shall be required to transmit the report of the births and deaths reported to him by physicians to the State Board of Health as often as said board may require.

Section 28. Any physician who makes or causes to be made a false certificate of death, or who makes any false statement in a certificate of death made by him, upon the body of a deceased person, shall be deemed guilty of a misdemeanor and shall upon conviction thereof be punished by a fine in the sum of one hundred dollars and ninety days in jail.

SPECIAL NOTICE.

Information called for in this blank must be furnished as provided. Attention is called to the instructions found on the margin. Also to hospital, institutions and transient or recent residents.

J. C. MAHR,
State Commissioner of Health

Cushing, Okla
Dec 23 1912

Mr. Horace J. Johnson
  Sir
    This is to certify that the baby of Martha Baker and Jim Scott Jr died Dec. 18, 1912
      Very Respt
        Arza B. Collins
          Addl. Farmer

Mr. M. Enter on Roll

Sac & Fox – Shawnee
1853-1933   Volume X

THE WESTERN UNION TELEGRAPH COMPANY.
INCORPORATED
25,000 OFFICES IN AMERICA.   **CABLE SERVICE TO ALL THE WORLD.**

This Company **TRANSMITS** and **DELIVERS** messages only on conditions limiting its liability, which have been assented to by the sender of the following message. Errors can be guarded against only by repeating a message back to the sending station for comparison, and the Company will not hold itself liable for errors or delays in transmission or delivery of **Unrepeated Messages**, beyond the amount of tolls paid thereon, nor in any case where the claim is not presented in writing within sixty days after the message is filed with the Company for transmission.
This is an **UNREPEATED MESSAGE**, and is delivered by request of the sender, under the conditions named above.

THEO. N. VAIL, PRESIDENT   **BELVIDERE BROOKS,** GENERAL MANAGER

RECEIVED AT   T 124   T 24   KM LB   GB   FILED 140 PM   19 PAID

WYANDOTTE, OKLA. DEC 25 1912

MR. BUNTIN,

    SHAWNEE INDIAN SCHOOL

        SHAWNEE, OKLA.

WILL ARRIVE AT R I DEPOT   WITH SONS BODY FRIDAY TWENTY
SEVENTH TEN AM PLEASE   MEET US WITH CARRIAGE

        W. P. HAWORTH

        441 PM.

****

THE WESTERN UNION TELEGRAPH COMPANY.
INCORPORATED
25,000 OFFICES IN AMERICA.   **CABLE SERVICE TO ALL THE WORLD.**

This Company **TRANSMITS** and **DELIVERS** messages only on conditions limiting its liability, which have been assented to by the sender of the following message. Errors can be guarded against only by repeating a message back to the sending station for comparison, and the Company will not hold itself liable for errors or delays in transmission or delivery of **Unrepeated Messages**, beyond the amount of tolls paid thereon, nor in any case where the claim is not presented in writing within sixty days after the message is filed with the Company for transmission.
This is an **UNREPEATED MESSAGE**, and is delivered by request of the sender, under the conditions named above.

THEO. N. VAIL, PRESIDENT   **BELVIDERE BROOKS,** GENERAL MANAGER

RECEIVED AT   T 3   KM LB   GB   FILED 8 20 PM   10 PAID

WYANDOTTE, OKLA. DEC 25 1912

MR. BUNTIN,

    INDIAN SCHOOL

        SHAWNEE, OKLA.

WILL ARRIVE ELEVEN TWENTY OVER   ROCK ISLAND INSTEAD OF TEN

        W. P. HAWORTH

        807 AM

Sac & Fox – Shawnee
1853-1933 Volume X

DEPARTMENT OF THE INTERIOR

UNITED STATES INDIAN SERVICE

Otoe Agency, Otoe, Okla., March 13, 1913.

Supt. H. J. Johnson,
 Sac & Fox Agency,
  Okla.

Dear Sir:-

 Will you kindly advise me as to the date of the death of Elwood a deceased allottee of your reservation who died in or about the year 1900 and also who are his heirs according to your records. If Mary Grant McGlaslin and Vestina Grant are not shown as his heirs and he was divorced from the said Mary Grant McGlaslin, please give me data bearing thereon, & oblige.

        Very respectfully,
        Ralph P. Stanion
        Supt. & S.D.A.

    ****

Heirship of
Elwood.

    Sac and Fox Indian Agency,
    Stroud, Okla., Mar. 17, 1913.

Supt. Ralph P. Stanion,
 Otoe Agency,
  Otoe, Oklahoma.

Dear Sir:-

 Referring to your letter of the 13th instant, concerning Elwood whom you say was a deceased allottee of this Reservation, I have to advise that we have no allottee by this name, neither can I find any one connected with Mary Grant McGlaslin and Vestina Grant who was known as Elwood. If you can give me any other names by which this person was known perhaps I can get the information concerning him which you desire.

 Regretting that I am unable to assist you in this matter, I am

Sac & Fox – Shawnee
1853-1933   Volume X

Very respectfully,

Supt. & S. D. A.

HJJ/CP

[Copy of original Death Certificate]

CERTIFICATE OF DEATH
OKLAHOMA STATE BOARD OF HEALTH
Bureau of Vital Statistics
OKLAHOMA, OKLA.

Form No. 1

1 PLACE OF DEATH
County: Pottawatomie
Township or Village: McLoud
City: .... (No. .... St. .... Ward)
Registered No. ....
(If death occurred in hospital or institution give the name instead of St. and No.)

2 FULL NAME: Jessie Jaunita Muchennene

Personal and Statistical Particulars

3 Sex: Female
4 COLOR OR RACE: Indian
5 SINGLE, MARRIED, WIDOWED or DIVORCED (Write the word): ....

6 DATE OF BIRTH: July 25 1914
(Month) (Day) (Year)

7 Age: .... yrs. 2 mos. 8 ds.
If less than one day, ... hrs. or .... mins.

8 OCCUPATION
(a) Trade, profession, or particular kind of work ....
(b) General nature of industry, business, or establishment in which employed (or employer) ....

9 BIRTHPLACE (State or country): Pottawatomie

10 NAME OF FATHER: Muchenenne

11 BIRTHPLACE OF FATHER (State or country): ....

12 MAIDEN NAME OF MOTHER: Wah-tws-ah-quah

13 BIRTHPLACE OF MOTHER (State or country): ....

14 THE ABOVE IS TRUE TO THE BEST OF MY KNOWLEDGE
Informant: Nellie G. Cdle
(Address): Shawnee, Oklahoma

Medical Certificate of Death

16 DATE OF DEATH: October 3 1914
(Month) (Day) (Year)

17 I HEREBY CERTIFY, That I attended deceased from .... 191 .... to .... 191 ....
that I saw h........ alive on .... 191 ....
and that death occurred, on the date stated above at .... m

THE CAUSE OF DEATH, was as follows:
....
.... (Duration) .... yrs. .... mos. .... ds
CONTRIBUTORY
.... (Duration) .... yrs. .... mos. .... ds
(Signed) .... M.D.
.... 191 ... (Address) ....

* State the disease causing death, or, in deaths from violent causes, state (1) means of injury and (2) whether accidental, suicidal or homicidal.

18 LENGTH OF RESIDENCE (for Hospitals, Institutions, Transients, or Recent Residents)
At place .... In the
death .... yrs. .... mos. .... ds. State .... yrs. .... mos. .... ds.
Where was disease contracted, if not at place of death ....
Former or usual residence ....

19 PLACE of BURIAL or REMOVAL | DATE of BURIAL
.... | Oct 4th 1914

20 UNDERTAKER | ADDRESS

****

Sac & Fox – Shawnee
1853-1933   Volume X

[Transcription of Death Certificate on page 60]

CERTIFICATE OF DEATH
OKLAHOMA STATE BOARD OF HEALTH
Bureau of Vital Statistics
Oklahoma, Okla.

PLACE OF DEATH:
Pottawatomie County
McLoud Village
FULL NAME: Jessie Jaunita Muchennene
Female – Indian
DATE OF BIRTH: July 25, 1914
AGE: 2 mos [??] da
BIRTHPLACE: Pottawatomie
NAME OF FATHER: Muchenenne
MAIDEN NAME OF MOTHER: Mah twa ah quah

INFORMANT: Nellie G. Odle, Shawnee, Oklahoma

DATE OF DEATH: October 3, 1914
DATE OF BURIAL: Oct. 4th 1914

Sac and Fox Indian School,
Stroud, Okla. Dec. 16th, 1915.

Mr. Arza B. Collins,
    Cushing, Okla.

Dear Sir:-
    Please ascertain the date of the death of Hiram Starr, and report to this office at as early date as practicable,

Very respectfully,
Horace J Johnson
Supt. & S.D.A.

BEK.

Sac & Fox – Shawnee
1853-1933 Volume X

Death of
Caroline Pickett.

Shawnee Oklahoma,
March 31st, 1916.

Horace J. Johnson, Supt.
  Sac and Fox Indian School,
    Stroud, Oklahoma.

Sir:-

    I wish to report that Cariline[sic] Pickett died on the 28th of this month at the home of Jackson Wakole where she has been sick for some time. And as instructed by you over the telephone I seen that she was given as decent a burial as circumstances would permit.

    I am also enclosing a bill from F.S. Irvine of Prague Okla, for the sum of $60.00 to pay for the casket purchased from him for the deceased which should be given early attention.

    I wish also to state that Caroline was paying Ester Wakole the sum of $20.0 per month for her care and keep, and the attention that this woman was giving her, and was paying same out of her monthly allowance, and I would respectfully ask that if it could be done that the sum of $20.00 be paid to this woman for the last months care she gave this woman.

                  Very Respectfully,
                    U.S. Farmer.

DEPARTMENT OF THE INTERIOR
UNITED STATES INDIAN SERVICE
Cushing, Okla.

RECEIVED
MAY 15 1916
SAC AND FOX INDIAN SCHOOL, OKLA.

May 13, 1916.

Mr. Horace J. Johnson,
  Dear Sir:

Sac & Fox – Shawnee
1853-1933   Volume X

Inclosed find list of those who Died recently, with Smallpox and other diseases.

Grace Lee, March 22, 1916.

Nona Grant died April 6, 1916.

Isaac Givens died April 8, 1916.

Jessie Smith, died April 9, 1916.

Clifford Wyman, died April 9, 1916.

Ollive Givens, died April 13, 1916.

Caroline Grant. died April 17, 1916.

Pearl Smit, died April 18, 1916.

Stella Grant. died April 24, 1916.

U.S. Grant, died April 24, 1916.

John Givens died April 26, 1916.

Clarence Logan, died April 26, 1916.

Walter Samuel ~~Emmerson~~ Falls died April 26, 1916.

Henry Appletree, died April 29, 1916.

Marie Appletree, died May 8, 1916.

Hopeing[sic] *this is a satisfactory report relative to deaths with Smallpox I am*

Very Respectfully,

.....Arza B. Collins........

Circular
No. 1096.

Sac and Fox Indian School,
Stroud, Okla. Sept. 30, 1916.

Commissioner Indian Affairs,
Washington, D. C.

Sir:

Referring to the above noted Circular, my reply thereto dated May 18, 1916, and Office letter dated June 9, 1816, and in compliance

Sac & Fox – Shawnee
1853-1933   Volume X

with instructions contained in the last noted letter. I have the honor to report that we continued our work along the lines indicated in my letter of May 18, 1916 with, I believe, fairly good results. I can best definitely report on results by asking the attention of the Office to the statistical report for the fiscal year 1916.

On page 4 thereof it will be noted that eight infants under the age of three years, died during the fiscal year and six of these were chargeable to the small-pox epidemic which we had on the reservation during the Spring. This leaves only two deaths of infants under three years of age chargeable to normal conditions. Our census roll prepared June 30, 1915, shows therein names of thirty-three children under three years of age. This would show a death rate under normal conditions of something slightly over six per-cent of children under three years of age which Supervisor Newborne said was very good.

Very respectfully,

Supt. & S. D. A.

HJJ-FAP

Department of the Interior
United States Indian Service

RECEIVED
APR 3 1917
SAC AND FOX INDIAN SCHOOL, OKLA.

Cushing, Okla.
April 2, 1917.

Mr. Horace J. Johnson,
　　Stroud Okla.
　　　　Dear Sir.
Inclosed find report of the Deaths which possibly have not been reported.
　　Grace Lee wife of Frank Smith died Mar. 22, 1916.
　　Stella Grant, died in April. ………….. 1916.
　　Sarah Bigwalker died in May some time. 1916.
　　Rachel Pate died July 2, 1916.
　　Benjamin Butler son of George and Edith Butler died Sept. 27, 1916.
　　Daniel Franklin Son of Harding and Minnie Franklin died Dec. 27, 1916.

Sac & Fox – Shawnee
1853-1933   Volume X

Fred Butler son of Edward and Ida Butler died Jan. 21, 1917.

Very Respectfully,

Arza B. Collins

DEPARTMENT OF THE INTERIOR
UNITED STATES INDIAN SERVICE
MEMORANDUM

THE UNITED STATES
To   Sac and Fox Trading Co.
         Stroud, Oklahoma.   10/31/18

Agency

Date of Delivery	Contents of Packages	Quantity	Unit	Amount
10/31	Coffin	1	No.	20.00
"	Pine Box	1	No.	5.00
				25.00

Letter B and
No. 4 – 6 of the methods of purchase.
Delivered at   Sac & Fox Ag'cy, Okla.
Approver for $ 25.00

Inspected 10/31/18

REFER IN REPLY TO THE FOLLOWING: ADDRESS ONLY THE
Ed-Health   COMMISSIONER OF INDIAN AFFAIRS
   N

DEPARTMENT OF THE INTERIOR,
OFFICE OF INDIAN AFFAIRS,
WASHINGTON,

11-22-18
Sac & Fox Indian School,
Stroud, Oklahoma.

NOV 19 1918

Mr. Horace J. Johnson,
   Supt., Sac and Fox Agency.

My dear Mr. Johnson:

Your request for allotment, November 8, 1918:

Your attention is invited to circular 1483, dated November 9, 1918,

Sac & Fox – Shawnee
1853-1933   Volume X

You may send in the bill for burying Julia Jones in the form of a claim to be liquidated when there are funds.

Very truly yours,

EB Meritt
Assistant Commissioner.

11-FL-14

****

Ed-Health
N

Sac and Fox Indian School,
Stroud, Oklahoma, Nov. 23. 1918

Commissioner of Indian Affairs.
Washington, D. C.

Sir:

I have the honor to acknowledge receipt of above noted communication, dated Nov. 19, 1918, and to furnish herewith claim for burial expenses of Julia Jones as requested.

Very respectfully,

Supt. & S.D.A.

HJJ/JD

Encl:Claim

****

REFER IN REPLY TO THE FOLLOWING:
Ed-Health
N
94878-18

DEPARTMENT OF THE INTERIOR,   12-14-18
OFFICE OF INDIAN AFFAIRS,
WASHINGTON,   DEC 11 1918

ADDRESS ONLY THE
COMMISSIONER OF INDIAN AFFAIRS

Mr. Horace J. Johnson,
Supt. Sac and Fox Agency.

My dear Mr. Johnson:

In connection with the claim for the burial expenses of Julia Jones, you are requested to forward a certificate that she was an Indian, giving such proof as will satisfy the Auditor

Sac & Fox – Shawnee
1853-1933 Volume X

for the Interior Department when the account goes to his office.

Very truly yours,

EB Meritt
Assistant Commissioner.

12-MLJ-9

****

Sac and Fox Indian School,
Stroud, Oklahoma, March 1st, 1919.

Mr. Carl F. Mayer, Supt.,
Seneca Indian Agency,
Wyandotte, Oklahoma.

Dear Mr. Mayer:

Julia Jones, wife of Henry Jones, an Indian who belongs under your jurisdiction died last December. It was necessary for us to pay her burial expenses, which amounted to $25.00. The Office requests that I give such proof as will satisfy the Auditor that she was an Indian. I can make up a certificate to that affect, but thought it would be better to have you do so if one was enrolled there. I can't tell from what Henry says whether she was or not, but believe she was, and if you will furnish me with a certificate to that effect, I shall be very much obliged.

Very respectfully,

Supt. & S. D. A.

HJJ/JD

****

Sac & Fox – Shawnee
1853-1933   Volume X

File 1145.

DEPARTMENT OF THE INTERIOR
UNITED STATES INDIAN SERVICE
Quapaw Indian Agency,
Wyandotte, Okla.
March 21, 1919.

RECEIVED
MAR 24 1919
SAC AND FOX INDIAN SCHOOL, OKLA.

Sup't. Horace J. Johnson,
Sac and Fox Indian School.
Stroud, Oklahoma.

Dear Mr. Johnson:

Replying to your letter of March 1st, 1919 regarding degree of blood of Julia Jones Dec'd wife of Henry Jones Ottawa Allottee No.1 of this Reservation. I have to advise that I am unable to find any record showing that this woman was ever allotted on this reservation. However, throught[sic] the correspondence in connection with the sale of land allotted to Henry Johnes[sic] I find Julia referred to as a mixed Blood Indian. If you will talk to Henry further and find out what Julia's name was prior to her marriage and advise me I will be glad to look further into the matter.

Yours very truly,

Carl F. Mayer
Superintendent.

GAR:WM.

****

Sac and Fox Indian School,
Stroud, Oklahoma, April 19, 1919.

Mr. A. R. Snyder, Supt.,
Potawotami[sic] Indian Agency,
Mayetta, Kansas.

Dear Mr. Snyder:

Julia Jones, wife of Henry Jones, and Ottawa allottee at the Quapaw Indian Agency, died some time ago, and it was necessary for us to bury her at Government expense.

Sac & Fox – Shawnee
1853-1933   Volume X

The Office has asked for a certificate that she was an Indian, giving such proof as will satisfy the Auditor for the Interior Department when this account goes to his office. Her husband, Henry, advises me that she was allotted under your jurisdiction, and if so, I should be obliged if you will furnish me with a certificate to that effect

Very respectfully,

Supt. & S.D.A.

HJJ/JD

****

Sac and Fox Indian School,
Stroud, Oklahoma, June 12, 1919.

Mr. A. R. Snyder, Supt.,
Potawatomi Indian Agency,
Mayetta, Kansas.

Dear Mr. Snyder:

Referring to your letter of May 26, and my letter of April 19 in which I asked for information concerning Julia Jones, I have finally secured the information that she was allotted under the name of Julia Davis near Ottowa[sic], Kansas, I believe. My informant said something about Chippewa Ridge, but this place is something I know nothing about. If you find she was allotted there, please furnish me with a certificate to that effect.

Very respectfully,

Supt. & S.D.A.

HJJ/JD

Mr. Deaver

Please take care of this claim. Letter in other lot from Snyder in answer to above

[Illegible]

****

Sac & Fox – Shawnee
1853-1933   Volume X

Department of the Interior

United States Indian Service

Potawatomi Agency,
Mayetta, Kansas,
May 26, 1919.

Supt. Horace J. Johnson,
   Stroud, Oklahoma.

Dear Mr. Johnson:

      This will acknowledge receipt of your letters of date April 19, 1919, and May 19, 1919, requesting a certificate showing that Julia Jones was an Indian, etc.

      You are advised that I have delayed answering your letter of April 19th and I have made an extended search of our files to find the name of Julia Jones, also have looked over all of the old Munsie and Nemaha files but failed to find any trace of this woman. I have also made inquiry here and no one seems to be able to identify this name. In your letter of April 19th, you state that "Julia Jones, wife of Henry Jones, an Ottawa allottee at the Qua-paw Indian Agency, died some time ago, etc." If Julia Jones is allotted here it is under some other name and I would suggest that you ascertain whether or not she had an Indian name and I will make a search of our records.

      I am sorry that I have delayed this matter so long for you, but I have made every effort to get the information you requested.

      Very truly yours,

      A. R. Snyder
ARS:MBS   Supt. & Sp'l. Disb. Agt.

****

Sac and Fox Indian School,
Stroud, Oklahoma, May 19, 1919.

Mr. A. R. Snyder, Supt.,
Potawotami[sic] Indian Agency,
   Mayetta, Kansas.

Dear Mr. Snyder:

Sac & Fox – Shawnee
1853-1933   Volume X

On April 14 I wrote you concerning Julia Jones, wife of Henry Jones, an Ottawa allottee at the Quapaw Agency, Oklahoma, asking that you would if possible furnish me with a certificate showing that she was an Indian, and giving such proof as would satisfy the Auditor to that effect, when the claim for burial expense for her was presented to him.

Very respectfully,

Supt. & S.D.A.

HHJ/JD

---

enrollment of
Sha-ma-ka
Wasekuk[sic].

Sac and Fox Indian School,
Stroud, Oklahoma, Nov. 23, 1918

Dr. R. L. Russell, Supt.
 Sac and Fox Sanatorium,
  Toledo, Iowa.

Sir:
In reply to your letter of Nov. 19, will say that advise that this child died in October is correct, but I have not as yet been able to ascertain the exact date in October.

Very respectfully,

Supt. & S.D.A.

JD

****

Sac and Fox Indian School,
Stroud, Oklahoma, Dec. 3, 1918.

R. L. Russell, Supt.
 Sac and Fox Sanatarium[sic],
  Toledo, Iowa.

Sac & Fox – Shawnee
1853-1933   Volume X

Dear Dr. Russell:

In reply to your inquiry concerning the date of death of the baby of Waseskuk, Sha-ma-ka by name, I have to advise that our information is that this child died Oct. 13, 1918.

Very Respectfully,

MJ.   Superintendent.

Death
Certificates
February   Sac and Fox Indian School,
                            Stroud, Oklahoma, March 10, 1919.

The Commissioner of Indian Affairs,
    Washington, D. C.

Sir:

There are forwarded, herewith, the following death certificates pertaining to the jurisdiction of <u>Sac & Fox, Okla.</u>

Current Certificates

Number of Certificates forwarded	For the month of	Year of	Serial numbers inclusive	Remarks
1	February	1919	1	

Supplemental or Corrected Certificates

Number	Month	Year	Serial Number	Annotations
None				

Delayed Certificates

Number	Month	Year	Serial Number	Annotation
None				

Very Respectfully,

MJ Encl: in duplicate.   Superintendent.

Edward Morris (Crane)

Sac & Fox – Shawnee
1853-1933   Volume X

****

March Report
of deaths.

Sac and Fox Indian School,
Stroud, Oklahoma, April 9, 1919.

The Commissioner of Indian Affairs,
Washington, D. C.

Sir:
  There are forwarded, herewith, the following death certificates pertaining to the jurisdiction of Sac and Fox, Oklahoma.

------------------------------ Current Certificates ------------------------------

Number of Certificates forwarded	for the month of	Year of	Serial numbers inclusive	Remarks
1	March	1919	1	

Supplemental or corrected certificates

Number	Month	Year	Serial Number	Annotations.
None				

Very Respectfully,

MJ encl: in dupl.   Superintendent.

****

Death Cer-
tificates
January, 1919

Sac and Fox Indian School,
Stroud, Oklahoma, April 19, 1919.

The Commissioner of Indian Affairs,
Washington, D. C.

Sir:
  There are forwarded, herewith, the following Death certificates pertaining to the jurisdiction of Sac & Fox, Okla.

------------------------------ Current Certificates ------------------------------

Number of Certificates	For the month of	Year of	Serial numbers inclusive.)	Remarks No deaths

Sac & Fox – Shawnee
1853-1933   Volume X

forwarded 0   January   1919.   0   in January.

Supplemental or corrected
Certificates

Number   Month   Year   Serial   Annotations.
0   numbers

Delayed Certificates

Number   Month   Year   Serial   Annotation
0   Numbers

Very Respectfully,

MJ   Superintendent.

****

April Report
of Deaths.

Sac and Fox Indian School,
Stroud, Oklahoma, May 15, 1919.

The Commissioner of Indian Affairs,
    Washington, D. C.

Sir:
    There are forwarded, herewith, the following Death certificates pertaining to the jurisdiction of Sac and Fox, Oklahoma.

                      Current Certificates
Number of   for the   Year   Serial   Remarks
certificates   month of   of   numbers
forwarded 3   April   1919   inclusive 1-13

Supplemental or corrected
certificates

Number   Month   Year   Serial   Annotation.
none   Numbers

74

Sac & Fox – Shawnee
1853-1933   Volume X

Very Respectfully,

MJ
   Isaac   Struble   1,
   Sophie Lincoln 2,   Supt. & S. D. A.
   Charles Grass   3.

[Copy of original Death Certificate]

STANDARD CERTIFICATE OF DEATH

1 PLACE OF DEATH
County: Lincoln   State: Oklahoma   Registered No. 2-
Township: Ponca   or Village
City: No.   St.   Ward

2 FULL NAME: Pearl Conger DeLausanne
(a) Residence: No.   Ponca Twp, Oklahoma   St.   Ward

PERSONAL AND STATISTICAL PARTICULARS   MEDICAL CERTIFICATE OF DEATH

3 SEX: Female   4 COLOR OR RACE: Indian   5 Single, Married, Widowed or Divorced: Married
16 DATE OF DEATH: May 28, 1919
I HEREBY CERTIFY, That I attended deceased from

5a If married, widowed, or divorced
HUSBAND of (or) WIFE of: Fred DeLausanne

6 DATE OF BIRTH: 10/5/95
7 AGE: 23 Years 7 Months 23 Days
The CAUSE OF DEATH was as follows:
No Physician at the time of death. Tubercular Trouble.
Also afflicted with Rheumatism

8 OCCUPATION OF DECEASED: Housewife

BIRTHPLACE: Ponca Township
NAME OF FATHER: Andrew Conger
BIRTHPLACE OF FATHER: Kansas
MAIDEN NAME OF MOTHER: Julia Conger
BIRTHPLACE OF MOTHER: Kansas

Informant: Arza " Collins
Cushing, Oklahoma

PLACE OF BURIAL: Indian Cemetery
Ponca Township
DATE OF BURIAL: May 30, 1919

****

Sac & Fox – Shawnee
1853-1933   Volume X

[Transcription of Death Certificate on page 75]

STANDARD CERTIFICATE OF DEATH

Registered No. 2

PLACE OF DEATH
    Lincoln County
    Ponca Township
    Oklahoma

FULL NAME
    Pearl Conger DeLausanne
RESIDENCE NO. Ponca Twp. Oklahoma
    Female – Indian - Married

HUSBAND
    Fred DeLausanne

DATE OF BIRTH
    10/5/95
AGE: 23 Years 7 Months 23 Days

OCCUPATION OF DECEASED
    Housewife

BIRTHPLACE
    Ponca Township

NAME OF FATHER
    Andrew Conger
BIRTHPLACE OF FATHER
    Kansas

MAIDEN NAME OF MOTHER
    Julia Conger
BIRTHPLACE OF MOTHER
    Kansas

INFORMANT
    Arza B Collins
    Cushing, Oklahoma

DATE OF DEATH
    May 28, 1919

CAUSE OF DEATH
    No Physician at the time
    of death, Tubercular Trouble,
    Also afflicted with Rheumatism
DURATION   1 year
CONTRIBUTORY
    Unknown
WHERE WAS DISEASE
CONTRACTED   Unknown
DID OPERATION PRECEDE
DEATH?   No
WAS THERE AN AUTOPSY?
    No
WHAT TEST CONFIRMED
DIAGNOSIS?   None
PLACE OF BURIAL,
CREMATION OR REMOVAL
    Indian Cemetery
    Ponca Township
DATE OF BURIAL
    May 30, 1919

Sac & Fox – Shawnee
1853-1933 Volume X

Death Reports
May 1919. Sac and Fox Indian School,
Stroud, Oklahoma, June 15, 1919.

Commissioner of Indian Affairs,
Washington, D. C.

Sir:
There are forwarded, herewith, the following death certificates pertaining to the jurisdiction of Sac & Fox Indian School, Oklahoma.

Current Certificates.

Number of Certificates forwarded	For the month of	Year of	Serial numbers inclusive.	Remarks
2	May	1919.	1-2	

Supplemental or corrected Certificates

Number	Month	Year	Serial Numbers	Annotations.
0	May			

Delayed Certificates.

Number	Month	Year	Serial Numbers	Annotations.
0				

Very Respectfully,

MJ
Encl:
Mary A. Keokuk,
Pearl Conger De Lausanne,

Superintendent.

****

Sac & Fox – Shawnee
1853-1933   Volume X

Death
certificates
June 1919.

Sac and Fox Indian School,
Stroud, Oklahoma, July 15, 1919.

Commissioner of Indian Affairs,
    Washington, D. C.

Sir:
    There are forwarded, herewith, the following Death certificates pertaining to the jurisdiction of Sac and Fox Indian School for the month of June, 1919.

---------------------------Current Certificates---------------------------------

None

Supplemental or corrected
---------------------------certificates.---------------------------------

None

Delayed Certificates

None

Very Respectfully,

MJ
                                        Special Supervisor.

Sac & Fox – Shawnee
1853-1933   Volume X

Shawnee Indian Agency
Shawnee, Oklahoma
December 9, 1921

Mrs. Eliza Panther
Tecumseh, Oklahoma
Route #2
c/o Billie Panther

Dear Madam:

In connection with the statement you sent to this office recently about the death of Rose Charley who was an heir in the John Taylor estate, you claim is your half brother, you are informed that proper record of his death has been made and filed for reference to the Examiner of Inheritance to take up when is assigned to this Agency in the future.

Very truly yours

J. L. Suffecool
Superintendent

JJ/JC

Shawnee Indian Agency,
Shawnee, Oklahoma,
Mar. 18, 1922.

Mrs. Sarah F. Starr,
1301 South First St.,
Terre Haute, Indiana.

Dear Madam:

Replying to your letter of the 12th instant in which you inquire about the address of the Kickapoo Reservation where you heard your grand mother as you claim, Mrs. Prudence Wilson, died.

You are informed that this office is the headquarters of this Tribe. Matters pertaining to these Indians are handled here.

An examination of the records shows that no one by your grandmother's names appears thereon. As nearly all of the Kickapoos are on record by their Indian names this may be true with your grandmother.

Sac & Fox – Shawnee
1853-1933   Volume X

Yours very truly,

3 od 18.
J. L. Suffecool,
Superintendent.

Shawnee Indian Agency,
Shawnee, Oklahoma,
September 23, 1922.

Dr. J. R. McLauchlin,
    Superintendent State Tub. Sanatorium,
        Clinton, Oklahoma.
Dear Dr. McLauchlin:-

　　　　This is to advise that it will not be necessary to consummate the papers in the case of John French, as Mr. French died September 22, 1922.

　　　　The blanks are enclosed and returned herewith.

Very respectfully,

J. L. Suffecool
Superintendent.

EV.
ENCLS.

Shawnee Indian Agency
Shawnee, Okla.
Aug. 20, 1923.

Mr. Fred Richmond,
    Ottawa, Kansas.
My dear sir:

　　　　Your letter of 18th at hand and in reply have to advise you that Mrs. Sarah Whistler died several years ago, but I am unable to advise you at what pace she was buried. Her daughter Gertie died in 1906, I

Sac & Fox – Shawnee
1853-1933 Volume X

believe and her son Leo is now living at Stroud, Okla. You may write him there, care of the Lynch Hotel and he can give you more information concerning his mother.

Returned herewith are you[sic] letter and card from the Indian Office.

Very truly yours,

Incls.
JLR.

J.L.Suffecool,
Superintendent.

Shawnee Indian Agency,
Shawnee, Okla.
October 4, 1923.

The Commissioner of Indian Affairs,

Washington, D.C.

Dear Mr. Commissioner:-

There are transmitted herewith the following death certificates pertaining to the jurisdiction of Shawnee Indian Agency.

CURRENT CERTIFICATES.

Number of certificates forwarded.	For the month of.	Year of.	Serial Numbers, Inclusive.	Remarks.
1	Sept.	1923.	1	

Incl.
JLR.

Very truly yours,

J. L. Suffecool,
Superintendent.

****

Sac & Fox – Shawnee
1853-1933   Volume X

Shawnee Indian Agency.

Shawnee, Oklahoma,
November 9, 1923.

The Commissioner of Indian Affairs,
Washington, D. C.

Dear Mr. Commissioner:

There are forwarded herewith the following death certificates pertaining to the jurisdiction of Shawnee Indian Agency,

Current certificates

Number of certificates forwarded.	For the month of	Year of	Serial[sic] numbers inclusive.	Remarks.
1	October	1923	1	

Very Truly Yours,

J. L. Suffecool,
Superintendent.

Incls.
AMS.

Shawnee Indian Agency.

Shawnee, Oklahoma,
November 12, 1923.

Dr. G. S. Baxter,
c/o Shawnee Clinic,
Mammoth Bldg.,
Shawnee, Oklahoma.

Dear Dr.:

In the month of November 1920 you waited on a Kansas Pottawatomie Indian in the Shawnee Hospital by the name of John Cadue or Hoke Smith Cadue who died while in the hospital. The Soldiers' Bonus

Sac & Fox – Shawnee
1853-1933 Volume X

Board is not requesting a death certificate signed by the attending Physician so I am enclosing a Certificate and requesting that you supply the sufficient information and return to me so that I may pass the same on to the proper department.

Very Truly Yours,

encl.

JLR:AMS

J. L. Suffecool,
Superintendent.

****

Shawnee Indian Agency.

Shawnee, Oklahoma,
November 30, 1923.

Mr. A. R. Snyder, Supt.,
Mayetta, Kansas.

Dear Mr. Snyder:

I am enclosing herewith, death certificate for Hoke Smith Cadue, who died from the result of Typhoid fever in the Shawnee Hospital, November 28, 1920, signed by Dr. G. S. Baxter.

Very Truly Yours,

J. L. Suffecool,
Superintendent.

JLR:AMS

Shawnee Indian Agency,
Shawnee, Oklahoma,
February 13, 1924.

Mr. Shade E. Wallen,
    Supt. Five Civilized Tribes,
        Muskogee, Oklahoma.

Dear Mr. Wallen:

Sac & Fox – Shawnee
1853-1933 Volume X

This is to advise that the baby of Mr. and Mrs. Te-ko-co-be-nay Squire died the 2d of January. The Gaskill Undertaking firm of Shawnee was engaged.

As Mr. Squire is from your jurisdiction you no doubt need this for your records.

Very truly,

J. L. Suffecool,
Suprintendent[sic].

--Mc

Shawnee Indian Agency,
Shawnee, Oklahoma.
February 27, 1924.

Mr. Orlando Johnson
   Cushing, Oklahoma.

My dear Friend:

This will acknowledge the receipt of your letter of February 25th in which you advise that on account of the death of Mrs. Milton Carter you were unable to attend the meeting last Thursday. I regret that you were not present and your absence was missed. We did not accomplish very much other than to get two or three pamphlets that some of the boys had. In fact I believe that is all that is necessary at this time. I forwarded the pamphlets to Mr. Kappler, the attorney at Washington, as he requested and he will make an examination of them and make a report. As soon as his report is received I will be glad to write you in full concerning the matter. You will be advised from time to time.

Your friend,

J. L. Suffecool,
Superintendent.

S-Mc

Sac & Fox – Shawnee
1853-1933   Volume X

                        Shawnee Indian Agency,
                        Shawnee, Oklahoma,
                        March 12, 1924.

Mr. A. R. Snyder,
  Supt. Potawatomi Agency,
    Mayetta, Kansas.

Dear Mr. Snyder:

    Replying to your letter of March 7th in which you state that Pack-to-neece died on your reservation a few years ago and who belonged under this jurisdiction you are advised that I am unable to locate any allotment or inherited interest belonging to one by the name given.

    It may be that he was known under some other name than that reported to you by Joe Turtle his nephew, who you state is making inquiry concerning the matter. If such be the same please advise me and I will look further into the matter.

                      Very truly yours,

                      J. L. Suffecool,
R/M   Superintendent.

                        Shawnee Indian Agency,
                        Shawnee, Oklahoma,
                        April 15, 1924.

The Commissioner of Indian Affairs,
Washington, D. C.

S i r:

    I am enclosing herewith a request for an allotment of $148.00 from "Relief of Distress and Prevention of Diseases, etc., among Indians" for the purpose of paying funeral expenses of Louis Bruno, Pottawatomie Indian boy who died at the Concho Indian School hospital on April 4th, and whose home was in Konawa, Oklahoma. The parents nor the child do not have funds in the office.

    The parents are almost destitute themselves and do not have much means for a livelihood. The mother of the child has an oil lease on her land which is due next winter in the amount of $92. This is an oil and gas lease on 80 acres of land and this represents all the money that they will get in the --urse[sic] of the year. In view of the family's financial circumstances I am recommending that this allotment be made for this purpose, if there are regulations permitting such. Attached hereto is statement from Mr. Thomas Benson, funeral director of El Reno, covering the price of casket and so on.

                Very truly yours,

                A. W. Leech,

R/Mc   Superintendent.

Incl.

Sac and Fox-Shawnee – CEMETERY
1875 - 1924

Sac & Fox – Shawnee
1853-1933   Volume X

August 24th 1875

Hon. J. H. Pickering
Dear Sir

I write you this letter that you may inform the Chiefs of the Sacs & Foxes that two certain graves of their distinguished men in Franklin County Kansas has been opened and the medals which were interred with them have been taken away and the bones of the deceased Chiefs have been thrown on the surface of the earth 1st grave is marked as follows with a marble slab, "Sacred to the memory of Ke o Kuck a distinguished Chief Born at Rock Island in 1788. Died in April 1848.

M. Park St Louis

The 2nd grave is marked also by a marble slab having the following inscription Sacred to the memory of Hard Fish a Sac Chief Born at Shock-o-ton in 1800. Died in 1851.

San [?]ony

About 2 months ago I returned the relics of these chiefs to their respective graves and also replaced the marble slabs to their places and would suggest that a piece of ground be purchased for the preservation of the relics of these men and should they so conclude to do so or any other plan which they might suggest I should take pleasure in preserving and secure them from insult Dear Sir a small appropriation would now preserve these slabs which I verily believe will also be stolen or taken away. Any suggestions or instructions relative to this matter will be promptly attended to by me

Yours respectfully
Edward McCoonse
Ottawa Franklin Co
Kansas

Refer in reply to the following:
LAND
32051-1904.

Department of the Interior.
OFFICE OF INDIAN AFFAIRS
Washington, May 18, 1904.

W. C. Kohlenberg, Esq.,
  Superintendent Indian School,
    Sac and Fox Agency, Nebraska.

Sir:

Sac & Fox – Shawnee
1853-1933 Volume X

Your report of May 7th is at hand. You advise that amicable arrangements can be made whereby certain Iowa Indians may obtain title to a half acre of land sold to Albert Kenworthy, this land being that conveyed by the heirs of Isaac Perry, deceased allottee, to Mr. Kenworthy, the half acre in question being used as a graveyard. You state that this half acre, with the right of entry from the section line, will cost $100, and say that the Indians are willing to pay for this burying ground out of their annuity payment, but state you think it should be paid direct from the funds to their credit with the Treasurer of the United States if it can be done. However, if neither of these propositions can be arranged, you state the land can be paid for from funds raised among the Indians by subscription, if desired.

This office is of the opinion that the purchase of this burying ground should be made by the parties of interest. It is hardly feasible to use money belonging to the tribe and now in the Treasury, for this purpose. Neither does it appear proper to deduct this amount from the annuity payments made to these Indians. You will therefore take such steps as may be necessary to raise the $100 from among the Indians interested in this matter. The deed from the heirs of Isaac Perry to Albert Kenworthy will be recommended for approval, and when it is returned to you, obtain a deed from Kenworthy covering the half acre and the right of ingress and egress, conveying to the United States in trust for the Indians who made contribution to the funds necessary to make the purchase, and forward it to this office, where it will be approved and recorded. It will then be returned to you to be recorded in the proper office of the Territory and then deposited in the files of your Agency.

Very respectfully,

A.C. Tonner
Acting Commissioner.

M.G.-L.C.

****

Sac & Fox – Shawnee
1853-1933   Volume X

Stillwater O T
Agent   Aug 2

Dear Sir

I expect to be down the 15 of August will be away until about that time
I guess Springer has the money for grave yard. I was told that if he had one more dollar he would have it all but 99 dollars. so I recken we can fix it up

yours with respect
Albert Kenworthy

****

Warranty Deed.

This Indenture Made this 18 day of April A.D., 190 5 between Albert Kenworthy and Agnes Kenworthy, his wife parties of the first part, and The United States of America in trust for the Iowa tribe of Indians in Oklahoma, party of the second part.

Witnesseth, That the said parties of the first part, for and in consideration of the sum of Twenty five………………….. and no Dollars the receipt whereof is hereby acknowledged, do… by these presents grant, bargain, sell and convey unto said party of the second part, all of the following described Real Estate, situated in the County of Payne and Territory of Oklahoma, to wit One-half (1/2) acre of land situated in the west half (W/2) of the Northwest (NW) quarter (1/4) of Section fourteen (14) Township seventeen (17) north of range three (3) east of the Indian meridian, more particularly described as follows: Beginning seventy-seven (77) rods south and twenty-one (21) rods east of the Northwest corner of the said section fourteen (14) township seventeen (17) north of range three (3) east of the Indian meridian, and from thence eight (8) rods south, thence ten (10) rods east, thence eight (8) rods north, thence ten (10) rods west to place of beginning

The said one-half acre of land to be used by the Iowa tribe of Indians for graveyard purposes, together with the right of ingress and egress at any and all times, from the section line t its nearest point west of the said one-half (1/2) acre of land.

Sac & Fox – Shawnee
1853-1933 Volume X

To Have and to Hold the Same, Together with all and singular the tenements, hereditaments and appurtenances thereunto belonging, or in any wise appertaining, forever.

And said Albert Kenworthy and Agnes Kenworthy, his wife for their heirs, executors, or administrators, do... hereby covenant, promise, and agree to and with said party of the second part, that at the delivery of these presents they are lawfully seized in their own right of an absolute and indefeasible estate of inheritance, in fee simple, of and in all and singular, the above granted and described premises, with the appurtances; that the same are free, clear, discharged and unencumbered of and from all former and other grants, titles, charges, estates, judgments, taxes, assessments, and incumbrances, of what nature of kind soever................. and that they will warrant and forever defend the same unto the said party of the second part against said parties of the first parties heirs, and all and every person or persons whomsoever lawfully claiming or to claim the same.

In Witness Whereof The said parties of the first part have hereunto set their hands and seals the day and year first above written.

Signed, Sealed and Delivered in Presence of (Signed) Albert Kenworthy [SEAL]

(Signed) Agnes Kenworthy [SEAL]

Territory of Oklahoma, County of Payne, SS.

Before me   W. E. Hodges a Notary Public within and for said county and territory, on this 18 day April 1905 personally appeared Albert Kenworthy and Agnes Kenworthy, his wife to me known to be the identical persons who executed the within and foregoing instrument and acknowledged to me that they executed the same as their free and voluntary act and deed for the uses and purposes thereto set forth.

Witness my hand and official seal the day and year above set forth.

(Signed) W. E. Hodges

COUNTY CLERK'S CERTIFICATE.

Territory of Oklahoma   )
) ss.
Payne County   )

Sac & Fox – Shawnee
1853-1933   Volume X

I, J. H. Donart, County Clerk, in and for the County and Territory aforesaid, do hereby certify that W. E. Hodges is a notary public duly commissioned and qualified; that his commission was dated June 27, 1901, and will expire on the 27th day of June 1905, and that his signature attached hereto is genuine.

Witness my hand and official seal this 29th day of May 1905.
Signed
J. H. Donart,
Signed   County Clerk.
W. E. Hodges.

****

Warranty Deed.

Albert Kenworthy and his wife

TO

The United States of America
in trust for the Iowa Indians

Territory of Oklahoma   )
                                              S.S
Payne County   )

This instrument was filed for record in the Recorder's office at Payne County aforesaid, on the 8th day of August, 1905, at 4 o'clock P.M; and recorded in Book 16 of ......Deeds on page 612-3
Signed
Ralph Smith
Register.
Indian Office
52501   1 9 0 5.
Incl. No. 5

****

Sac & Fox – Shawnee
1853-1933   Volume X

Indian Office
38242   ----------   1 9 0 5

Office of Indian Affairs
6964   May 15, 1905.

The within deed is respectfully submitted to the Secretary of the Interior with recommendation that it be approved.
Signed.
C. F. Larrabee
Acting Comm'r.

Department of the Interior.
July 7, 1905.
The within deed is hereby approved.
Signed,
E. A. Hitch[paper torn]
Secr[paper torn]

****

DEPARTMENT OF THE INTERIOR

UNITED STATES INDIAN SERVICE

Sac and Fox Agency, O.T.
May 27, 1905.

Mr. Albert Kenworthy,
   Stillwater, O.T.

Dear Sir:

Referring to acknowledgment taken on the deed from yourself to the Iowa tribe of Indians for cemetery, situated on the W/2 of the NW/4 of Sec. 14-17-3, the Indian Office states that there is no record of Mr. Hodges official character on file and requests that a certified copy of the report of his appointment be submitted at the earliest convenience.

Sac & Fox – Shawnee
1853-1933   Volume X

Will you please have Mr. Hodges send me a certified copy of his appointment, which can be secured from the county clerk for twenty-five cents? If you will tell him to send this, and pay the mount, the first time you come to the agency, (or I see you) I will refund the same. I do not know where Mr Hodges lives, but I have written to Stillwater and requested this.

                      Very respectfully,

                      W.C. Kohlenberg
                      Supt. & Spl. Disb. Agent.

      Cushing June 4=1905
Dear Sir I will see that you get certificate soon as I go to Stillwater. I am at work here on the Ida Monsur Place
I also enclose receipts
               yours with respect   Albert Kenworthy

[The letter below typed as given]

J. E. OGROSKY   *A. E. MARR*   *J. W. MARR*

RECEIVED
Capital City JUN 7 1909
Marble and Granite Works SAC & FOX AGENCY,
316 WEST OKLAHOMA OKLAHOMA.

Estimates Furnished Free.   Write for Catalogue.

            Guthrie, Okla., _____June 4_____, 190 9

Mr Colenburg
     Sach & Fox Agency   O.K.
Gentlemen   Yours of May 15 at hand and noted no we do not intend to finish any work on the order of Mr John Pettit and would halfto have some kind of an approval from you we would like verry much to get a chance at the work and would be pleased to give you prices on same as soon as you get things in shape for it or on any other work in our line if there is any thing at present plese let us know and we will send you [illegible] of any thing you may want or call on you we will give you a fair deal and it would pay you to give us a chance.
                    Yours J.E. Ogrosky

                    ****

Sac & Fox – Shawnee
1853-1933   Volume X

J. E. OGROSKY   *A. E. MARR*   *J. W. MARR*

Capital City
Marble and Granite Works
316 WEST OKLAHOMA

RECEIVED
MAY 14 1909
SAC & FOX AGENCY,
OKLAHOMA.

Estimates Furnished Free.   Write for Catalogue.

Guthrie, Okla., _____May 12_____, 190 9

Mr Kohlenberg
    Sac and Fox
        Okla
Dear sir:-
    John Pettit placed an order for a monument with us and asked us to write you in regards to the money enclosed please find order if Ok.
    Please sign and return by [illegible] mail for he is in a hurry for the monument.
                Yours truly
                J.E. Ogrosky
316 W. Okla Ave.

****

Capital City Marble & Granite Works
GUTHRIE, OKLA.

_____Red Rock_____ P.O., _____ County, O.K. _____May 12_____ 1909

I do hereby order of Capital City Marble & Granit Works one ____Monument____ of ____Blue Marble____ to be finished according to design No. __3474__ and for the following dimensions Di 8 x 8 x 2:8 B. 1:0 x 1.0 x 0.6 B.B. 1:6 x 1:6 x 1:2 Cross 1:3 x 1:3 x 0:[?] -3 foot marker 1.6 x 1.2 x 0:6 Base 1.6 x 1:0 x 1.0 = with lamb on top.

Inscription to be as follows: __C H A R L I E M O H E E__
_____Died MAR. 7, 1909 – Saturday Evening Six_____
_____age 19._____

To be delivered at _____Red Rock_____ about _____May 30_____ 190 9 or as soon thereafter as is possible. For which consideration I agree to pay to the Capital City Marble & Granite Works or order the sum of _____Seventy five $75.00_____ Dollars on delivery
This order not subject to countermand.
Attest:_____Signed,_____

Sac & Fox – Shawnee
1853-1933 Volume X

REFER IN REPLY TO THE FOLLOWING:
Education-
Purchase
27658-1910
W A P

DEPARTMENT OF THE INTERIOR,
OFFICE OF INDIAN AFFAIRS,
WASHINGTON,

RECEIVED APR 11 1910
SAC & FOX AGENCY, OKLAHOMA.

ADDRESS ONLY THE COMMISSIONER OF INDIAN AFFAIRS

APR -8 1910

Resolution of former
Sac and Fox Council

W. C. Kohlenberg, Esq.,

    Superintendent Sac and Fox Indian School,

        Sac and Fox Agency, Oklahoma.

Sir:

    The copy of the resolution passed by the former Sac and Fox Council, authorizing an expenditure of $500 for repairing cemetery, etc., submitted by you on March 30, is herewith returned so that it can be attached to the proper vouchers.

        Very respectfully,

        J H [Illegible]

        Chief Education Division.

EH-7
9197

[Copy of original]

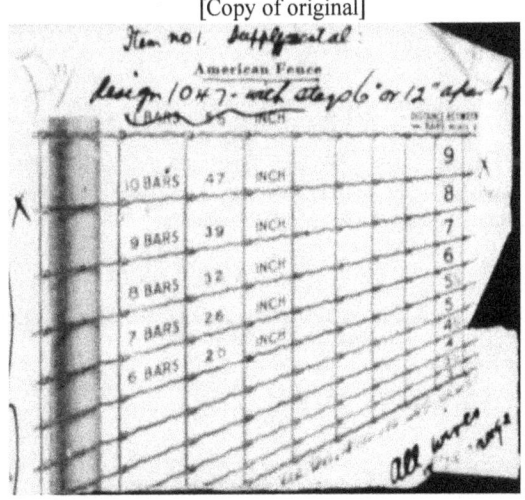

Sac & Fox – Shawnee
1853-1933 Volume X

****

ADVERTISEMENT.

Department of the Interior,
UNITED STATES INDIAN SERVICE.

Sac and Fox Agency, Okla.,

February 26, 1910.

Proposals on the blank below will be received at this office until __12__ o'clock ____ m., March 12, 1910, xxx , for furnishing the following articles for immediate delivery, or service for the ~~period commencing~~ ****************** 190 ** ~~and ending~~ ***************** 190 *.

The right is reserved to reject any and all bids, to accept one part and reject the other, and to waive technical defects as the interests of the service may require. Bidders are invited to be present. W. C. Kohlenberg,

Supt. & Spl. Disb. Agt.

	ITEM NO.	ARTICLE OR SERVICE REQUIRED	PRICE PER UNIT (To be filled in by [illegible])	TOTAL AMOUNT
		~~73 Rods 50" Ellwood Lawn fence, 4" mesh~~		
x	1	1200 ft fencing fabric, 48 in. high	68¢ per Rod	
	2	150 no. intermediate line posts, iron, to set 2'	cannot furnish	
	3	4 no. double corner posts,	" "	
	4	4 no. single end gate posts,	" "	
x	5	1 no. double drive gate, 10 ft. 50" high	$6^{25}	
x	6	1 no. single walk gate, 3 ft. 50" high	$1^{75}	
		Prices f.o.b. Stroud, Okla., on Frisco Rwy.		
		Cuts of fencing bid upon desired.		
		Wanted for fencing cemetery on uneven ground.		

PROPOSAL.

The undersigned hereby agree to furnish the __Sac and Fox Agency, Okla.,__ in conformity with this proposal, any or all of the foregoing articles or service at the prices affixed thereto, and will deliver the articles or service as above states.

American Steel & Wire Co
By HA Parks, Asst Mg Fence Dpt.
Chicago Ill

ACCEPTANCE.

Approved and accepted as to items numbered _____ *at the prices specified.*

Dated _____, 190 ____ _____

Sac & Fox – Shawnee
1853-1933   Volume X

[Opposite side of form on page 98]

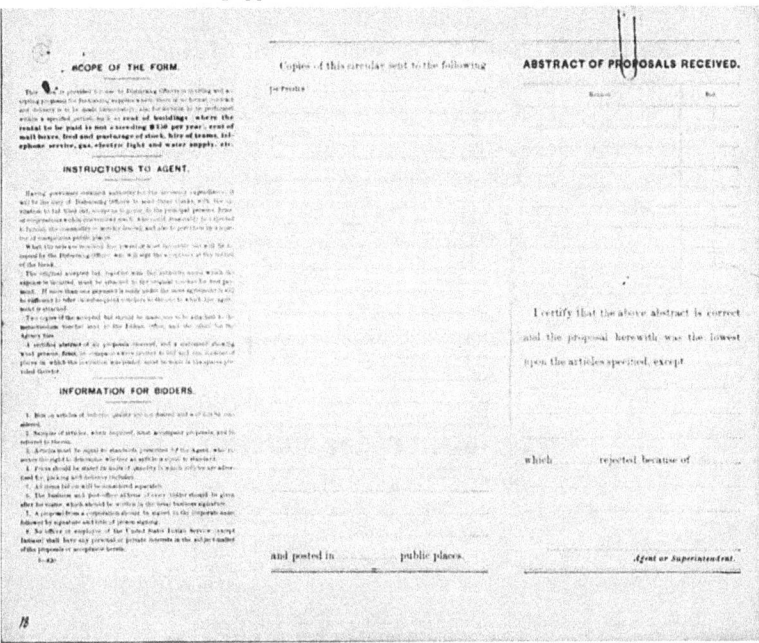

****
[Copy of original]

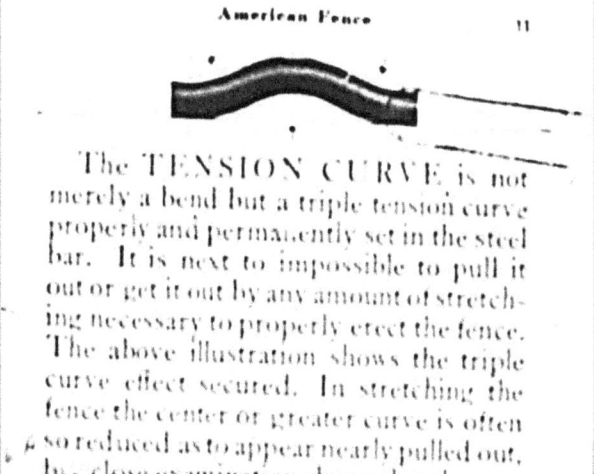

Sac & Fox – Shawnee
1853-1933 Volume X

****

[Transcription of Article on page 99]
The TENSION CURVE is not merely a bend but a triple tension curve properly and permanently set in the steel bat. It is next to impossible to pull it out or get it out by any amount of stretching necessary to properly erect the fence. The above illustration shows the triple curve effect secured. In stretching the fence the center or greater curve is often so reduced as to appear nearly pulled out, but close examination shows that the ten-
[end of article].

ADVERTISEMENT.

Department of the Interior,
UNITED STATES INDIAN SERVICE.

Sac and Fox Agency, Okla.,

June 2, 1910.

Proposals on the blank below will be received at this office until _____ o'clock ___ m., Immediately , ___, for furnishing the following articles for immediate delivery, or service for the period xxxxxxxxxxxxxxxxxxxxxxxxxxxx190x xxxxxxxxxxxxxxxxxxxxxxxx190x.

The right is reserved to reject any and all bids, to accept one part and reject the other, and to waive technical defects as the interests of the service may require. Bidders are invited to be present.

W. C. Kohlenberg,

Supt. & Spl. Disb. Agt.

Item No.		Article or Service Required	Price Per Unit (To be filled in by [illegible])	Total Amount
	1	Dynamite Caps		.10
	2	50 ft. Fuse,		.45
	3	2 lbs. Dynamite.	.25	.50
	4	50 lbs. smooth wire Galv. No. 12	.04	2.00
	5	20 lbs. Short staples, wire, Galv.	.04	.80
				3.85

PROPOSAL.

Sac & Fox – Shawnee
1853-1933 Volume X

The undersigned hereby agree to furnish the __Sac and Fox Agency, Okla.,__ in conformity with this proposal, any or all of the foregoing articles or service at the prices affixed thereto, and will deliver the articles or service as above states.

_____R. J. Miller,_____
_____Stroud, Okla._____

ACCEPTANCE.

Approved and accepted as to items numbered __1 to 5__ *at the prices specified.*

Dated __June 2, 1910__, 190   __W.C. Kohlenberg,__
Supt. & Spl. Disb. Agt.

****

[Opposite side of form on page 101]

SCOPE OF THE FORM.

INSTRUCTIONS TO AGENT.

INFORMATION FOR BIDDERS.

Copies of this circular sent to the following persons:

R. J. Miller, Stroud, Okla.

and posted in __0__ public places.

ABSTRACT OF PROPOSALS RECEIVED.

	Amount	Bid
R. J. Miller		3.85

I certify that the above abstract is correct and the proposal herewith was the lowest upon the articles specified, except force of men were at work on fence & material was needed without delay hence same was bought from claimant. he being only x̶x̶x̶x̶x̶x̶x̶x̶x̶x̶x̶x̶x̶x̶x̶x̶x̶x̶x̶x̶x̶ dealer who could furnish same at once.

W.C. Kohlenberg,
X̶X̶X̶ *Agent or Superintendent.*

****

Sac & Fox – Shawnee
1853-1933 Volume X

MEMORANDUM.

VOUCHER FOR PURCHASES.

The United States, June 25, 1910. *190*
To R. J. Miller, Dr.
(Give post-office address.) Stroud, Okla.

DATE 1910	ITEMS	AMOUNT.
June 2	To 12 Dynamite caps, G	.10
" 2	" 50 ft. Fuse, G	.45
" 2	" 2 lbs. Dynamite @25¢ per lb.	.50
" 2	" 50 lbs. Smooth wire, galv. No. 12, @ 4¢ per lb.	2.00
" 4	" 20 lbs. Short Staples, wire galv. @ 4¢ per lb.	.80
	TOTAL.................... $	3.85

The above is a true copy of original voucher, except as to certificates.

PAID IN CASH, UNLESS OTHERWISE NOTED AT THE BOTTOM HEREOF.

Delivered at Sac and Fox Agency, Okla., on June 2 & June 4, 1910, 190 ;
Required for Fencing Indian Cemetery, Agency,
Purchase made under authority dated November 26, 1909, 190 , attached to original or to voucher No. 38 to account for 2nd quarter, 190 , and in accordance with sections B and 2 of the methods stated on original.
Certificate as to quantity and quality signed by H. C. Shelton, Financial Clerk.

Dated June 25, 1910, 190

Paid by Check No. 735956, dated June 25, 1910, 19 , for $3.85,
on Asst. Treasurer, U. S. St. Louis, Mo., to order of claimant.

****

Sac & Fox – Shawnee
1853-1933 Volume X

MEMORANDUM

CASH

Voucher No. __37__ __4th__ Quarter, 1910

FOR

PURCHASES

IN FAVOR OF

R. J. Miller.

For $ 3.85

Paid by W. C. Kohlenberg,

Supt. & Spl. Disb. Agt.

Sac and Fox Agency, Okla.

****

ADVERTISEMENT.

Department of the Interior,
UNITED STATES INDIAN SERVICE.

Sac and Fox Agency, Okla.,

February 26, 1910.

Proposals on the blank below will be received at this office until __12__ o'clock ___ m., __March 12__, 19__10__, for furnishing the following articles for immediate delivery, or service for ~~the period commencing~~ **************190** *~~and ending~~********************190**.

The right is reserved to reject any and all bids, to accept one part and reject the other, and to waive technical defects as the interests of the service may require. Bidders are invited to be present. __W. C. Kohlenberg,__

__Supt. & Spl. Disb. Agt.__

Item No.	Article or Service Required	Price Per Unit (To be filled in by [illegible])	Total Amount
1	1100 ft. fencing fabric. 48 in. high (No.58)		159.55
2	135 No. intermediate line post iron to set 2'#12		78.61
3	4 No. double corner posts, #10, Ex. Hvy.,		23.64
4	2 No. single end gate posts, #11 Ex. Hvy.,		4.63
5	1 No. double drive gate, 10 ft, B fabric (Ornamental................		6.29
			$276.72
	Prices f.o.b. Stroud, Okla., on Frisco Rwy.		
	Cuts of fencing bid upon desired.		
	Wanted for fencing cemetery on uneven ground.		

PROPOSAL.

The undersigned hereby agree to furnish the __Sac and Fox Agency, Okla.,__ in conformity with this proposal, any or all of the foregoing articles or service at the prices affixed thereto, and will deliver the articles or service as above states.

__The Ward Fence Co.__

Decatur, Indiana

__L. E. Steele,__

Secy.

ACCEPTANCE.

Approved and accepted as to items numbered __1 to 5__ at the prices specified.

Dated __March 26, 1910__, 190   __W. C. Kohlenberg__

Supt. & Spl. Disb. Agt.

****

Sac & Fox – Shawnee
1853-1933   Volume X

[Opposite side of form on page 104]

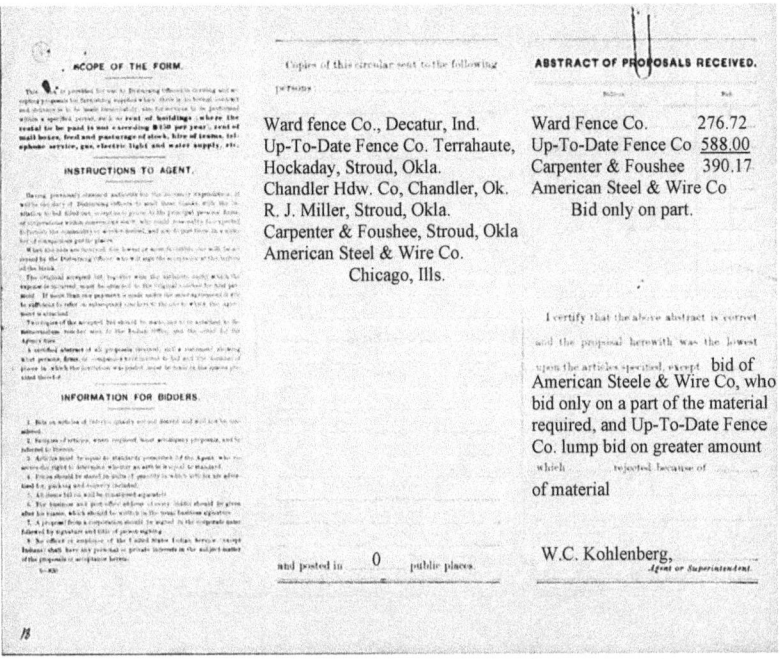

****

UNITED STATES INDIAN SERVICE.   TRIPLICATE.

WEIGHER'S RETURN.

Sac and Fox Agency, Okla.

May 23, 1910   190

RETURN of fencing material _____ *received*

from The Ward Fence Company _____ *, and weighed*

by W. H. Layton, Laborer _____ *, for*

W. C. Kohlenberg, Supt. & Spl. Disb. Agt.

    3 rolls wire fencing fabric   2910 lbs. Net weight.

    141 No.   posts   1580 "   "   "

    10 "   Braces.   510 "   "   "

              Total   5000 lbs. Net weight.

Sac & Fox – Shawnee
1853-1933   Volume X

--R. Sparks.---------------------

    The tare was arrived at by weighing ___there was no tare since each piece was___
___taken at the invoice weight.___---
    ---------I-------- *certify on honor that the above is a true return of weights as weights by*
----me---------

                                              --------W.H. Layton--------------
                                                          --------------Laborer.--------------

    *I certify on honor that the above named articles have been properly weighed by the party who ha*__s__ *signed*__his__ *name hereto, and that the weights, as above given, are correct.*
                                            ----W. C. Kohlenberg,----------------
                                                  Supt. & Spl. Disb. Agt.

                                             ****

DUPLICATE

WEIGHER'S RETURN

OF

----------Wire fencing Material----------

Delivered------May 23, 1910.--------, *190*

------Sac and Fox Agency, Okla.---------

Sac & Fox – Shawnee
1853-1933   Volume X

****

MEMORANDUM.

VOUCHER FOR PURCHASES.

The United States,　　　　　　　　　　　　　May 24, 1910. *190*
　　　　　　　　　To　The Ward Fence Co.　　　　　　, Dr.
　　　(Give post-office address.)　　　Decatur, Indiana.

DATE 1910	ITEMS	AMOUNT.
May 23	To 1100 ft. Fencing fabric 48 in high. (No. 58)	159.55
	" 135 No. intermediate line posts, Ex. Hvy iron to set 2' #12	78.61
	" 4 No. double corner posts. #10 Ex. Hvy..	23.64
	" 2 No. single end gate posts, #11 Ex.Hvy.,	8.63
	" 1 No. Double drive gate, 10 ft. B Fabric, Ornamental	6.29
	(Note: See Voucher N. 25, 4th quarter 1910 for freight from R.R. station.)	
	TOTAL......................	$276.72

The above is a true copy of original voucher, except as to certificates.

PAID IN CASH, UNLESS OTHERWISE NOTED AT THE BOTTOM HEREOF.

Delivered at __Stroud, Okla._____, on _____May 23, 1910_____, 190 ;
Required for _____Fencing Indian Cemetery. (Agency)_____
Purchase made under authority dated __November 28,_____, 190 9 , attached to original or to voucher No. __38_____ to account for _2nd___ quarter, 1910__, and in accordance with sections __B_ and __2___ of the methods stated on original.
Certificate as to quantity and quality signed by _____W. H. Layton, Laborer._____

Dated __May 24, 1910_____, 190

Paid by Check No. __735945__, dated __June 3, 1910_____, 19 , for $__276.72_____,
on __Asst. Treasurer, U. S. St. Louis, Mo.__, to order of claimant.

****

MEMORANDUM

CASH

Voucher No. **24**   **4th** Quarter, 19**10**

FOR

PURCHASES

IN FAVOR OF

The Ward Fence Co.

For $**276.72**

Paid by W. C. Kohlenberg,

Supt. & Spl. Disb. Agent. Spl. Disb. Agt.

Sac and Fox Agency, Okla.

****

[Copy of original]

****

Sac & Fox – Shawnee
1853-1933   Volume X

[Copy of original]

[Transcription under fence]
Illustrating Our Style A 36" Fabric Fence Complete
Rated March 28 1899

****

ADVERTISEMENT.

Department of the Interior,
UNITED STATES INDIAN SERVICE.

Sac and Fox Agency, Okla.,

February 26, 1910.

Proposals on the blank below will be received at this office until __12__ o'clock ____ m., __March 12, 1910__, xxx, for furnishing the following articles for immediate delivery, or service for the period commencing*****************190** and ending*********************190**.

The right is reserved to reject any and all bids, to accept one part and reject the other, and to waive technical defects as the interests of the service may require. Bidders are invited to be present.

W. C. Kohlenberg,

Supt. & Spl. Disb. Agt.

Item No.	Article or Service Required	Price per Unit (To be filled in by [illegible])	Total Amount
1	1200 ft. fencing fabric, 48 in. high	250⁰⁰	
2	150 no. intermediate line posts, iron, to set 2'	150⁰⁰	
3	4 no. double corner posts	9⁰⁰	
4	4 no. single end gate posts,	9⁰⁰	
5	1 no. double drive gate, 10 ft.	8⁰⁰	

6	1 no. single walk gate, 3 ft.		4⁰⁰	430⁰⁰
	Prices f.o.b. Stroud, Okla., on Frisco Rwy. Cuts of fencing bid upon desired.			
	Wanted for fencing cemetery on uneven ground.			

PROPOSAL.

The undersigned hereby agree to furnish the ___Sac and Fox Agency, Okla.,___ in conformity with this proposal, any or all of the foregoing articles or service at the prices affixed thereto, and will deliver the articles or service as above states.

___Carpenter & Foushee___

___Stroud   Okla___

ACCEPTANCE.

Approved and accepted as to items numbered_____at the prices specified.

Dated _____, 190   _____

****

ADVERTISEMENT.

𝕯epartment of the 𝕵nterior,
UNITED STATES INDIAN SERVICE.

Sac and Fox Agency, Okla.,

February 26, 1910.

Proposals on the blank below will be received at this office until __12__ o'clock ____ m., __March 12,_____, 1910, for furnishing the following articles for immediate delivery, or service for ✱the✱period✱commencing✱✱✱✱✱✱✱✱✱✱✱✱190✱✱ and ending✱✱✱✱✱✱✱✱✱✱✱✱✱✱✱✱✱190✱✱

The right is reserved to reject any and all bids, to accept one part and reject the other, and to waive technical defects as the interests of the service may require. Bidders are invited to be present.   ___W. C. Kohlenberg,_____

___Supt. & Spl. Disb. Agt.___

ITEM No.	ARTICLE OR SERVICE REQUIRED	PRICE PER UNIT (To be filled in by [illegible])	TOTAL AMOUNT

Sac & Fox – Shawnee
1853-1933   Volume X

1	1200 ft. 49 in Fabric fence, Style No. 84		
2	150 no. posts intermediate line, set 2 ft. deep		
3	4 no. double corner posts		
4	4 no. single end gate posts,		$588^{00}
5	1 double drive gate, 10 ft., ornamental		
6	1 single walk gate, 3 ft., "		
	1200 angle line [illegible]		
	1200 Braided [illegible]		

Prices f.o.b. Stroud, Okla., on
Frisco Rwy.

Cuts of fence bid on desired.
Wanted for fencing cemetery on uneven ground.

PROPOSAL.

The undersigned hereby agree to furnish the ___Sac and Fox Agency, Okla.,___
in conformity with this proposal, any or all of the foregoing articles or service at the prices affixed
thereto, and will deliver the articles or service as above states.Up-to-Date Mfg. Co.,
___[Name Illegible]___

___Terre Haute Ind___

ACCEPTANCE.

Approved and accepted as to items numbered_____at the prices specified.
Dated _____, 190   _____

****

THE WARD FENCE COMPANY
DECATUR, IND. U.S.A.

4/5/10.

W. C. Kohlenberg,
    Sac & Fox Agency, Okla.

Dear Sir:

    We have started the manufacture of your order for 1100 ft. of Style B, 48" Fence. We find that it will be impossible for us to weave this in one roll. Kindly let us know the size rolls that will be most convenient for you to handle.

    Trusting that you will give this your early attention, we remain,

Sac & Fox – Shawnee
1853-1933   Volume X

Yours truly,

THE WARD FENCE CO.,

Per-J. O'Brien

O'B-RCV.

****

THE WARD FENCE COMPANY
DECATUR, IND. U.S.A.

4/13/10

W. C. Kolenburg[sic],
Sac & Fox Agency, Okla.

Dear Sir:

We have your valued favor of April 8th, and in reply beg to adcise[sic] you g[sic] that we have instructed our factory to make up the Fabric in 2 sections at 380' each, and 2 sections of 170' each.

We have also instructed them to let this shipment go forward at the earliest possible moment, and we trust that you will receive it without any serious delay, and that you will find it entirely satisfactory when we erected upon your property.

Thanking you for your past favors, we remain,

Yours truly,

THE WARD FENCE CO.,

Per E H Shoemaker

EHS/EMC

****

Sac & Fox – Shawnee
1853-1933 Volume X

THE WARD FENCE COMPANY
DECATUR, IND. U.S.A.

5/11/10.

W. C. Kohlenberg,
   Sac & Fox Agency, Okla.

Dear Sir:

It is our pleasure to hand you, herewith, the original bill of lading, invoice and instructions, covering the shipment of your valued order for Posts, Fabric only and 1 Double Drive Gate.

This shipment went forward, freight collect on May 10th, consigned to yourself.

We trust it will arrive without delay, in perfect condition and prove entirely satisfactory to you.

Taking this occasion to again thank you for past favors, and to solicit your further needs in our line, to our mutual pleasure and profit, we remain,

Yours truly,

THE WARD FENCE COMPANY.,

Per- [Name Illegible]

313   Secretary.
LES-AAT
Enc. B-B/L.-116.

****

THE WARD FENCE COMPANY
DECATUR, IND. U.S.A.

6-2-10.

W. C. Kohlenberg,
   Sac & Fox Agency, Okla.
Dear Sir:-

We are just in receipt of your favor of May 28th, in reference to the fastening of the fabric to the line posts which we recently shipped you. For your information, would state that it is our custom to furnish small tie wires to be placed around the posts and the line wires of the fabric. We find, however that our shipping department failed to send these tie wires with the shipment.

We not also that you did not receive any hinges for the gates. It is however, out[sic] custom to wire the hinges to the gates when we make shipment of this kind of material. They no doubt have been lost in transit and we are therefore sending you by express prepaid a sufficient quantity of the tie wires and hinges to complete the fence.

We trust upon receipt of this material that you will be able to erect the fence to your entire satisfaction.

Thanking you for past favors, we remain,

Yours truly,

EHS-AS.   THE WARD FENCE CO.

Per-   E.H. Shoemaker

HOWELL & MILEY
LAW OFFICES
SHAWNEE, OKLA.

EDWARD HOWELL
J. M. MILEY
A. M. WIDDOWS

September 20, 1912.

Mr. John A. Buntin,

Shawnee Indian Mission,

Shawnee, Oklahoma.

Dear Sir:-

The Catholic Church in Shawnee desires to establish a cemetery for the burial of its people and are trying to ascertain where they can buy a piece of land which will be within the law. In other words they want the land as near to Shawnee as possible, but under the law it must be at least three-fourths of a mile from any land platted in which lots have been sold for residence purposes. They have noticed that Section 11, Township 10, Range 3, East of the Indian Meridian, is the most satisfactory, and find that this land is now the property of Kickapoo Indians. Will you kindly let me know whether there is any way of which the Catholic Church could buy a portion of this land for the purpose above indicated.

                                              Yours very truly,

H/V   Howell & Miley

****

HOWELL & MILEY
LAW OFFICES
SHAWNEE, OKLA.

EDWARD HOWELL
J. M. MILEY
A. M. WIDDOWS

                                              September 24, 1912.

Mr. J. A. Buntin,

    Shawnee Indian Agency,

        Shawnee, Oklahoma.

Dear Sir:-

Referring to your letter of the 23rd inst., with reference to cemetery for the Catholic Church on Section 11, Township 10, North of Range 3, East of the Indian meridian, we beg to state that we have taken the matter up with the church people and they will have a plat drawn showing the place that they desire and we will then take the matter up further with you.

Thanking you for the information given us, we are,

                                              Yours very truly,

H/V   Howell & Miley

****

Sac & Fox – Shawnee
1853-1933   Volume X

EMERY A. FOSTER
ATTORNEY AT LAW
Chandler - Oklahoma

RECEIVED
JUN 21 1916
SAC AND FOX INDIAN SCHOOL, OKLA.

June
Nineteenth,
Nineteen Hundred Sixteen.

Mr. Horace J. Johnson, Supt.,
   Sac & Fox Agency, Okla.
Friend Johnson:

   The Ft. Smith & Western Railway runs through a piece of land near Fallis. The Iowa Indians have a graveyard near Fallis on the land of Adolph Baer.

   What I wish to know is whether your office shows a graveyard there belonging to the Indians or held by the Government in trust for them.

   I enclose a slip of paper which client left for me as I was not in my office when he came.

                 Yours truly,
                     Emery A Foster

EAF/FF.

   Lot 6   19-15-2   10 acres

****

                Mr Emroy[sic] Foster

Dear Sir I been here for to see you about the land deal wht the F S & W

   The Indians claim the land the grave yard the land the government Farm Admin

RECEIVED
JUN 21 1916
SAC AND FOX INDIAN SCHOOL, OKLA.

The Indians Names are Robert Small & Dave Tohee at Perkins

So the R.R. got nothing you can get the information at the Sac & Fox Agency

                Your truly
                Adolf Baier

****

Sac & Fox – Shawnee
1853-1933 Volume X

Sac and Fox Indian School,
Stroud, Okla. July 5, 1916.

Emory A. Foster
Chandler, Oklahoma.

Sir:

Referring to your letter of June 19th concerning the Iowa Indian grave-yard near Fallis, I have to advise that a tract of land was set aside for this purpose for the Iowa Indians near Fallis. It is described as Lot 6 of Section 19-15-2 and contains 10 acres.

Very respectfully,

Supt. & S. D. A.

HJJ/AM

Shawnee Indian Agency,
Shawnee, Oklahoma,
May 13, 1924.

County Clerk, Payne County.
Ex. Of. Register of Deeds,
Stillwater, Oklahoma.

Dear Sir:

It appears that there may be a cemetery reservation within the NW/4 of Section 14, Twp., 17, Range 3 East. probably owned by Mr. Kenworthy. We would be pleased to have information pertaining to any record in your office showing this to be a fact or not.

Very truly yours,

A. W. Leech,
Superintendent.

D/Mc

Sac and Fox-Shawnee – VITAL STATISTICS
1896 & 1908

Sac & Fox – Shawnee
1853-1933 Volume X

Sac & Fox Agency, Oklahoma.
May 8th, 1896.

We, the undersigned chiefs of the Sac and Fox tribe of Indians, certify that Shelah Guthrie is the daughter of John Brown.

WITNESS.   Chief McKosito   his x mark

  J. H. Lawrence   Chief Moses Keokuk   his x mark

  Peter Soocey

I, William Hurr, U.S. Interpreter, certify that the foregoing certificate was explained to and fully understood by the parties signing hereto by making their mark.

Wm Hurr
U.S. Interpreter.

****

Sac & Fox Agency, Oklahoma.
May 8th, 1896.

We, the undersigned Head men of the Iowa Tribe of Indians, certify that Theresa Bigrat and Theresa Bigear are one and the same person.

WITNESS.   Chief McKosito   his x mark

  J. H. Lawrence   Chief Moses Keokuk   his x mark

  Peter Soocey

I, William Hurr, U.S. Interpreter, certify that the foregoing certificate was explained to and fully understood by the parties signing their names by making their marks.

Wm Hurr
U.S. Interpreter.

****

Sac & Fox – Shawnee
1853-1933   Volume X

Sac & Fox Agency, Oklahoma.
May 8th, 1896.

We, the chiefs of the Sac and Fox Tribe of Indians, certify that Cassie Eaton and W.F. Rogers are one and the same person.

WITNESS.   Chief McKosito   his x mark

J. H. Lawrence   Chief Moses Keokuk his x mark

Peter Soocey

I, William Hurr, U.S. Interpreter, certify that the foregoing certificate was explained to and fully understood by the parties signing the same by making their marks.

Wm Hurr
U.S. Interpreter.

****

Sac & Fox Agency, Oklahoma.
May 8th, 1896.

We, the undersigned chiefs of the Sac & Fox Tribe of Indians, certify that Henry Miller is the Father and Ann Barker is the Mother of Ruth Miller.

WITNESS.   Chief McKosito   his x mark

J. H. Lawrence   Chief Moses Keokuk his x mark

Peter Soocey

I, William Hurr, U.S. Interpreter, certify that the foregoing certificate was explained to and fully understood by the parties signing the same by making their marks.

Wm Hurr
U.S. Interpreter.

****

Sac & Fox – Shawnee
1853-1933 Volume X

U.S. INDIAN AGENCY
RECEIVED
AUG 23 1908
Ans M Vol 14 p 297
SHAWNEE, OKLA.

DEPARTMENT OF THE INTERIOR
UNITED STATES INDIAN SERVICE
Ponca, &c. Agency,
Whiteagle, Okla Aug. 22, 1908.

Supt. F.A. Thackeray[sic],
Shawnee, Okla.

Dear Sir:

  Will you kindly furnish this office with the age of Anna B. Rhodd, as it appars[sic] on your Census rolls

  Thanking you in advance for the information, I remain

    Very respectfully,
    J.H. McIntyre

JWB   Clerk In Charge

Sac and Fox-Shawnee – BIRTHS
Undated and 1892 - 1923

Sac & Fox – Shawnee
1853-1933   Volume X

Mr Leroy Jones
high to home
and ade on his
Role on Jan 5th
Leroy Jones Jr
Born

Boy Born Yesterday
Kah Kaque   No 78
Take increase off Naw Naw-que
It was a mistake   No 7
The child was enrolled last
Payment
       John [Illegible]

UNITED STATES INDIAN SERVICE

Sac & Fox (O. Ty.) Agency,
September 26th, 1892.

Oliver Martel,
  Louisville,
    Pott. County,
      Kansas.

Dear Sir:-

Please send me the exact date of your daughter, Viola B. Martel. And return same to me in enclosed envelope which does not require a stamp.

Very Truly,
      Samuel L Patrick
      U. S. Indian Agent.

Affidavit of Mrs W F. Rogers
July 6th 1894

Giving notice to this office of
the birth of Beulah [Illegible] Rogers,
daughter of Mrs. W. F. Rogers, Santa Rosa Cal

Sac & Fox – Shawnee
1853-1933   Volume X

RECEIVED
DEC 31 1913
SAC & FOX AGENCY,
OKLAHOMA.

Shawnee Okla
Dec 30 – 13

Mr Horace J Johnson
    Sac & Fox Agent
        Stroud
            Okla
Dear Sir
    We wish to have our daughter Ruth H Kenyon enrolled, born Dec 9-1913 Also do you know where Mr [illegible…]
        Yours Very Truly
            Albert D.Kenyonfff

Sugar Grove, Ark.
9-24-1904

Mr. Kohlenberg, Agent.
I will write you in regard to my new born baby boy You can enroll him by the name of William Theadore[sic] Brown Born Sept the 17, 1904. Now in regard to William Jefferson he is with me yet he is stout and Harty and well pleased. That is all

        Yours Truly
        Julia Brown

Territory of Oklahoma)
) ss.
County of Pottawatomie)

    I __J. E. Coyle M.D._____, a regular practicing physician according to the laws of Oklahoma Territory and also being the physician who waited on Mrs Cassie Williams during her confinment[sic] which occurred October 2o[sic], 1904, do hereby upon oath state that there was born to the said Cassie Williams a boy on the said date; and that the child is a healthy one and still living; it and the mother both doing well.

                J. E. Coyle M.D.

Sac & Fox – Shawnee
1853-1933   Volume X

Subscribed and sworn to before me this the 22 day of October, 19o4.

       S. T [Illegible]
       Notary Public.

My Commission Expires
Jany 9th 1908

Department of the Interior.
UNITED STATES INDIAN SERVICE.

....

....................................., *190*...

Births

John B McClellan son Jan 9-1906
John McClellan Father
Fanny McClellan Mother

Mary Givens dau Jan 5-1906
Eveline Givens Father
Matilda Givens Mother

Mabel Walker dau Feb 3-06
Ben Walker Father
Dora Walker Mother

Emma Logan dau Feb 27 06
Clarence Logan Father
Mattie Logan Mother

Harriet Longshore dau Nov 30-1905
Charley Longshore Father
Annie Longshore Mother

William Shaw	Feb 5-1906	
Emma Logan	Mar 10-1906	Infant
Theodore R Longshore	Mar 14-1906	Infant
Anna Butler	Mar 16, 1906	Infant
Julia Clay	Mar 11, 1906	
Naomi Sullivan	Mar 19, 1906	
Roger Mathews	Jan 17, 1906	
Judith Houston	Dec 31-1906	

Sac & Fox – Shawnee
1853-1933 Volume X

Louis Cuppahe son Mar 1-1906
Lee Cuppahe Father

JOHN DAVIS,
Attorney and Counselor At Law,
PRAGUE, OKLAHOMA.

Jan. 26, 1906.

Mr. W.C. Kohlenberg, Agent,

Sac & Fox Agency, Okla.

Dear Sir:

Please find enclosed affidavits of myself and wife duly executed as per your instructions. We are unable to get the affidavit of the attending Physician for the reason that he has moved away and we do not know his present post office address.

Yours very truly

Ed Rider

DEPARTMENT OF THE INTERIOR
UNITED STATES INDIAN SERVICE

Sac and Fox School, Iowa.

Toledo, August 16, 1906.

Hon. W. C. Kohlenberg,
 Supt. & Spl. Disb. Agent,
  Sac and Fox Agency,
   Okla.

Sir:-

I have the honor of herewith enclosing receipts in triplicate, signed by Emma Hunter and signature duly witnessed. Her child, (F) born July 12, is enrolled at this agency.

Sac & Fox – Shawnee
1853-1933 Volume X

Very respectfully,

W.G. Malin

Supt. & Spl. Disb. Agent.

RECEIVED
FEB 27 1907
SAC & FOX AGENCY,
OKLAHOMA.

Shawnee Ok. Terr.
Feb 4 1907

Mr. W.C. Kohlenburg[sic],

I write to inform you we have an addition of another little girl in our family.
Miss Ella Beattrice Meek
Born Feb. 19, 1907

Respectfully.
Mrs. Jennie Meek

RECEIVED
AUG 3 1907
SAC & FOX AGENCY,
OKLAHOMA.

Delaware I.T.
July 31 07

Mr. W. C. Kohlenberg
Supt. Spl Dis Agent
Dear Sir:-

Enclose find statement from the doctor
The baby was born June 24 a boy baby
Its name is
Lenard White

Very Respy
James Tyner White

****

OFFICE PHONE 193.
RESIDENCE PHONE 140.

E. F. COLLINS,
PHYSICIAN AND SURGEON.

NOWATA, I.T. _7/29_ 190 7

RECEIVED
LAWSON BUILDING
AUG 3 1907
SAC & FOX AGENCY,
OKLAHOMA.

This is to certifil[sic] that I did wate[sic] on Mrs Ada White on June 24 1907 when she gave birth to a male child on date above and the same is in my presence this date and is in good health

E F Collins MD

Sac & Fox – Shawnee
1853-1933 Volume X

RECEIVED
SEP 23 1907
SAC & FOX AGENCY,
OKLAHOMA.

W.C. Kohlenburg
Sac & Fox

Stroud Ok
Sept 21 07

Dear Sir:- Please give me credit for one D. Dennis Keokuk on Sac & Fox Roll & oblige

J.E. Keokuk

10 Pounds   Born Sept 19th 07

[The letter below typed as given]

Cushing Okla
Nov. 16 – 07

RECEIVED
NOV 18 1907
SAC & FOX AGENCY,
OKLAHOMA.

W.C. Kohlenberg,

Agent

Well I heard you was haveng payment if so please send the vouchers down and Julia can sign them and I can bring them back for she is sick in bead. We have another little Indian girl at our house. born Nov. 11 – 07.

Yours Truly
G. T. Brown

****

Cushing Okla
March 10 – 08

W. C. Kohlenberg

Dear Agent

I recd my check yesterday and was glad you sent it for we are very busy and have no time to come down. and our Baby Girl was born Nov. the 11 – 07 and her name is Elcie F Brown

Yours Very Truly
Julia Brown

Sac & Fox – Shawnee
1853-1933   Volume X

Territory of Oklahoma)
) ss.
County of Pottawatomie)

Dr. JB Ellis[sic] being of lawful age, a regular practicing physician of and according to the law of the above name territory, and duly sworn, deposes and says that there was born to Cassie Williams a baby girl on April 8, 1906, he being the physician who waited on the said Cassie Williams during her confinement on the aforesaid date.

J.B. Tellis MD

Subscribed and sworn to before me this the 12 day of April 1906.

Jesse F. Dickson
Notary Public.

My commission expires Sept 13th 1908

WILLIAM M. TAYLOR,
LAWYER
OFFICE OVER FIRST NAT'L BANK

SHAWNEE, OKLAHOMA.   April 12, 1906.

Hon. W. C. Kohlenberg,
    Sac and Fox Agency, Oklahoma.

    Dear Sir—: Enclosed you will find certificate and affidavit of the birth of my little girl who was born on the 6 inst.

    Please have her placed on the roll for her Annuity the same as other Sac and Fox Indians. Her name is Hazel Faye Williams.

Very respectfully,
Cassie Williams

****

Sac & Fox – Shawnee
1853-1933 Volume X

FRANK WILLIAMS
ATTORNEY-AT-LAW

SHAWNEE, OKLA._____ April 13, 1908.

RECEIVED
APR 14 1908
SAC & FOX AGENCY,
OKLAHOMA.

Hon. W. C. Kohlenberg,

    Sac and Fox, Oklahoma.

Dear Sir:

    Enclosed you will find Physician's Affidavit, stating that there was born to me a baby girl on the morning of the 12 day of April 1908.

    Her name is Elsie Marie Williams.

    Please enroll her as are other Sac and Fox Children for her Annuities.

                              Cassie Williams

****

State of Oklahoma)
) ss.
Pottawatomie County)

RECEIVED
APR 14 1908
SAC & FOX AGENCY,
OKLAHOMA.

W.R. Williams, a regular practicing physician according to the laws of Oklahoma, his Office in Shawnee, Oklahoma, being by me duly sworn, deposes and says that he was the physician who waited on Cassie Williams during her Confirment[sic] on the Morning of the 12 day of April, 1908 and that there was born to her a Baby Girl on the said date, that the said confinment was in Shawnee, Oklahoma.

                              W. R. Williams M.D.
                                   Physician.

Subscribed and sworn to before me this the 13, day of April 1908.

                              [Name Illegible]
                                  Notary Public.

My Commission epires[sic] Nov. 10th 1909.

Sac & Fox – Shawnee
1853-1933   Volume X

[The letter below typed as given]

Mr Kohlenberg
if my son in Law as not report thire Babys name is Lenard ~~m~~ Crain, & date childs birth, soon as m Crain same lack me will report it to you he will be back tomorrow or next day
yours
H C Jr

PLANTERS' STATE BANK
PAID UP CAPITAL $10,000.00

RECEIVED AUG 6 1908
SAC & FOX AGENCY, OKLAHOMA.

Ripley, Okla.

RECEIVED
APR 14 1908
SAC & FOX AGENCY, OKLAHOMA.

W.C. Kohlenburg[sic] Agent Sac & Fox, Okla.
Dear Sir
I wish to advise you of the birth of a baby girl at my home, born August 3rd 1908. Mother and daughter, both doing well, and I am feeling better. I talked with Chief Dave Tohee, yesterday. He told me to write to you and put her name on the rolls it is Bessie Kent, if you have any lease money for me, send it right away, send it to me in care of The Planters State Bank, at Ripley
Very Truly Yours   Frank Kent
   Rec, Aug 7 08

RECEIVED
AUG 7 1908
SAC & FOX AGENCY, OKLAHOMA.

Prague, Okla.
Aug. 6, 1908

W.C. Kohlenberg
    Sac & Fox, Okla.
Dear Sir:-
    A Baby Girl came into our family at eleven oclock P.M., Aug. 5. We have named her Frances Oralee. Kindly enter her name on the roll as a member of the Sac & Fox tribe and greatly oblige.
            Yours Truly
                Leroy Jones.
    Rec 8-7-08

Sac & Fox – Shawnee
1853-1933   Volume X

RECEIVED
MAR 26 1908
SAC & FOX AGENCY,
OKLAHOMA.

Payson, Okla
March 24th 09

Agt Kholenberg[sic]
    Sac & Fox Agcy
        Okla
Dear Sir
    I take this opportunity of enforming[sic] you that their[sic] was born to John and Bertha Goodell a little Daughter on Monday 22nd inst (name) Lavona Madesta Goodell
        Yours Resp
        John J Goodell

[The letter below typed as given]

Mr. W C Kolenberg
    Sac & Fox Agency Okla

Kind Sir This is to inform you that Mrs Mammie Jennings was confirmed & gave birth to a girl 5 lbs at $2^{\underline{30}}$ pm June the 8th 1898 at my Sanitarium 323 E M Sawnee Okla
        Respectfully your friend
        N.P. Keene MD

    Ps   Pearl Elithebeth Jennings
            is Babe name

****

Sac & Fox – Shawnee
1853-1933   Volume X

[The letter below typed as given]

June 9   190 9

Mr W. C. Kolenberg[sic]
        Sac & Fox Agency Okla
Dear Sir:-
        As my wifes child had Berth at 2:30 P.M. on the 8 of June 1909 I will ask you if you will mail this to the Goverment as soon as you receive it and if he sees fit for the payment to go through let it come and if not no harm done But it would be a great faver to us both.
                Yours resptfully
                        Edgar Jennings
Box 383 Shawnee Okla

I am writing this for my wife as she is not able to at up and write   By By
Please do this for Hir
gov rec'd check all ok.

BART. W. FREER, M. D.
ELUM M. RUSSELL, M. D.
MEDICINE AND SURGERY

NOWATA, OKLAHOMA

(DR. FREER
(DR. RUSSELL
RECEIVED
AUG 5 1909
SAC & FOX AGENCY,
OKLAHOMA.

        State of Oklahoma,
           County of Nowata.)ss

                B. W. Freer, being duly sworn, upon his oath, states: That he is a practicing physician, located at Nowata, Nowata County, Oklahoma, duly licenses to practice medicine and surgery in said county and state; that on the 6th day of July, 1909, he was called upon to attend Mrs. James T. White, of Delaware, Oklahoma, in child birth; that a child was born to said Mrs. James T.

Sac & Fox – Shawnee
1853-1933   Volume X

White, alive and is still living; that the name of said child is Lahoma Edith White.; that said child, born as aforesaid, is a girl; and your affiant further sayeth not.

..B. W. Freer..............

Subscribed and sworn to before me this 4th day of Aug., 1909.

..W. J. Campbell........
Notary Public.

My com. exp.

Nov. 24th, 1912.

****

[The letter below typed as given]

Aug. 4, 1909

RECEIVED
AUG 5 1909
SAC & FOX AGENCY,
OKLAHOMA.

Mr. W.C. Kholenberg

Sir, would it be possible for you to send these children money to me after this as Jim justs drinks it up when he get it I need the money for other purposes. Thanking you in advance

I remain yours Truly   Ida M. White

[The letter below typed as given]

Shawnee OK
Oct. 4 1909

RECEIVED
OCT 7 1909
SAC & FOX AGENCY,
OKLAHOMA.

Mr Kolhenburg
I write to tell you of a birth of a girl in our family name
   Frances Cecelia Meek
   Born Aug. 21. 09
              Respectfully
              Mrs Jennie Meek

Sac & Fox – Shawnee
1853-1933 Volume X

RECEIVED
OCT 21 1909
SAC & FOX AGENCY,
OKLAHOMA.

Flathead Agency, Jocko, Montana.

October 16, 1909.

Mr. W.C. Kohlenberg,
Supt. and Spl. Disb. Agent,
Sac and Fox Agency, Okla.

Dear Mr. Kohlenberg,-

I have to advise you that we have a baby girl at our home, born this date. Please take her up on your rolls as Paulena Montana Lewis. Mother and child are doing nicely. With best wishes for your continued success in your work I am as ever,

Very sincerely,

Omen Lewis

****

Flathead Agency, Jocko, Montana.

October 16, 1909.

To whom it may concern;

I hereby certify on honor that there was born unto Mrs. Pauline Lewis a baby girl.

John H. [Illegible]
Agency Physician.

O. B. ELMORE   W. J. RICE.

ELMORE & RICE
DEALERS IN
DRY GOODS and GROCERIES

RECEIVED
FEB 19 1910
SAC & FOX AGENCY,
OKLAHOMA.
2-16 1910

Red Rock, Okla.,

Mr. WC Collenburg[sic]
Dear Friend   I Have Got a Boy I want you to put on Roll
Born Victor Dupee 26 of Dec 1909. And oblige

139

Sac & Fox – Shawnee
1853-1933   Volume X

Ps Pleas[sic] Let me know if My wifes land is sold yet
Respectfully
Victor & [Illegible] Dupee

LYNDON, KANSAS.

State of Kansas, |
                    | SS.
County of Osage, |

RECEIVED
FEB 18 1910
SAC & FOX AGENCY,
OKLAHOMA.

    R. H. Miles, being by me first duly sworn upon oath, deposes and says that he is a regular practising[sic] physician residing at Lyndon in the county and State aforesaid; that he did on the 15th day of February, 1910, deliver of Mrs. John T. Capper, wife of John T. Capper. one living baby boy, names Alfred Rodell Capper.
    And affiant further says that the BIRTH RETURN attached hereto is true.

                                  R H Miles M D

Subscribed and sworn to before me this 16" day of February, 1910.

                          O.B. Hartley
                Clerk of District Court, Osage County, Kans.

****

Sac & Fox – Shawnee
1853-1933   Volume X

BIRTH RETURN.

NOTE. – Send this without delay to County Health Officer. Write further remarks on back. Report stillbirths (on and after seventh month; under seventh month, no report) as births, and

1. Name of child __Alfred Rodell Copper__
2. Sex __Male__   3. Color __white__   4. No. of child of this mother __1st__
5. Date of birth __Feb 15   1910__
6. Place of birth __Lyndon Kas__
7. Born alive __yes__   8. Legitimate __yes__
9. Natural labor __yes__
10. Difficult labor __yes__
11. Cause of difficult labor __small pelvis and large child__
12. Means of relief ____
13. Mother's maiden name __Nobel Haggerty__
14. Mother's age __25__   15. Nationality __American__
16. Father's name ____
17. Father's age __32__   18. Occupation __Real estate__
19. Father's nationality __American__
20. Returned by __R. H. Miles__, M. D.
21. Post-office address __Lyndon Kas__
22. Date of return __Feb 16__, 1910
23. Remarks: ____

[The letter below typed as given]

RECEIVED
FEB 25 1910
SAC & FOX AGENCY,
OKLAHOMA.

Red Rock, Okla
February 22, 1910

Mr MCAhenenney
Sac and Fox Agency
Okla.
Dear Friend,
    I rec'd your welcome letter today.
I have make a mistake in month of baby birth
Baby was born Nov. 26 day of 1909. and his
name is Louise Dupee.
    I'll close.
    I remain your's
    Victor Dupee

Sac & Fox – Shawnee
1853-1933   Volume X

[The letter below typed as given]

RECEIVED
FEB 24 1910
SAC & FOX AGENCY,
OKLAHOMA

Prague Okla

Feb 22 – 1910

Born to Thersa Wood a baby girl on the 18th of Feb 1910 name Ethelyn Gladys Wood

      Yours Truly
      HC Jones

****

H. C. Jones

      Prague, Okla. Feb 22 1910

W. C. Kohlenberg
 Supt & Sp Dis Agent
I here with Inclosed name Thresas Baby Thresa been Pretty sick not any Better yet

      Yours Truly
      Henry C Jones

DEPARTMENT OF THE INTERIOR
UNITED STATES INDIAN SERVICE

RECEIVED
MAR 2 1910
SAC & FOX AGENCY,
OKLAHOMA.

    Sac and Fox Agency, Okla.,

    Feb. 26, 1910.

Mr. Victor Dupee,
 Red Rock, Okla.
Dear sir,-

  I am in receipt of your letter of the 22nd instant in which you give some information regarding your child. In order that the record of the birth may be correctly recorded in full on our roll, I shall have to ask you to inform me as to the sex of the child. You wrote, "His name is Louise". Is the child a boy named Louis or a girl name Louise? It is difficult to be sure from your letter.

Sac & Fox – Shawnee
1853-1933   Volume X

                        Very respectfully,
                            W.C. Kohlenberg
RS   Supt. & Spl. Disb. Agt.

Dr Sur
   In reply to above inquiry, would state <u>his</u> name is Louis Dupee as the child is a boy.
                        Yours Truly
                            Victor Dupee
Red Rock Okla   2/28/10   _____

                              RECEIVED
                              MAY 3 1910
                          SAC & FOX AGENCY,
                             OKLAHOMA.
                        Sparks Oklahoma

                        May 1, 1910

Mr. W.C. Kohlenberge[sic],

            I drop you a letter in regards of getting my baby girl on the roll she was born on the 29th of April her name is Myrtle May McKinney.

    Thanking you for your kindness in this matter. Answer soon so I will know   Yours Respt.

        Aaron McKinney
           Sparks
            Okla
    Rout No 2 Box 45 A

Sac & Fox – Shawnee
1853-1933   Volume X

[The letter below typed as given]

RECEIVED
MAY 16 1910
SAC & FOX AGENCY,
OKLAHOMA.

Potrillo New Mex
May 5/11-10

Dear Sir   W.C. K.
Sac and Fox Agency, Okla

On the day of this Sat we Glad and happy because we have a news. we have a [illegible] baby girl   She is born on this day of may at 9 clock and so we let you know her name is Rosie Boyd and this is all

you bary trouly

Joe. A. Boyd

Earlsboro Okla
Sept 21 1910

RECEIVED
SEP 23 1910
SAC & FOX AGENCY,
OKLAHOMA.

W.C. Kohlenberg
Dear Sir
I have a little girl born in Dec. 22 of 1909. Which you please put her on the roll. Her name is Alice Tyner

Very Respectfully,
Maggie Tyner

H. C. Jones

Prague, Okla.   Sept 8

RECEIVED
SEP 9 1910
SAC & FOX AGENCY,
OKLAHOMA.

W. C. Kohlenberg
Supt & Sp Dis Agent

Dear sir   Please let go on Roll new comer Henry Lee Jones Born Sept 4th   Another Jones Boy

Yours Truly
HC Jones

Sac & Fox – Shawnee
1853-1933 Volume X

RECEIVED
NOV 8 1910
SAC & FOX AGENCY,
OKLAHOMA.

Sparks Okla
Oct. 7, 1910

Mr. W. C. Kohlenberg

Dear Sir

Please enrole our babie girl Edith Clarence Casteel born this seventh of Oct ninten hundred & ten

And Oblige

Lizzie Casteel

****

[Copy of original Birth Certificate]

****

Sac & Fox – Shawnee
1853-1933 Volume X

[Transcription of Birth Certificate on page 145]

Color __White__   RECORD OF BIRTH   File No. _____

OKLAHOMA STATE BOARD OF HEALTH
BUREAU OF VITAL STATISTICS
GUTHRIE, OKLA.

Full name of Child __Edith Clarence Casteel__
Place of Birth __3½ mi   S.W. Sparks   Lincoln__
Sex of Child __Female__   Single or ~~Multiple~~ __yes__   Legitimate __yes__   Date of Birth __11-7-1910__
Born Alive __yes__   Natural Labor __yes__   If difficult labor Cause ⸺ Means of relief ⸺

FATHER	MOTHER
Full Name __James Clarence Casteel__	Full Name __Elizabeth McKinney Casteel__
Post office address __Sparks Okla__	Postoffice address __Sparks Okla__
Color or race __White__ Age __24__ Years	Color or race __½ Sac & Fox Indian__ Age __26__ Years
Birthplace __Goffs[sic] Kansas__	Birthplace __Lincoln Co Okla__
Occupation __Farmer__	Number of children __3__ Number now living __3__

CERTIFICATE OF ATTENDING PHYSICIAN OR MIDWIFE

I hereby certify that I attended the birth of the above child and that it occurred on __Nov 7__, 19__10__, *at* __10AM__
*Signature*____ __H C Brown__ _____   *Dated* ____ __Nov 7__ _____ 19__10__   __Sparks__

****

[Other side of Birth Certificate]

SENATE BILL NO. 188

[Text of Senate Bill No. 188 is too faded to transcribe clearly, containing Sections 7, 24, 25 regarding duties of the State Commissioner of Health, physicians reporting births, deaths, marriages, and divorces, and penalties for false certificates.]

Sac & Fox – Shawnee
1853-1933   Volume X

RECEIVED APR 19 1911 SAC & FOX AGENCY, OKLAHOMA.

Cushing, Okla.

April 17, 1911.

W.C. Kohlenberg.

Well Mr Kohlenberg We have got another baby here at our house. You can put him on the roll. Boy Baby.
He was born April 13, 1911. His name Elmer Gokey
He is doing fine.

Resp yours

Leo Gokey

RECEIVED JUN 7 1911 SAC & FOX AGENCY, OKLAHOMA.

Prague Okla
June 6th 1911

Mr W.C. Kholenburg [sic]

Dear Sir

Please send me application blank for which I would like to draw out.

Have you got out baby's name on the roll if not his name is Eugene Lewis Taylor. Born August 5th 1910

Yours respectfully

Mrs. Gertie Taylor

Sparks Okla
Sept 9-11

RECEIVED SEP 12 1911 SAC & FOX AGENCY, OKLAHOMA.

W. C. Kohlenberg,
   Sir

i see By Application you have Isaac Longshore Birth 1898, it is not correct his exact date of Birth is July 3 – 1897
Isaac was 14 years old July 3- 1911

Resp

Annie Longshore

Sac & Fox – Shawnee
1853-1933   Volume X

DEPARTMENT OF THE INTERIOR

UNITED STATES INDIAN SERVICE

RECEIVED DEC 27 1911 SAC & FOX AGENCY, OKLAHOMA.

Sac and Fox Indian Agency,
Stroud, Okla. RFD#2.
December 20, 1911.

Mr. O. A. Williams,
      Pottawatomie Agency,
          Hoyt, Kansas.

Dear Sir:-

    Will you kindly advise me the year in which Mj-ish-ke was born. This information is required in order to satisfy the Department in respect to the lease roll which now require the year of birth instead of the age.

                Very respectfully,
                W.C. Kohlenberg
                Supt. & Spl. Disb. Agent.

WCK/WMH

    Our records show she was born in 1850. The day and month not known.

            Respt
            G.L. Williams
            Supt.

DEC 23 1911 Nadeau, Kans.

4---12---297.

Department of the Interior.
United States Indian Service.

MISCELLANEOUS.

In re date of birth
Fannie Grayson.

OFFICE OF
DISTRICT AGENT.

RECEIVED DEC 29 1911 SAC & FOX AGENCY, OKLAHOMA.

Okmulgee, Oklahoma, December 27, 1911.

W. C. Kohlenberg,
    Supt. & Spl. Disb. Agent,
        Sac & Fox Indian Agency.

S[sic]   Stroud Okla. RFD#2.,

Sac & Fox – Shawnee
1853-1933 Volume X

Dear Sir:-

Your letter of December 20, 1911, addressed to Mrs. Fannie Grayson, Okmulgee, Oklahoma, in which she was requested to give you the date of her birth has been referred to this office by the addressee for reply. Mrs. Grayson states that the date of her birth was May 16, 1881.

Respectfully,

C E Bearse

CEB.   Acting District Agent.

DEPARTMENT OF THE INTERIOR
UNITED STATES INDIAN SERVICE

RECEIVED JAN 6 1912
SAC & FOX AGENCY, OKLAHOMA.

Shawnee, Oklahoma.
January 4, 1912.

Mr. W. C. Kohlenberg.
　　Superintendent.
　　　　Sac and Fox Agency, Oklahoma.

Dear Sir:

I have your letter of December 19, 1911, relative to the exact age of Tom Pe-ne-shee and in reply you are advised after a considerable delay I have obtained the information desired in that Tom Pe-ne-shee states he was born on the 15th day of August, 56 years ago, being in the year 1855.

I hope this will remove the exception taken by the Department.

Very respectfully,

J.A. Buntin

RS   Superintendent.

Sac & Fox – Shawnee
1853-1933 Volume X

DEPARTMENT OF THE INTERIOR

UNITED STATES INDIAN SERVICE

RECEIVED
JAN 16 1912
SAC & FOX AGENCY,
OKLAHOMA

Otoe Agency, Otoe, Okla.
January 16, 1912.

W.C. Kohlenberg,

Stroud, Okla.

Dear Sir:

In answer to your letter dated December 20, 1911, asking for the year of birth of certain Indians, I will state that we do not have any record of births of these Indians, but have noted the ages as we have them. We are required to note ages instead of births on our lease rolls.

Very respectfully,

Ralph P. Stanion
Supt. & S. D. A.

Date of Birth required for lease roll.

RECEIVED
JAN 16 1912
SAC & FOX AGENCY,
OKLAHOMA.

Otoe Agency.

Lease roll [Illegible] Jr. 1912

NAME.	Age.	
Harvey Atkins.	7	1904
William Atkins Jr..	9	1902
Josephine Atkins	29	
Baxter Atkins.	1	
Mark Burgess,	6	1904
Roy Burgess,	9	1901
Ralph Frank Burgess,	14	1896
William Burgess,	39	(872)
~~John Deroin,~~	~~31~~	
William Deroin,	10	1901

Sac & Fox – Shawnee
1853-1933   Volume X

Name	Age	Year
Joseph Deroin,	12	1899
Mitchell Deroin,	50	1861
Sam Ellis.	52	
Vestina Grant,	12	1902
Frank Grant,	16	1895
Anna Grant,	18	1893
Thelma Grant,	13	1898
Mary Green Grant, ..	50 Mary Ely Green Grant Brown MC Glasli[sic]	
Ralph Green, .	Horton, Kansas	
Mary Harragara.,	33	1879
Tom Hartico.	38	
Lizzie Hallowell.	31	1881
Eva B. Hoogradora,	here but age not known	
Dora Jones, Hudson	39	1871
~~Eliza Morr~~is,	~~Not here Horton, Kansas~~ Ok.	
Richard Roubideaux.	87	1823

Alice Duncan – Born Jan 2 – 1912

Dickson Duncan   father –
Lilly Neal   mother –

[The letter below typed as given]

RECEIVED
JAN 30 1912
SAC & FOX AGENCY,
OKLAHOMA.

Shawnee
Jan 28, 1912

W.C. Kohlenberg
Dear Sir

Sac & Fox – Shawnee
1853-1933   Volume X

I recieved your letter which I am in notion of Drawing out. I have a baby boy borned Thursday Jan 25 we have named the boy Levi Walker

Hoping too [illegible] soon

I am

Elma Walker

P.S.

I guess you know I am legally married.

RECEIVED
JAN 31 1912
SAC & FOX AGENCY,
OKLAHOMA.

Prague, Okla
1/29, 1912

Mr. W. C. Kohlenberg
Sir,

Please enrolle my little girl, her name
Minnie Thorpe
Born the 26, 1912

Yours Respt.
Frank Thorp

[Copy of original – Reverse side of Birth Certificate on page 153]

SENATE BILL NO. 188

SECTION 2. The State Commissioner of Health shall have power to make and enforce any and all needful rules and regulations for the prevention and cure, and to prevent the spread of any contagious, infectious or malarial diseases among persons. To establish quarantine and isolate any persons affected with contagious and infectious diseases. To remove or cause to be removed any dead or putrid body, or any decayed, putrid or other substance that may endanger the health of persons or domestic animals. To condemn or cause to be destroyed any impure or diseased article of food that may be offered for sale. To superintend the several boards of health in counties, cities, villages, towns and townships. To establish rules and regulations for the keeping and reporting of all vital statistics, births, deaths, marriages and divorces, as prescribed by this act.

SECTION 24. It shall be the duty of all physicians practicing in each county in this state to within thirty days report to the County Superintendent of Public Health, all births, and deaths, and the diseases with which said person died, and the age and sex, which said report shall be verified by affidavit of the said physician, and for each and every such report shall receive as compensation therefore the sum of ten cents, to be paid from the contingent fund of such county. It shall be the duty of the Clerk of the District Court to report to the State Board of Health the record of all divorces had in said court upon the close of the term of which said divorce is granted. The said County Superintendent of Public Health shall be required to transmit the report of the births and deaths reported to him by physicians to the State Board of Health as often as said Board may require.

SECTION 25. Any physician who makes or causes to be made a false certificate of death, or who makes any false statement in a certificate of death made by him, on the body of a deceased person, shall be deemed guilty of a misdemeanor, and shall, upon conviction thereof, be punished by a fine in the sum of one hundred dollars and ninety days in jail.

****

Sac & Fox – Shawnee
1853-1933   Volume X

[Copy of original Birth Certificate]

****

[Transcription of above Birth Certificate]

STANDARD CERTIFICATE OF BIRTH
OKLAHOMA STATE HEALTH DEPARTMENT
BUREAU OF VITAL STATISTICS
OKLAHOMA CITY, OKLAHOMA

PLACE OF BIRTH
County of Pottawatomie
Township of Earlboro
FULL NAME OF CHILD   Loa Marie Greenfeather
Sex of Child – Female   Legitimate? Yes   Date of birth Sept. 16, 1912

FATHER	MOTHER

FATHER
Full Name: Luther Greenfeather
Residence: R.R. #3, Shawnee, Okla
Color: Copper
Age at Last Birthday: 34 years

MOTHER
Full Maiden Name: Hattie Washington
Residence R.R. #3, Shawnee, Okla
Color: Copper
Age at Last Birthday: 32 years

Sac & Fox – Shawnee
1853-1933   Volume X

Birthplace: Whiteoak[sic], Oklahoma   Birthplace: Shawnee, Oklahoma
Occupation: Farmer   Occupation: Housekeeper
Number of Children born to this mother including present birth: 3
Number of children of this mother now living: 3

CERTIFICATE OF ~~ATTENDING PHYSICIAN OR MIDWIFE~~
I hereby certify that ~~I attended the birth of~~ this child, ~~who~~ was born alive at .... M., on the date above stated.

J A Buntin
Supt. & Spl. Disb. Agt.
Shawnee Indian Agency
(No physician in attendance)

****

[The letter below typed as given]

Shawnee Okla
Sept. 17, 1912.

Mr. John A Buntin
Dear Sir
Well my understanding is to report. When ever a new chile comes. Hattie Washington – or Greenfeather has a little girl. Born yesterday on the 16th. We haven't named her yet.
So long.
Switch Little Ax

RECEIVED
DEC 1 1912
SAC & FOX AGENCY,
OKLAHOMA.

Asher Okla
Nov 28-12

Mr. Horace J. Johnson
Sac and Fox Agency
Okla
Dear Sir:
Please enroll Jewel Virginia Kenyon Born to Albert D Kenyon and Isabel Kenyon Nov 25-12
Yours Truly
Isabel Kenyon
Asher Okla

Sac & Fox – Shawnee
1853-1933   Volume X

****

Asher Okla
Jan 10 – 13

Mr Horace J Johnson
Sac and Fox Agency
Okla

Dear Sir:

Will the Dept push the charges of perjury against Wm Seaborn in regard to the Lena Seaborn heirship case. The records plainly shows it with motive. We wrote sometime ago sending names and date of our girl. And recd no reply. Jewel Virginia Kenyon born Nov. 25 1912   daughter of Isabel and AD Kenyon

Hoping to her from you soon
  I am
    Your's[sic] Truly
      A.D. Kenyon
       Asher
        Okla

****

Verification of birth.

Sac and Fox Indian School,
Stroud, Okla., Dec. 6, 1912.

Mr. Maurice R. Gayle,
  U. S. Expert Framer[sic],
    Prague, RFD#1, Oklahoma.

Dear Sir,-

  I am in receipt of a letter from Isabel Kenyon, nee Barney, reporting the birth of a daughter Nov. 25, 1912. Kindly make your usual report in verification of same.

      Very respectfully,

TPM   Supt. & S. D. A.

****

Lena Seaborn
heirship

Sac & Fox – Shawnee
1853-1933   Volume X

Sac and Fox Indian School,
Stroud, Okla., Jan. 17, 1913.

A. D. Kenyon,
    Asher, Okla.,

Sir:-

   Your letter of the 20th. inst., has been received; as the Lena Seaborn heirship matter is still in abeyance, I can not tell what action can or will be taken against Mr. Seaborn, on account of his testimony, in the matter.
   The matter of the birth of your daughter is having proper attention.

Very respectfully,

Supt. & S. D. A.

HJJ/AM

****

   For letter relative to birth of Jewel Virginia Kenyon see jacket of this child. Jacket No. 714 1/2.

RECEIVED
OCT 14 1913
SAC & FOX AGENCY,
OKLAHOMA.

Cushing Okla
Oct. 11, 1913

Mr. Horace J Johnson
   Dear Sir
         This is to report the birth of Robert Charles Pate born Aug 27, 1913. Male
         Father   Robert Pate
         Mother Nellie Pate

Very Respt

Arza B Collins

Sac & Fox – Shawnee
1853-1933   Volume X

DEPARTMENT OF THE INTERIOR

UNITED STATES INDIAN SERVICE

Sac & Fox Indian School,
Stroud, Okla., Dec. 17, 1914.

I certify on honor that the records in the office of the Sac & Fox Indian School, Sac and Fox Agency, Oklahoma, show that Edward L. Morris, a Sac and Fox Indian, was born on July 15. 1893.

Horace J Johnson
Supt. & S. D. A.

[Copy of original Birth Certificate]

****

Sac & Fox – Shawnee
1853-1933   Volume X

[Transcription of Birth Certificate on page 157]
STANDARD CERTIFICATE OF BIRTH
OKLAHOMA STATE HEALTH DEPARTMENT
BUREAU OF VITAL STATISTICS
OKLAHOMA CITY, OKLAHOMA

PLACE OF BIRTH
County of Pottawatomie
Village of McLoud
FULL NAME OF CHILD   Jessie Jaunita Muchenenne
Sex of Child – Female   Twin, Triplet, or others? Twin   Number in order of birth: 2
Legitimate? Yes   Date of birth: July 25, 1914

FATHER   MOTHER

Full Name: Muchenenne   Full Maiden Name: Mahtwaahquah
Residence: Near McLoud   Residence near McLoud
Color: Indian   Color: Indian
Number of Children born to this mother including present birth: 3
Number of children of this mother now living: 2

****

[Transcription of Birth Certificate on page 159]
STANDARD CERTIFICATE OF BIRTH
OKLAHOMA STATE HEALTH DEPARTMENT
BUREAU OF VITAL STATISTICS
OKLAHOMA CITY, OKLAHOMA

PLACE OF BIRTH
County of Pottawatomie
Village of McLoud
FULL NAME OF CHILD   Bessie Wi nona Muchenenne
Sex of Child – Female   Twin, Triplet, or others? Twin   Number in order of birth: 1
Legitimate? Yes   Date of birth: July 25, 1914

FATHER   MOTHER

Full Name: Muchenenne   Full Maiden Name: Mah twa ah quah
Residence: near McLoud   Residence near McLoud
Color: Indian   Color: Indian
Number of Children born to this mother including present birth: 3
Number of children of this mother now living: 2

Sac & Fox – Shawnee
1853-1933   Volume X

[Copy of original Birth Certificate]

STANDARD CERTIFICATE OF BIRTH
OKLAHOMA STATE HEALTH DEPARTMENT
Bureau of Vital Statistics

County: Pottawatomie
Township of
Village of McLoud
City of

OKLAHOMA CITY, OKLAHOMA
Registered No.

FULL NAME OF CHILD: Bessie Mi nona Muchenenne

Sex of Child: Female   Twin   1   Yes   Date of Birth: July 25, 1914

FATHER
Full Name: Muchenenne
Residence: near McLoud
Color: Indian

MOTHER
Full Maiden Name: Mah twa ah quah
Residence: near McLoud
Color: Indian

Number of Children: 3   Number of children of this mother now living: 2

Sac and Fox Indian School
Stroud, Okla., Dec. 8, 1915.

Claud Chandler
Shawnee, Oklahoma

Sir:

Maggie Tyner has reported the birth of a daughter November 28, 1915, to whom she has given the name Ida Susan Tyner.

Please verify this in the usual manner.

Sac & Fox – Shawnee
1853-1933 Volume X

Very respectfully,

Horace J Johnson
Supt. & S. D. A.

HJJ/ND

[The letter below typed as given]

Supt. O. J. Green
Shawnee Okla

Sir Enclosed you will find names & birth of myself and children & my oldest sons family for to put on the Roll as we were informed to send them in to get the Roll in shape for the payment due us

Your respt
Effie M Dike Coder
Wamego Kans.

Effie M Dike Coder
born Mch 7 1873

Ralph Albert Coder
Born Mch 31st 1894

Frederick Clyde Coder
Born July 31st 1895

Hazel Francis Coder
born Sept 14th 1897

Wm Jefferson Coder
Born May 15th 1912

this is a correct statement of myself & childrens birth

My oldest son children

Muriel Lafern Coder
Born December 20th 1912

Sac & Fox – Shawnee
1853-1933   Volume X

Ralph Junior Coder
Born April 15th 1917

Children of Ralph Albert Coder
son of Effie M Coder

Births of Sac and Fox Indian Children reported since Jan. 1, 1917.

Father.	Mother.	Child.	Sex.	Date Born.
Jacob Wyman.	Mary Wyman.	Florine Wyman.	F.	3/16/17.
George Butler.	Edith Butler.	Benjamin Butler.	M.	8/7/16.
Harding Franklin	Minnie Franklin.	Daniel Franklin.	M.	10/19/16.
Edward Butler.	Ida Butler.	Fred Butler.	M.	1/7/17.
Robert Roubidoux.	Emily Roubidoux.	Arch Roubidoux.	M.	1/23/17
Elmer Manatowa.	Grace Manatowa.	Joseph Manatowa.	M.	2/3/17.
Austin Grant.	Alice Grant.	(Grover Grant.	M.	4/8/17.
" "	" " -Twins	(Mamie Grant.	F.	4/8/17.
Grover Morris.	Clara Morris.	Samuel Morris.	M.	5/8/17
Benjamin Walker.	Dora Walker.	Mary Walker.	F.	6/4/17

Death of Sac and Fox Indians reported since Jan. 1, 1917.
XXXXXXXXXXXXXXXXXXXXXXXXXXXXXXXXXXXXXXXXXXXX

Name	Sex.	Age.	Date.
Pearl Bessie Grant.	F.	1 Yr.	2/21/17.
Benjamin Butler.	M.	1 "	9/27/16.
Daniel Franklin.	M.	2 Mo.	12/27/16.
Fred Butler.	M.	7 Mo.	1/21/17.
Viola May Foster.	F.	2 Yr.	10/30/16.
Ople Murray	F.	4 mo 5 days	4/1/17.
Grover Grant.	M.	21 days	4/29/17

Department of the Interior

UNITED STATES INDIAN SERVICE **RECEIVED**

APR 3 1917

SAC AND FOX INDIAN SCHOOL, OKLA.

Cushing, Okla.

April 2, 1917.

Mr. Horace J. Johnson,
    Stroud Okla.
Dear Sir.

    Inclosed find report of Births[sic] among the Sac and Fox and Iowa, which I have not a record as to the report of.

    Benjamin Butler son of George and Edith Butler.
born Aug. 7, 1916.

    Fannie Harris Daughter of Benjamin and Grace Harris
born Sept. 27, 1916.

    Florena Wyman. Daughter of Mary and Jacob Wunan[sic].
born Mar. 18, 1917.

    Matilda Grass. Daughter of Ada and Silas Grass.
born Dec. 12, 1916.

    Aron Roubidoux, Son of Robert and Emily Roubidoux.
born Jan. 23, 1917.

    Vera Kent, Daughter of Frank and Emma Kent.
born Nov. 26, 1916.

    Fred Butler Son of Edward and Ida Butler.
born Jan. 7, 1916.

    Joseph Springer. Son of John and Gertrude Springer.
born Dec. 27, 1916.

    Ople Murry, Daughter of Kerwin and Alice Murry.
born Dec. 24. 1916.

    This includes some that have already been reported.

    Daniel Franklin son of Harding and Minnie Franklin
born Oct. 19, 1916.

    Very Respectfully,
    Arza B Collins

Sac & Fox – Shawnee
1853-1933   Volume X

[The letter below typed as given]

September – 10 – 1917
Wamego Kansas

Mr. Green   Shawnee mishion
Agent   Pott indian
i will send you the names of My children to place on the indian Roll of the Pottawatomie here are the Names

	ages
Margret Louan Dike	13
Jerrie Warren Dike	10
Pearl Josephene Dike	8
Joseph Edward Jr Dike	6
Reason Thomas Dike	4
Edith Marll[sic] Dike	2
{ Dean Howard } Dike	1 Month
{ Dale Eugene } Dike	1 Month
J E Dike Sr	

Please return Mail with me

[The letter below typed as given]

San Antonio Texas
Sept 23-1917

Mr. O. J. Green
   Shawnee Okla
      Dear Sir.
In Complyance with new request we are pleased to inform you of the Birth of our little Boy, his name, William Franklin Morris Hindman Jr. A Citizen Pottowatomie Born July 7-1917. doing nicely

Very Resp
Mr. & Mrs L. M. Hindman.

Sac & Fox – Shawnee
1853-1933   Volume X

Birth
Certificate
March, 1919
                Sac and Fox Indian School,
                  Stroud, Oklahoma, April 18, 1919.

The Commissioner of Indian Affairs,
    Washington, D. C.

Sir:

    There are forwarded, herewith, the following birth certificates pertaining to the jurisdiction of Sac & Fox, Okla.

Current Certificates

Number of Certificates forwarded	for the month of	Year of	Serial numbers inclusive	Remarks
1	March	1919	1	

Supplemental or corrected Certificates.

Number	Month	Year	Serial Number	Annotations
None				

Delayed Certificates.

Number	Month	Year	Annotation

                                Very Respectfully,

MJ- encl: 1
                                Superintendent.

Patsy Harris.

Sac & Fox – Shawnee
1853-1933   Volume X

Birth Certi-
ficate, February.   Sac and Fox Indian School,
  Stroud, Oklahoma, April 18, 1919.

The Commissioner of Indian Affairs,
 Washington, D. C.

Sir:
 There are forwarded, herewith, the following birth certificates pertaining to the jurisdiction of Sac & Fox, Okla.

Current Certificates.

Number of Certificates forwarded	For the month of February	Year of 1919	Serial numbers inclusive	Remarks

Supplemental or corrected Certificates.

Number	Month	Year	Serial	Annotations
0	Feb.	1919	Number	

Delayed Certificates.

Number	Month	Year	Serial	Annotations
1	February	1919	number 3	Enclosed certificate filed 4/16/19

Very Respectfully,

MJ   Superintendent.
  encl: 1

George Maxwell Hodsdon.

Sac & Fox – Shawnee
1853-1933   Volume X

Sac and Fox Indian School,
Stroud, Oklahoma,
July 14, 1919.

Arza B. Collins,
Cushing, Oklahoma.

Dear Mr Collins:

I hand you herewith a waiver and certificate of allegation in the matter of Harrison Hunter Jr., child of Carrie H. Hunter.

Please have this signed by John Thompson and Carrie Hunter and return it to this office at an early date as practicable, also obtain from Carrie H. Hunter a sworn statement concerning the parents of this child. Such statement is enclosed herewith. You may insert the data where it has been omitted.

Very respectfully,

Horace J Johnson
Supervisor in charge.

HJJ-ELB

Enclo.

Birth certificates for June, 1919.

Sac and Fox Indian School,
Stroud, Oklahoma, July 15, 1919.

Commissioner of Indian Affairs,
Washington, D. C.

Sir:

There are forwarded, herewith, the following birth certificates pertaining to the jurisdiction of the Sac and& Fox Indian School, Stroud, Oklahoma.

Current Certificates.

Number of Certificates forwarded	For the Month of	Year of	Serial Numbers inclusive	Remarks
	June	1919	1.	

Sac & Fox – Shawnee
1853-1933   Volume X

Supplemental or corrected certificates.

None

Delayed Certificates.

None

Very Respectfully,
Horace J Johnson
MJ- encl: 2.   Special Supervisor.

Clarence Grant Rice # 1.

DEPARTMENT OF THE INTERIOR   auth. 78

Bartlesville Okla
Aug 24 – 1920

Pottawatomie Indian Agent.
What date of birth does your records show
Reuben H Pappan
wire collect.
Worrlow.

Ans   Aug 24 – 1920

Worrlow
Bartlesville, Okla
        Your wire   Reuben H Pappan
        Not enrolled here.   Confer with Pawnee Agency
Pawnee, Oklahoma
                    Deane
                    Indian Agt.

Sac & Fox – Shawnee
1853-1933 Volume X

DEPARTMENT OF THE INTERIOR   auth. 78
Office of Indian Affairs
Washington

September 17, 1921.

Order No. 90.

To all Disbursing Officers of the Indian Service:

Paragraph 6 of Order No. 32, approved June 25, 1917, which confers general authority upon disbursing officers to incur liabilities and make disbursements that are legal and proper from funds allotted to them, is hereby amended so that the clause, "not to exceed $500 in any one case" shall read, "not to exceed $100 in any one case."

Paragraphs 7, 8, 13, 14, 18, and 19 of said order and any subsequent amendments or orders, wherein the sum of $500 appears as the limit of disbursements or liabilities allowed under general authority are also hereby amended so as to reduce said limit to $100. Provided, that all authorities involving liabilities and disbursements above $100 and not exceeding $500 shall require only the approval of the Commissioner of Indian Affairs.

CHAS. H. BURKE,

Commissioner.

September 19, 1921.

Approved:

F. M. GOODWIN,

Assistant Secretary.

Shawnee Indian Agency
Shawnee, Oklahoma
December 10, 1921

Mr. Irwin H, Spooner
Ottawa, Kansas

Dear Sir:

Sac & Fox – Shawnee
1853-1933   Volume X

In reply to your letter of December 5, requesting us to give you certificate of the dates of births of each of your children, you are informed that a certificate under the signature of the Superintendent has been made out and it is herewith enclosed, which I trust will serve the purpose for which you want it.

The letter from the Treasury Department to you, which you sent us, is returned herewith.

                                 Very truly yours,

                                 J. L. Suffecool
                                 Superintendent.

JJ/JC

****

                                 Shawnee Indian Agency
                                 Shawnee, Oklahoma
                                 December 9, 1921

CERTIFICATE

This is to certify that the undersigned is the duly appointed Superintendent of the Shawnee Indian Agency at Shawnee, Oklahoma; that he has the custody of the records pertaining to the Indians of the Shawnee Indian Agency jurisdiction, that such records show the family history of Ida Miller Spooner, the wife of Irwin Spooner to have had the following children, with dates of births as indicated.

        Mary Elizabeth Spooner..born March 13, 1912
        Bernice Henrietta Spooner " Nov. 12, 1913.
        Evangeline Miller Spooner " Oct. 8, 1915
        Lena Josephine Spooner   " July 11, 1917
        Edward Spooner   "   1919

                                 J. L. Suffecool
                                 Superintendent

JJ/JC

Sac & Fox – Shawnee
1853-1933 Volume X

Shawnee Indian Agency
Shawnee, Oklahoma
December 22, 1921

Mrs. Lizzie Casteel Porter
Sparks, Oklahoma

My dear friend:

I am in receipt of your letter of December 20, in which you advise of the birth of your son, named Scottie Alexendria[sic] Porter, and request that he be placed on the rolls at this Agency.

In reply, you are advised that an examination of the rolls has been made and we are unable to identify you by the name given. If you will kindly advise us of your maiden name, I will be pleased to comply with your request.

Your friend,

J. L. Suffecool
Superintendent

JLS/JC

Shawnee Indian Agency,
Shawnee, Oklahoma,
March 27, 1922.

Mrs. Elsie F. Kenny,
Pershing, Okla.

My friend:-

Replying to your letter of March 22, asking that your little girl, Frances Jay Kenny, 1/16th Pottawatomie Indian, born Nov. 5, 1921, be placed on the family register in this office; you are advised that your baby's name has been noted under your card and will be of record in the future. This is the first time that it has come to our notice that you were married.

At your convenience, we will be glad to have you forward to this office, the name of your husband, whether he is white or Indian, if Indian of what Tribe, and when you were married; so that we may make permanent record of your family history for future use.

Sac & Fox – Shawnee
1853-1933 Volume X

Very truly yours,

J. L. Suffecool
Superintendent

JJ:EV

Shawnee Indian Agency,
Shawnee, Oklahoma,
May 15, 1922.

Mr. John Tohee,
Perkins, Oklahoma.

Dear Sir;

    I am returning herewith your Certificate of Baptism as it gives us no record of your birth. It will be necessary for you to furnish this office with a certificate showing the date of your birth.

Very truly yours,

J. L. Suffecool
Superintendent

MPG-encl

****

Shawnee Indian Agency,
Shawnee, Oklahoma,
May 29, 1933[sic].

Mr. John Tohee,
Perkins, Oklahoma.

My friend:-

    This will acknowledge the receipt of your affidavit with reference to your birth and also a Certificate of Baptism, the same is returned herewith for the reason that the affidavit does not bear the personal signature of the Notary Public but only has his typewritten signature; also, in the Certificate of Baptism it is noted that you were baptized on the 16th day of April, 1922. This must be a mistake, if you were baptized on the 16th day of April, 1922, the Certificate is of no value and should be returned, however, if you can ascertain the exact date that you were baptized on, you may return the same.

    Please see that this affidavit is properly signed and returned, and upon receipt of same, the matter will be referred to the Indian Office.

                          Very respectfully,

                                J. L. Suffecool
                                Superintendent.

JLS:EV.
ENCL. 3

                   Shawnee Indian Agency,
                       Shawnee, Okla.
                       May 5, 1923.

Mr. A. R. Snyder, Supt.,
    Mayetta, Kansas.

Dear Mr. Snyder:-

    I am returning the birth certificates you sent me for the child of Leona Wiles Zhuckkahosee. These have been filled out from information gathered by the farmer. No physician's signature appears thereon as none was in attendance. This is the second child and is named James. The first child is named Frank and you have him enrolled with the Kickapoos at your agency.

    It is proposed to close the Sac & Fox Indian Roll here soon and if any interested parties reside within your jurisdiction please notify them of the anticipated action.

Incls.   Very truly yours,
JLR.

                                J. L. Suffecool,
                                Superintendent.

                     ****

Sac & Fox – Shawnee
1853-1933   Volume X

Frank Zhuck ko ho see   11/15/19
James   "   7/31/21

Mr. R.
Above two are the only children –
Ed –

****

Department of the Interior

United States Indian Field Service

RECEIVED
APR 23 1923
SHAWNEE INDIAN AGENCY

Potawatomie Indian Agency
Mayetta, Kansas
April 21, 1923.

Supt. J. L. Suffecool,
Shawnee Indian Agency,
Shawnee, Oklahoma.

Dear Mr. Suffecool:

I find in our files, a letter which you wrote this office, on May 5, 1922, requesting that the nine months old baby of Leona Wiles Zhuckkahosee, be placed on the Kickapoo Roll with its father, John Zhuckkahosee. This child's name was given as James.

We have no birth certificate of this child on file here, and I am inclosing two blank copies which I would thank you to have her fill out and return to this office. We are preparing our annuity roll now and wish to have the birth certificate.

We have enrolled here, a child of Leona Wiles, under the name of Frank Zhuckkahosee, but presume this is another child.

Very truly yours,
AR Snyder AW
A. R. Snyder
Superintendent.
AW

James
7/31/21 – Morning.

How many children, <u>living</u> have these people & names?
J.R.R.

173

Sac & Fox – Shawnee
1853-1933 Volume X

****

Shawnee Indian Agency,
Shawnee, Okla.
May 5, 1923.

Mr. A. R. Snyder, Supt.,
Mayetta, Kansas.
Dear Mr. Snyder:-

I am returning the birth certificates you sent me for the child of Leona Wiles Zhuckkahosee. These have been filled out from information gathered by the farmer. No physician's signature appears thereon as none was in attendance. This is the second child and is named James. The first child is named Frank and you have him enrolled with the Kickapoos at your agency.

It is proposed to close the Sac & Fox Indian Roll here soon and if any interested parties reside within your jurisdiction please notify them of the anticipated action.

Incls. Very truly yours,
JLR.
J. L. Suffecool,
Superintendent.

Shawnee Indian Agency,
Shawnee, Oklahoma,
June 12, 1923.

Mrs. Roseann Dean Lee,
1122 N. Tyler St.,
Topeka, Kansas.

Dear Madam:-

This is to acknowledge receipt of your letter under date of June 7, 1923, in which you advised that you were a member of the Pottawatomie Tribe of Indians and that you had two children which you desired to enroll with this Tribe.

Sac & Fox – Shawnee
1853-1933   Volume X

In reply I have to request that you will please inform us of your maiden name and of the names of your two children. Also, fill out the enclosed birth certificates in duplicate and have the physician attending at birth of child sign same.

Very truly yours,

J. L. Suffecool,
Superintendent.

EV.
enclos.

Shawnee Indian Agency,
Shawnee, Oklahoma,
Sept. 22, 1923.

Mrs. Rilla Meek De Porte,
Los Angeles, Cal California.

Dear Mrs. De Porte:-

I was informed yesterday that a son has made his arrival at your home. I am inclosing birth certificates which you will please fill out and have signed by your physician, then return to me at your earliest convenience in the inclosed penalty envelope. This is necessary in order that the proper report may be made to the Indian Office at Washington concerning vital statistics.

Thanking you, I am,

Yours Very truly,

J. L. Suffecool,
Superintendent.

JLR:EV
encls.

Sac & Fox – Shawnee
1853-1933   Volume X

Shawnee Indian Agency,
Shawnee, Okla.
October 4, 1923.

The Commissioner of Indian Affairs,
    Washington, D. C.

Dear Mr. Commissioner:-

    There are transmitted herewith the following birth certificates pertaining to this jurisdiction.

CURRENT CERTIFICATES.

Number of Certificates forwarded	For the month of	Year of	Serial numbers inclusive.	Remarks
1	September	1923.	1	

SUPPLEMENTAL CERTIFICATES.

1-x	August	1923	1-A	Delayed report of birth by her people.

Incls.
JLR.

                Very truly yours,

                    J. L. Suffecool,
                      Superintendent.

Sac & Fox – Shawnee
1853-1933   Volume X

Shawnee Indian Agency.

Shawnee, Oklahoma,
November 9, 1923.

The Commissioner of Indian Affairs,
Washington, D. C.

Dear Mr. Commissioner:

There are forwarded herewith the following birth certificates pertaining to the jurisdiction of the Shawnee Indian Agency.

Current Certificates.

Number of certificates forwarded.	For the month of	Year of	Serial numbers, inclusive.	Remarks.
1	October	1923	1-2	

Delayed Certificates.

Number	Month	Year	Serial number	Annotations.
2	September	1923	2-3	Delay in being reported to the office.
Delayed report # 1	November	1922	1	Same as above
Delayed report # 1	September	1917	1	Delay in being reported to the office.

Very Truly Yours,

J. L. Suffecool,
Superintendent.

AMS.

Sac and Fox-Shawnee – MARRIAGES
Undated

Sac & Fox – Shawnee
1853-1933 Volume X

MARRIAGE CARD.

Marriage. Sex _____ Census or Allotment No. _____
Name _____ Tribe _____
Married _____ How _____
Married to whom _____ Census or Allotment No. _____
If divorced, When _____ Where _____
If divorced, How _____

CHILDREN BORN OF THIS MARRIAGE.

Census or Allotment No.	Sex	Name	Born	Blood / Died
	F	Ozetta Bourbonnais Jinks	1876	1/16 Pott
		Husband		white
		Carl "		1/32 Pott
		Artesia New Mex.		
ADDRESS				

See Marriage Cards Nos. _____ and _____ for half-brothers and half-sisters of these children.

CONGREGATIONAL INDIAN MISSION,
Darlington, Oklahoma,
R. H. HARPER, MISSIONARY.

Supt. Geo. W. H. Stouch

Marriage Returns.

****

Sac & Fox – Shawnee
1853-1933   Volume X

WALTER C. ROE,
COLONY, OKLA.

Marriage Ctf

Mrs. George Hocheni,

Colony,

Okla.

****

MARRIAGE CARD.

Marriage. Sex ___ Census or Allotment No. ___
Name ___ Tribe ___
Married ___ How ___
Married to whom ___ Census or Allotment No. ___
If divorced, When ___ Where ___
If divorced, How ___

CHILDREN BORN OF THIS MARRIAGE.

CENSUS OR ALLOTMENT NO.	SEX	NAME	BORN	BLOOD / DIED
	M	Clerence[sic] Peltier	1883	5/8 Pott
	F	wife		white
	M	Jack "	1911	5/16 "
	M	Edmond "	1913	5/16 "
	F	Floydie[sic] "	1915	5/16 "
	F	Ida "	1917	5/16 "
	F	Jessie M "	1919	5/16 "
	F	Helen "	1921	5/16 "
	M	Henry A. "	1924	5/16 "
	M	-------- ---- "	1926	5/16 "

Lexington # 3

address ___

See Marriage Cards Nos. ___ and ___ for half-brothers and half-sisters of these children.

Sac & Fox – Shawnee
1853-1933 Volume X

MARRIAGE CARD.

Name _____ Marriage. Sex _____ Census or Allotment No. _____
Married _____ Tribe _____
Married to whom _____ How _____
If divorced, When _____ Census or Allotment No. _____
If divorced, How _____ Where _____

CHILDREN BORN OF THIS MARRIAGE.

CENSUS OR ALLOTMENT NO.	SEX	NAME	BORN	BLOOD / DIED
		Husband		white
	F	Margariette Peltier Nicholes[sic]	Dec 4 1908	5/16 Pott
		Lexington #2		
address				

See Marriage Cards Nos. _____ and _____ for half-brothers and half-sisters of these children.

MARRIAGE CARD.

Name _____ Marriage. Sex _____ Census or Allotment No. _____
Married _____ Tribe _____
Married to whom _____ How _____
If divorced, When _____ Census or Allotment No. _____
If divorced, How _____ Where _____

CHILDREN BORN OF THIS MARRIAGE.

CENSUS OR ALLOTMENT NO.	SEX	NAME	BORN	Blood / DIED
	M	John B Peltier	1877	5/8 Pott
		wife		white
	F	Ella "	1907	5/16 Pott
	M	George "	1912	"
		Neb "		
		Mable "		
		Maud "		
		Ruby "		
address				

See Marriage Cards Nos. _____ and _____ for half-brothers and half-sisters of these children.

Sac & Fox – Shawnee
1853-1933 Volume X

MARRIAGE CARD.

.... Marriage. Sex .... Census or Allotment No. ....
Name .... Tribe ....
Married .... How ....
Married to whom .... Census or Allotment No. ....
If divorced, When .... Where ....
If divorced, How ....

CHILDREN BORN OF THIS MARRIAGE.

Census or Allotment No.	Sex	Name	Born	Blood	Died
	M	Husband		1/2 Cherokee and white	
	F	Ida Peltier Robinson	1904	5/16 Pott	
	F	------ ------ "	1927	5/32 Pott	

address

See Marriage Cards Nos. .... and .... for half-brothers and half-sisters of these children.

MARRIAGE CARD.

.... Marriage. Sex .... Census or Allotment No. ....
Name .... Tribe ....
Married .... How ....
Married to whom .... Census or Allotment No. ....
If divorced, When .... Where ....
If divorced, How ....

CHILDREN BORN OF THIS MARRIAGE.

Census or Allotment No.	Sex	Name	Born	Blood	Died
	F	Elsie Peltier Kenney		5/16	
	M	Husband		white	
	F	Joy "	1923	5/32 Pott	

address

See Marriage Cards Nos. .... and .... for half-brothers and half-sisters of these children.

Sac & Fox – Shawnee
1853-1933   Volume X

MARRIAGE CARD.

Name _____ Marriage. Sex _____ Census or Allotment No. _____
Married _____ Tribe _____
Married to whom _____ How _____
If divorced, When _____ Census or Allotment No. _____
If divorced, How _____ Where _____

CHILDREN BORN OF THIS MARRIAGE.

Census or Allotment No.	Sex	Name	Born	Blood (Died)
	M	James Peltier	1881	5/8 Pott
		wife		white
	M	James Jr "	May 1907	5/16 Pott
	M	Homes M "	1901	5/16 "
	F	Lily M "	1913	5/16 "
	M	George "	1915	5/16 "
	M	Halley "	1917	5/16 "
	F	Joy "	1921	5/16 "
address	Lexington # 2			

See Marriage Cards Nos. _____ and _____ for half-brothers and half-sisters of these children.

MARRIAGE CARD.

Name _____ Marriage. Sex _____ Census or Allotment No. _____
Married _____ Tribe _____
Married to whom _____ How _____
If divorced, When _____ Census or Allotment No. _____
If divorced, How _____ Where _____

CHILDREN BORN OF THIS MARRIAGE.

Census or Allotment No.	Sex	Name	Born	Blood (Died)
	F	Zoa Bruno Rhodd	1842	1/2 Pott
address	Konawa # 3			

See Marriage Cards Nos. _____ and _____ for half-brothers and half-sisters of these children.

Sac & Fox – Shawnee
1853-1933 Volume X

MARRIAGE CARD.

.................................Marriage. Sex........ Census or Allotment No.........................
Name... Tribe......Pott.................................
Married... How...
Married to whom...................................... Census or Allotment No......................
If divorced, When.................................... Where......................................
If divorced, How...

CHILDREN BORN OF THIS MARRIAGE.

Census or Allotment No.	Sex	Name	Born	Blood / Died
	M	Baptiste Curley	Jan 10 1899	29/32 Pott
		Wife		white
		Pawhuska Okla		
address				

See Marriage Cards Nos. _____ and _____ for half-brothers and half-sisters of these children.

MARRIAGE CARD.

.................................Marriage. Sex........ Census or Allotment No.........................
Name... Tribe......Pott.................................
Married... How...
Married to whom...................................... Census or Allotment No......................
If divorced, When.................................... Where......................................
If divorced, How...

CHILDREN BORN OF THIS MARRIAGE.

Census or Allotment No.	Sex	Name	Born	Blood / Died
	M	Husband		White
	F	Mary Curley Cavender	Dec 3 1901	29/32 Pott
		Konawa		
address				

See Marriage Cards Nos. _____ and _____ for half-brothers and half-sisters of these children.

Sac & Fox – Shawnee
1853-1933   Volume X

MARRIAGE CARD.

_____Marriage. Sex_____ Census or Allotment No._____
Name_____ Tribe_____
Married_____ How_____
Married to whom_____ Census or Allotment No._____
If divorced, When_____ Where_____
If divorced, How_____

CHILDREN BORN OF THIS MARRIAGE.

Census or Allotment No.	Sex	Name	Born	Blood	Died
	M	Joseph A Nona	Aug 12 1880	Full Pott	
	F	Tilda Curley "	1891	15/16 Pott	
	M	Thomas A "	Jan 7 1911	32/33 Pott	
	M	W^{m} "	July 3 1914	32/33 "	
	M	Iquatious[sic] "	Aug 10 1917	32/33 "	
	F	Cecilia "	May 29 1920	32/33 "	

address Konawa #2

See Marriage Cards Nos._____ and _____ for half-brothers and half-sisters of these children.

MARRIAGE CARD.

_____Marriage. Sex_____ Census or Allotment No._____
Name_____ Tribe_____
Married_____ How_____
Married to whom_____ Census or Allotment No._____
If divorced, When_____ Where_____
If divorced, How_____

CHILDREN BORN OF THIS MARRIAGE.

Census or Allotment No.	Sex	Name	Born	Blood	Died
	M	John LeClaire	Dec 5 1901	1/2 Pott	
	F	Gertrude Wana "	1907	1/2 "	
	M	John Jr. "	May 7 1928	1/2 "	

address Sacred Heart

See Marriage Cards Nos._____ and _____ for half-brothers and half-sisters of these children.

Sac & Fox – Shawnee
1853-1933   Volume X

MARRIAGE CARD.

Name _____ Marriage. Sex _____ Census or Allotment No. _____
Married _____ Tribe _____
Married to whom _____ How _____
If divorced, When _____ Census or Allotment No. _____
If divorced, How _____ Where _____

CHILDREN BORN OF THIS MARRIAGE.

Census or Allotment No.	Sex	Name	Born	Blood Died
	M	Henry LeClair	Sept 12 1898	1/2 Pott
		wife		white
	F	Bobie J "	May 12 1929	1/4 Pott

address Konawa # 2

See Marriage Cards Nos. _____ and _____ for half-brothers and half-sisters of these children.

MARRIAGE CARD.

Name _____ Marriage. Sex _____ Census or Allotment No. _____
Married _____ Tribe _____
Married to whom _____ How _____
If divorced, When _____ Census or Allotment No. _____
If divorced, How _____ Where _____

CHILDREN BORN OF THIS MARRIAGE.

Census or Allotment No.	Sex	Name	Born	Blood Died
	M	George A Lehman	July 13 1905	1/4 Pott
		wife		white
	F	Odela M "	Aug 11 1927	1/8 Pott

address Cogan Okla # 1 c/o J.W. Sanders

See Marriage Cards Nos. _____ and _____ for half-brothers and half-sisters of these children.

Sac & Fox – Shawnee
1853-1933 Volume X

MARRIAGE CARD.

Name .... Marriage. Sex .... Census or Allotment No. ....
Married .... Tribe .... Pott ....
Married to whom .... How ....
If divorced, When .... Census or Allotment No. ....
If divorced, How .... Where ....

CHILDREN BORN OF THIS MARRIAGE.

Census or Allotment No.	Sex	Name	Born	Died Blood
	F	Belle B Lehman	Feb 9 1885	1/2 Pott
	M	Husband		white
	~~M~~	~~George A. "~~	~~July 13 1905~~	~~1/4 Pott.~~
	M	Edgar W. "	Oct 2 1918	1/4 "
	F	Grace C "	Dec 27 1922	1/4 "

address Konawa #2

See Marriage Cards Nos. .... and .... for half-brothers and half-sisters of these children.

MARRIAGE CARD.   see Mary Cavender

Name .... Marriage. Sex .... Martha [Illegible]   n-Doc Rhodd
                                                    Census or Allotment No. ....
Married .... Tribe .... Pott ....
Married to whom .... How ....
If divorced, When .... Census or Allotment No. ....
If divorced, How .... Where ....

CHILDREN BORN OF THIS MARRIAGE.

Census or Allotment No.	Sex	Name	Born	Died blood
	M	Joe ([Illegible]) Curley	1872	[?] Pott
	F	Katherine Bennett "	1882	Full Pott
	M	Andrew "	1902	29/32
	M	Robert "	1905	
	F	Theresia "	1907	
	F	Margret "	1912	
	F	Florence "	1915	

address Pershing Okla

See Marriage Cards Nos. .... and .... for half-brothers and half-sisters of these children.

Sac & Fox – Shawnee
1853-1933   Volume X

MARRIAGE CARD.

_____ Marriage. Sex _____ Census or Allotment No. _____
Name _____ Tribe _____
Married _____ How _____
Married to whom _____ Census or Allotment No. _____
If divorced, When _____ Where _____
If divorced, How _____

CHILDREN BORN OF THIS MARRIAGE.

CENSUS OR ALLOTMENT NO.	SEX	NAME	BORN	DIED blood
	M	Husband		white
	F	Lucile Haas Lehman	Aug 18 1911	1/4 Pott
	M	Leo F "	Sept 16 1927	1/8 "
address	Konawa Okla #1			

See Marriage Cards Nos. _____ and _____ for half-brothers and half-sisters of these children.

MARRIAGE CARD.

_____ Marriage. Sex _____ Census or Allotment No. _____
Name _____ Tribe _____
Married _____ How _____
Married to whom _____ Census or Allotment No. _____
If divorced, When _____ Where _____
If divorced, How _____

CHILDREN BORN OF THIS MARRIAGE.

CENSUS OR ALLOTMENT NO.	SEX	NAME	BORN	DIED blood
	M	Joseph Negahuquet	Oct 19 1878	
		Wife		white
	M	Joseph Jr. "	Nov 2 1915	1/2 Pott
	M	Anthony "	Dec 14 1917	"
	F	Madeline "	Aug 23 1919	"
	M	James "	Dec 19 1922	"
	F	Thelma "	Mar 14 1923	"
	F	Maxine "	Feb 22 1925	"
	F	Louise "	Nov 23 1927	"
address	Pearson Okla.			

See Marriage Cards Nos. _____ and _____ for half-brothers and half-sisters of these children.

Sac & Fox – Shawnee
1853-1933 Volume X

MARRIAGE CARD.

Name _____ Marriage. Sex _____ Census or Allotment No. _____
Married _____ Tribe _____
Married to whom _____ How _____
If divorced, When _____ Census or Allotment No. _____
If divorced, How _____ Where _____

CHILDREN BORN OF THIS MARRIAGE.

Census or Allotment No.	Sex	Name	Born	Died blood
	M	Albert Negahuquet	1875	full
address				

See Marriage Cards Nos. _____ and _____ for half-brothers and half-sisters of these children.

MARRIAGE CARD.

Name _____ Marriage. Sex _____ Census or Allotment No. _____
Married _____ Tribe _____
Married to whom _____ How _____
If divorced, When _____ Census or Allotment No. _____
If divorced, How _____ Where _____

CHILDREN BORN OF THIS MARRIAGE.

Census or Allotment No.	Sex	Name	Born	Died blood
	M	Alowishes Negahuquet	1897	full Pott
	F	Wife		white
		Macomb #1		
address				

See Marriage Cards Nos. _____ and _____ for half-brothers and half-sisters of these children.

Sac & Fox -- Shawnee
1853-1933   Volume X

MARRIAGE CARD.

Marriage. Sex _____ Census or Allotment No. _____
Name _____
Married _____ Tribe _____
Married to whom _____ How _____
If divorced, When _____ Census or Allotment No. _____
If divorced, How _____ Where _____

CHILDREN BORN OF THIS MARRIAGE.

Census or Allotment No.	Sex	Name	Born	blood DIED
	F	Rosa Negahuquet Philips	1893	full Pott
	M	Husband		white
		Albert "	1925	1/2 Pott

address Davis #2

See Marriage Cards Nos. _____ and _____ for half-brothers and half-sisters of these children.

MARRIAGE CARD.

Marriage. Sex _____ Census or Allotment No. _____
Name _____
Married _____ Tribe _____
Married to whom _____ How _____
If divorced, When _____ Census or Allotment No. _____
If divorced, How _____ Where _____

CHILDREN BORN OF THIS MARRIAGE.

Census or Allotment No.	Sex	Name	Born	blood DIED
	M	Husband		white
	F	Katherine Negahuquet Debolt	1888	full Pott

address Davis #2

See Marriage Cards Nos. _____ and _____ for half-brothers and half-sisters of these children.

Sac & Fox – Shawnee
1853-1933   Volume X

MARRIAGE CARD.

Name _____ Marriage. Sex _____ Census or Allotment No. _____
Married _____ Tribe _____
Married to whom _____ How _____
If divorced, When _____ Census or Allotment No. _____
If divorced, How _____ Where _____

CHILDREN BORN OF THIS MARRIAGE.

Census or Allotment No.	Sex	Name	Born	Died blood
	M	Stephen Negahuquet	1853	full Pott
	M	Stephen Jr "	1890	"
	M	Thomas "	1895	"

address   Davis #2

See Marriage Cards Nos. _____ and _____ for half-brothers and half-sisters of these children.

MARRIAGE CARD.

Name _____ Marriage. Sex _____ Census or Allotment No. _____
Married _____ Tribe _____
Married to whom _____ How _____
If divorced, When _____ Census or Allotment No. _____
If divorced, How _____ Where _____

CHILDREN BORN OF THIS MARRIAGE.

Census or Allotment No.	Sex	Name	Born	Died blood
	M	Jerome Slatting	1894	10/16 Pott
	F	wife white		

address   Asher #2

See Marriage Cards Nos. _____ and _____ for half-brothers and half-sisters of these children.

Sac & Fox – Shawnee
1853-1933 Volume X

MARRIAGE CARD.

Name .... Marriage. Sex .... Census or Allotment No. ....
Married .... Tribe ....
Married to whom .... How ....
If divorced, When .... Census or Allotment No. ....
If divorced, How .... Where ....

CHILDREN BORN OF THIS MARRIAGE.

Census or Allotment No.	Sex	Name	Born	Died blood
	M	Frank Davis	Jan 5 1869	3/4 Pott
	F	Alice Pelky "	1871	5/18 "
	M	Robert "	Jan 8 1899	11/16 "
	F	Rosa "	Mar 1904	11/16 "
	F	Isabell "		11/16 "
	M	Carl "	March 15 1915	11/16 "
		(step children of Frank Davis)		
	F	Nora Slatting	May 28 1894	10/16 "
	M	Jerome "	1895	10/16
		(Father white)		
		Victor Cope	Dec 13 1928	11/32
		(Grand child)		
address		Asher #2		

See Marriage Cards Nos. .... and .... for half-brothers and half-sisters of these children.

MARRIAGE CARD.

Name .... Marriage. Sex .... Census or Allotment No. ....
Married .... Tribe ....
Married to whom .... How ....
If divorced, When .... Census or Allotment No. ....
If divorced, How .... Where ....

CHILDREN BORN OF THIS MARRIAGE.

Census or Allotment No.	Sex	Name	Born	Died blood
	M	Husband (white)		white
	F	Isabell Davis Cope		11/16 Pott
address		Asher #2		

See Marriage Cards Nos. .... and .... for half-brothers and half-sisters of these children.

Sac & Fox – Shawnee
1853-1933   Volume X

MARRIAGE CARD.

_____ Marriage. Sex _____ Census or Allotment No. _____
Name _____ Tribe _____
Married _____ How _____
Married to whom _____ Census or Allotment No. _____
If divorced, When _____ Where _____
If divorced, How _____

CHILDREN BORN OF THIS MARRIAGE.

CENSUS OR ALLOTMENT NO.	SEX	NAME	BORN	DIED blood
	M	Claud Castleberry	1883	1/8 Pott
		wife		white
	F	Beatrice "	1912	1/16 Pott
address	Ada Okla			

See Marriage Cards Nos. _____ and _____ for half-brothers and half-sisters of these children.

MARRIAGE CARD.

_____ Marriage. Sex _____ Census or Allotment No. _____
Name _____ Tribe _____
Married _____ How _____
Married to whom _____ Census or Allotment No. _____
If divorced, When _____ Where _____
If divorced, How _____

CHILDREN BORN OF THIS MARRIAGE.

CENSUS OR ALLOTMENT NO.	SEX	NAME	BORN	DIED blood
		Peter Buchanan		Part Indian?
	F	Edna Castleberry Buchanan	1885	1/8 Pott
		5 children names will be mailed in		
address	Ada Okla			

See Marriage Cards Nos. _____ and _____ for half-brothers and half-sisters of these children.

Sac & Fox – Shawnee
1853-1933   Volume X

Jesse } Give names
Earl   } to Agency
Ruben }

MARRIAGE CARD.

This name should be 1894 instead of 1891

_____ Marriage. Sex _____ Census or Allotment No. _____
Name _____ Tribe _____
Married _____ How _____
Married to whom _____ Census or Allotment No. _____
If divorced, When _____ Where _____
If divorced, How _____

CHILDREN BORN OF THIS MARRIAGE.

CENSUS OR ALLOTMENT NO.	SEX	NAME	BORN	blood	DIED
	M	John Edward French	1917	7/8 Pott ~~Shawnee~~	
	G	Mary Ann "	1918	7/8 "	
		Father and mother dead live G.W. Haas			
address					

See Marriage Cards Nos. _____ and _____ for half-brothers and half-sisters of these children.

MARRIAGE CARD.

_____ Marriage. Sex _____ Census or Allotment No. _____
Name _____ Tribe _____
Married _____ How _____
Married to whom _____ Census or Allotment No. _____
If divorced, When _____ Where _____
If divorced, How _____

CHILDREN BORN OF THIS MARRIAGE.

CENSUS OR ALLOTMENT NO.	SEX	NAME	BORN	blood	DIED
	M	Jesse Haas	1891	1/4 Pott	
	F	wife			
		J. R. "	1916	1/8 Pott	
		James "	1920	1/2 "	
address	Asher #1				

See Marriage Cards Nos. _____ and _____ for half-brothers and half-sisters of these children.

Sac & Fox – Shawnee
1853-1933   Volume X

MARRIAGE CARD.

```
_____Marriage. Sex_____ Census or Allotment No._____
Name_____   Tribe_____
Married_____   How_____
Married to whom_____   Census or Allotment No._____
If divorced, When_____   Where_____
If divorced, How_____
```

CHILDREN BORN OF THIS MARRIAGE.

Census or Allotment No.	Sex	Name	Born	Died blood
	M	Husband		white
	F	Viola Castleberry Cox	1898	1/8 Pott
	M	Homer Julian	1921	1/16 "
		by 1st husband		
address		Konawa # 1		

See Marriage Cards Nos. _____ and _____ for half-brothers and half-sisters of these children.

MARRIAGE CARD.

```
_____Marriage. Sex_____ Census or Allotment No._____
Name_____   Tribe_____
Married_____   How_____
Married to whom_____   Census or Allotment No._____
If divorced, When_____   Where_____
If divorced, How_____
```

CHILDREN BORN OF THIS MARRIAGE.

Census or Allotment No.	Sex	Name	Born	Died blood
	M	John Castleberry	1881	1/8 Pott
		wife		white
	M	Webster "	1917	1/16 Pott
address		Asher		

See Marriage Cards Nos. _____ and _____ for half-brothers and half-sisters of these children.

Sac & Fox – Shawnee
1853-1933   Volume X

MARRIAGE CARD.

Marriage. Sex _____ Census or Allotment No. _____
Name _____
Married _____   Tribe _____
Married to whom _____   How _____
If divorced, When _____   Census or Allotment No. _____
If divorced, How _____   Where _____

CHILDREN BORN OF THIS MARRIAGE.

Census or Allotment No.	Sex	Name	Born	Died blood
	M	James Castleberry		white
	F	Josephine Haas "	1874	1/4 Pott
	M	John "		
	F	Edna "		
	M	Claud		
	F	Viola "		

address _____

See Marriage Cards Nos. _____ and _____ for half-brothers and half-sisters of these children.

MARRIAGE CARD.

Marriage. Sex _____ Census or Allotment No. _____
Name _____
Married _____   Tribe _____
Married to whom _____   How _____
If divorced, When _____   Census or Allotment No. _____
If divorced, How _____   Where _____

CHILDREN BORN OF THIS MARRIAGE.

Census or Allotment No.	Sex	Name	Born	Died blood
	M	Joseph Haas	1897	1/8 Pott
		wife		white
		will mail in names of 2 children		

address Lindsay Okla

See Marriage Cards Nos. _____ and _____ for half-brothers and half-sisters of these children.

Sac & Fox – Shawnee
1853-1933   Volume X

MARRIAGE CARD.

Marriage. Sex .... Census or Allotment No. 555
Name .... Tribe .... Pott
Married .... How ....
Married to whom .... Census or Allotment No. ....
If divorced, When .... Where ....
If divorced, How ....

CHILDREN BORN OF THIS MARRIAGE.

Census or Allotment No.	Sex	Name	Born	Blood / Died
	F	Laura J Baylis Nedeau	1873	1/8 Pott
555	M	Eli J. Nedeau	Aug 15 1869	1/4 Pott
	M	Daniel A "	1893	"

address Tecumseh # 1

See Marriage Cards Nos. ____ and ____ for half-brothers and half-sisters of these children.

MARRIAGE CARD.

Marriage. Sex .... Census or Allotment No. ....
Name .... Tribe .... Pott
Married .... How ....
Married to whom .... Census or Allotment No. ....
If divorced, When .... Where ....
If divorced, How ....

CHILDREN BORN OF THIS MARRIAGE.

Census or Allotment No.	Sex	Name	Born	Blood / Died
		~~Re~~		white
	M	James C. Hollingsworth		
	F	Rena A Nedeau Hollingsworth	1895	1/4 Pott
	M	James C. " Jr	age 22 1917	1/8 "
	M	Daniel L "	Jan 1 1919	"
	F	Laura "	Nov 6 1922	"
	F	Dilla J "	Dec 31 1923	"
	F	Sarrah "	Oct 25 1925	"
	M	Glen V "	Aug 17 1928	"

address Tecumseh # 1

See Marriage Cards Nos. ____ and ____ for half-brothers and half-sisters of these children.

Sac & Fox – Shawnee
1853-1933   Volume X

MARRIAGE CARD.

Name .... Marriage. Sex ...... Census or Allotment No. ....
Married .... Tribe .... Pott ....
Married to whom .... How ....
If divorced, When .... Census or Allotment No. ....
If divorced, How .... Where ....

CHILDREN BORN OF THIS MARRIAGE.

Census or Allotment No.	Sex	Name	Born	Died / Blood
	M	Louis Acton	July 8 1995[sic]	3/4 Pott
		Address Harjo		

See Marriage Cards Nos. _____ and _____ for half-brothers and half-sisters of these children.

MARRIAGE CARD.

Name .... Marriage. Sex ...... Census or Allotment No. ....
Married .... Tribe .... Pott ....
Married to whom .... How ....
If divorced, When .... Census or Allotment No. ....
If divorced, How .... Where ....

CHILDREN BORN OF THIS MARRIAGE.

Census or Allotment No.	Sex	Name	Born	Died ~~Blood~~
	~~M~~	~~Clarence~~		
		Bell Cummings Clary	Mother Dead	
	M	Lawrence "	July 16 1910	Part Pott
	M	Jack "	1912	" "
ADDRESS		~~Maud~~		

See Marriage Cards Nos. _____ and _____ for half-brothers and half-sisters of these children.

Sac & Fox – Shawnee
1853-1933   Volume X

MARRIAGE CARD.

Name .... Marriage. Sex .... Census or Allotment No. ....
Married .... Tribe .... Pott ....
Married to whom .... How ....
If divorced, When .... Census or Allotment No. ....
If divorced, How .... Where ....

CHILDREN BORN OF THIS MARRIAGE.

CENSUS OR ALLOTMENT NO.	SEX	NAME	BORN	BLOOD
	F	Ellen M Cummings	Jan 12 1873	1/16 Pott

ADDRESS   Maud # 1

See Marriage Cards Nos. .... and .... for half-brothers and half-sisters of these children.

MARRIAGE CARD.

Name .... Marriage. Sex .... Census or Allotment No. ....
Married .... Tribe .... Pott ....
Married to whom .... How ....
If divorced, When .... Census or Allotment No. ....
If divorced, How .... Where ....

CHILDREN BORN OF THIS MARRIAGE.

CENSUS OR ALLOTMENT NO.	SEX	NAME	BORN	DIED VLOOD[sic]
		Husband		white
	F	Fama Cummings Brookover	Jan 26 1896	1/32 Pott
	F	Hazel "	May 14 1921	1/64 "
	M	Clinton S "	March 20 1928	1/64 "

ADDRESS   Colorado Texas

See Marriage Cards Nos. .... and .... for half-brothers and half-sisters of these children.

Sac & Fox – Shawnee
1853-1933   Volume X

MARRIAGE CARD.

Name _____ Marriage. Sex _____ Census or Allotment No. _____
Married _____ Tribe _____ Pott _____
Married to whom _____ How _____
If divorced, When _____ Census or Allotment No. _____
If divorced, How _____ Where _____

CHILDREN BORN OF THIS MARRIAGE.

Census or Allotment No.	Sex	Name	Born	Blood	Died
	M	Chas S Cummings	July 8 1893	1/32	
		wife		white	
	F	Normalee "	Oct 26 1919	1/64	

address   Maud # 1

See Marriage Cards Nos. _____ and _____ for half-brothers and half-sisters of these children.

MARRIAGE CARD.

Name _____ Marriage. Sex _____ Census or Allotment No. _____
Married _____ Tribe _____ Pott _____
Married to whom _____ How _____
If divorced, When _____ Census or Allotment No. _____
If divorced, How _____ Where _____

CHILDREN BORN OF THIS MARRIAGE.

Census or Allotment No.	Sex	Name	Born	Blood	Died
by 1st husband		Husbands white			
	F	Cora A. Cummings Harrison	June 22 1890	1/32	Pott
	M	Thomas H Tisby	Oct 11 1910	1/64	"
	M	Chas Harrison	Oct 7 1924	1/64	"

address   Ripley Okla

See Marriage Cards Nos. _____ and _____ for half-brothers and half-sisters of these children.

Sac & Fox – Shawnee
1853-1933 Volume X

MARRIAGE CARD.

```
                        Marriage. Sex_____  Census or Allotment No._____
Name_____       Tribe_____Pott_____
Married_____       How_____
Married to whom_____        Census or Allotment No._____
If divorced, When_____        Where_____
If divorced, How_____
```

CHILDREN BORN OF THIS MARRIAGE.

Census or Allotment No.	Sex	Name	Born	Died / Blood
	M	Andy J. Cummings	1868	1/16 Pott
	F	Theresa "	1869	white

address Maud # 1

See Marriage Cards Nos. _____ and _____ for half-brothers and half-sisters of these children.

MARRIAGE CARD.

```
                        Marriage. Sex_____  Census or Allotment No._____
Name_____       Tribe_____Pott_____
Married_____       How_____
Married to whom_____        Census or Allotment No._____
If divorced, When_____        Where_____
If divorced, How_____
```

CHILDREN BORN OF THIS MARRIAGE.

Census or Allotment No.	Sex	Name	Born	Died / Blood
	M	Halby C Willmett	1903	Part Pott
		wife		white
	M	Lessie F "	1924	Part Pott

address Lexington # 2

See Marriage Cards Nos. _____ and _____ for half-brothers and half-sisters of these children.

Sac & Fox – Shawnee
1853-1933   Volume X

7 children

MARRIAGE CARD.

Name _____ Marriage. Sex _____ Census or Allotment No. _____
Married _____ Tribe _____ Pott _____
Married to whom _____ How _____
If divorced, When _____ Census or Allotment No. _____
If divorced, How _____ Where _____

CHILDREN BORN OF THIS MARRIAGE.

CENSUS OR ALLOTMENT NO.	SEX	NAME	BORN	DIED Blood
	F	Dora Willmette Cheatwood	June 5 1895	Part
		Husband		white

address Lexington # 4

See Marriage Cards Nos. _____ and _____ for half-brothers and half-sisters of these children.

MARRIAGE CARD.

Name _____ Marriage. Sex _____ Census or Allotment No. _____
Married _____ Tribe _____ Pott _____
Married to whom _____ How _____
If divorced, When _____ Where _____
If divorced, How ____ sometimes called Susan May _____

CHILDREN BORN OF THIS MARRIAGE.

CENSUS OR ALLOTMENT NO.	SEX	NAME	BORN	DIED Blood
	M	Joseph A Willmett	1864	1/8 Pott
		~~Susan~~ Mary "	1871	3/4 French Pott 1/32
		Clarence L "	Nov 4 1898	"

address Lexington # 2

See Marriage Cards Nos. _____ and _____ for half-brothers and half-sisters of these children.

Sac & Fox – Shawnee
1853-1933 Volume X

MARRIAGE CARD.

```
_____Marriage. Sex_____  Census or Allotment No._____
Name_____  Tribe_____ Pott_____
Married_____  How_____
Married to whom_____  Census or Allotment No._____
If divorced, When_____  Where_____
If divorced, How_____
```

CHILDREN BORN OF THIS MARRIAGE.

CENSUS OR ALLOTMENT NO.	SEX	NAME	BORN	DIED blood
	M	Arthur [?] Pratt	Apr 30 1877	1/32
		wife	July 10 1912	white
	F	Myrtle "		1/64 Pott
	F	Verie J "	Apr 17 1914	1/64 "
	M	Bernard F "	Aug 1917	1/64 "
	F	Zelma M "	Feb 9 1919	1/64
	M	Valentine A "	Feb 14 1923	1/64
address		Maud #2		

See Marriage Cards Nos. _____ and _____ for half-brothers and half-sisters of these children.

MARRIAGE CARD.

```
_____Marriage. Sex_____  Census or Allotment No._____
Name_____  Tribe____ Pott_____
Married_____  How_____
Married to whom_____  Census or Allotment No._____
If divorced, When_____  Where_____
If divorced, How_____
```

CHILDREN BORN OF THIS MARRIAGE.

CENSUS OR ALLOTMENT NO.	SEX	NAME	BORN	DIED Blood
		Husband white		
	F	Ruth D. Pratt Lucy	1910	Part Pott
	M	Garland L. "	1927	"
	M	Terry E. "	April 23 1929	"
address		Maud #2		

See Marriage Cards Nos. _____ and _____ for half-brothers and half-sisters of these children.

Sac & Fox – Shawnee
1853-1933 Volume X

MARRIAGE CARD.

```
_____Marriage. Sex_____ Census or Allotment No._____
Name_____ Tribe_____Pott_____
Married_____ How_____
Married to whom_____ Census or Allotment No._____
If divorced, When_____ Where_____
If divorced, How_____
```

CHILDREN BORN OF THIS MARRIAGE.

Census or Allotment No.	Sex	Name	Born	Died Blood
		Louis Pratt (Dead)		Part Pott
		Gertrude Pratt (Mother)		white
	F	Maggie E Pratt Cheatwood	1904	Part Pott
	F	Jaunatia[sic] "	1924	"
	M	Robert "	1926	"
	M	James W. "	1928	"

address Maud

See Marriage Cards Nos. _____ and _____ for half-brothers and half-sisters of these children.

MARRIAGE CARD.

```
_____Marriage. Sex_____ Census or Allotment No._____
Name_____ Tribe_____Pott_____
Married_____ How_____
Married to whom_____ Census or Allotment No._____
If divorced, When_____ Where_____
If divorced, How_____
```

CHILDREN BORN OF THIS MARRIAGE.

Census or Allotment No.	Sex	Name	Born	Died Blood
		Husband white		
	F	Mabel Pratt Miller	1908	Part Pott
	M	Owen P "	1926	"
	M	Cloyd "	1928	"

address Maud

See Marriage Cards Nos. _____ and _____ for half-brothers and half-sisters of these children.

Sac & Fox – Shawnee
1853-1933 Volume X

MARRIAGE CARD.

```
                        Marriage. Sex          Census or Allotment No.
Name                                           Tribe         Pott
Married                                        How
Married to whom                                Census or Allotment No.
If divorced, When                              Where
If divorced, How
```

CHILDREN BORN OF THIS MARRIAGE.

CENSUS OR ALLOTMENT NO.	SEX	NAME	BORN	Blood DIED
	M	Ben M. Nadeau	1891	1/2 Pott
	F	Gladis Hains "		white
	M	Benjiman[sic] " Jr.	1921	1/4 Pott
	F	May "	1923	1/4 "
	F	Anzio "	1925	1/4 "

address Tecumseh # 1

See Marriage Cards Nos. ____ and ____ for half-brothers and half-sisters of these children.

MARRIAGE CARD.

```
                        Marriage. Sex          Census or Allotment No.
Name                                           Tribe
Married                                        How
Married to whom                                Census or Allotment No.
If divorced, When                              Where
If divorced, How
```

CHILDREN BORN OF THIS MARRIAGE.

CENSUS OR ALLOTMENT NO.	SEX	NAME	BORN	blood DIED
	M	Husband		white
	F	Lucy Higbee Angle	Nov 1869	1/16 Pott
		Julia " Loraine	1887	1/32 "
		Agness "	1892	1/32 "
		John "	1895	1/32 "
		W<u>m</u> "	1898	1/32 "

adress[sic] Burbank Cal.

See Marriage Cards Nos. ____ and ____ for half-brothers and half-sisters of these children.

Sac & Fox – Shawnee
1853-1933 Volume X

MARRIAGE CARD.

Name _____ Marriage. Sex _____ Census or Allotment No. _____
Married _____ Tribe _____
Married to whom _____ How _____
If divorced, When _____ Census or Allotment No. _____
If divorced, How _____ Where _____

CHILDREN BORN OF THIS MARRIAGE.

Census or Allotment No.	Sex	Name	Born	Died Blood
	M	Horace H Higbee	Apr 4 1902	1/32 Pott
	F	wife		white
	F	Elwanda "	Nov 9 1925	1/64 Pott
	F	Mary L. "	Nov 7 1929	"

Lexington # 4

See Marriage Cards Nos. _____ and _____ for half-brothers and half-sisters of these children.

MARRIAGE CARD.

Name _____ Marriage. Sex _____ Census or Allotment No. _____
Married _____ Tribe _____
Married to whom _____ How _____
If divorced, When _____ Census or Allotment No. _____
If divorced, How _____ Where _____

CHILDREN BORN OF THIS MARRIAGE.

Census or Allotment No.	Sex	Name	Born	Died blood
	M	Fabine S. Vieux	1889	1/2 Pott
	F	wife		white

address   Asher # 2

See Marriage Cards Nos. _____ and _____ for half-brothers and half-sisters of these children.

Sac & Fox – Shawnee
1853-1933   Volume X

MARRIAGE CARD.

```
_____Marriage. Sex_____  Census or Allotment No._____
Name_____       Tribe_____
Married_____       How_____
Married to whom_____        Census or Allotment No._____
If divorced, When_____        Where_____
If divorced, How_____
```

CHILDREN BORN OF THIS MARRIAGE.

CENSUS OR ALLOTMENT NO.	SEX	NAME	BORN	DIED Blood
	M	Nicholas Vieux	Feb 27 1891	1/2 Pott
	F	wife		white
	M	Chas F "	Sept 2 1925	1/4 Pott
	F	Ines[sic] M "	Nov 18 1916	"
address	Asher #2			

See Marriage Cards Nos. _____ and _____ for half-brothers and half-sisters of these children.

MARRIAGE CARD.

```
_____Marriage. Sex_____  Census or Allotment No._____
Name_____       Tribe_____
Married_____       How_____
Married to whom_____        Census or Allotment No._____
If divorced, When_____        Where_____
If divorced, How_____
```

CHILDREN BORN OF THIS MARRIAGE.

CENSUS OR ALLOTMENT NO.	SEX	NAME	BORN	DIED blood
	M	Chas Rhodd	1851	1/2 Pott
address		Macomb		

See Marriage Cards Nos. _____ and _____ for half-brothers and half-sisters of these children.

Sac & Fox – Shawnee
1853-1933   Volume X

MARRIAGE CARD.

Name .... Marriage. Sex .... Census or Allotment No. ....
Married .... Tribe ....
Married to whom .... How ....
If divorced, When .... Census or Allotment No. ....
If divorced, How .... Where ....

CHILDREN BORN OF THIS MARRIAGE.

Census or Allotment No.	Sex	Name	Born	Blood DIED
	F	Maggie Rhodd Silver	Oct 1 1902	3/4 Pott
	M	Chas D. Rhodd	May 18 1895	1/2 Pott
address	Macomb #2			

See Marriage Cards Nos. .... and .... for half-brothers and half-sisters of these children.

MARRIAGE CARD.

Name .... Marriage. Sex .... Census or Allotment No. ....
Married .... Tribe ....
Married to whom .... How ....
If divorced, When .... Census or Allotment No. ....
If divorced, How .... Where ....

CHILDREN BORN OF THIS MARRIAGE.

Census or Allotment No.	Sex	Name	Born	DIED blood
	M	Thos. Rhodd	May 17 1891	1/2 Pott
	F	Mary Ma-tah-Ru Rhood[sic]	Feb 28 1882	full
	F	Helen "	July 20 1909	3/4 Pott
	F	Zoa "	Dec 18 1910	3/4 "
	M	Henry "	Oct 21 1913	"
	M[sic]	Margrette "	July 22 1915	"
	M	Albert "	April 21 1917	"
	M	Benjamin "	Apr 27 1919	"
	M	Delbert "	Aug 26 1923	"
	M	Aldon "	July 19 1924	"
address	Macomb #2			

See Marriage Cards Nos. .... and .... for half-brothers and half-sisters of these children.

Sac & Fox – Shawnee
1853-1933 Volume X

MARRIAGE CARD.

Marriage. Sex _____ Census or Allotment No. _____
Name _____ Tribe _____
Married _____ How _____
Married to whom _____ Census or Allotment No. _____
If divorced, When _____ Where _____
If divorced, How _____

CHILDREN BORN OF THIS MARRIAGE.

Census or Allotment No.	Sex	Name	Born	blood / Died
	F	Rosa Yatt	April 10 1882	1/4 Pott
		Asher # 1		
	address			

See Marriage Cards Nos. _____ and _____ for half-brothers and half-sisters of these children.

MARRIAGE CARD.

Marriage. Sex _____ Census or Allotment No. _____
Name _____ Tribe _____
Married _____ How _____
Married to whom _____ Census or Allotment No. _____
If divorced, When _____ Where _____
If divorced, How _____

CHILDREN BORN OF THIS MARRIAGE.

Census or Allotment No.	Sex	Name	Born	blood / Died
		Janean Mitchell	Feb 25 1857	1/32 Pott
		Asher # 1		
	address			

See Marriage Cards Nos. _____ and _____ for half-brothers and half-sisters of these children.

Sac & Fox – Shawnee
1853-1933   Volume X

[Copy of original]

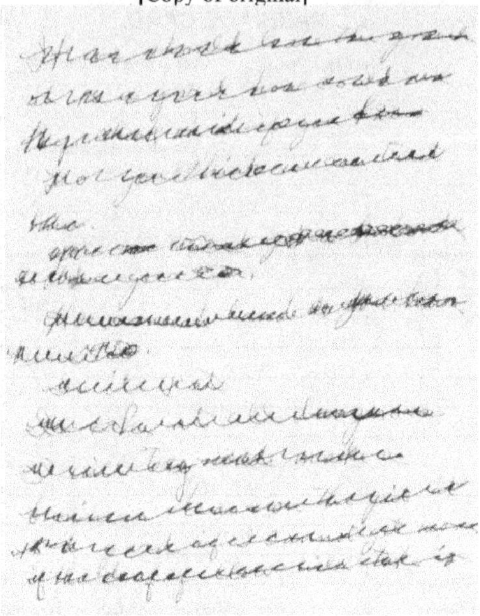

[handwritten note, illegible]

MARRIAGE CARD.

.... Marriage. Sex .... Census or Allotment No. ....
Name .... Tribe ....
Married .... How ....
Married to whom .... Census or Allotment No. ....
If divorced, When .... Where ....
If divorced, How ....

CHILDREN BORN OF THIS MARRIAGE.

Census or Allotment No.	Sex	Name	Born	Died / blood
		Janean Mitchell	Feb 25 1857	1/32 Pott
		Asher # 1		
	address			

See Marriage Cards Nos. _____ and _____ for half-brothers and half-sisters of these children.

Sac & Fox – Shawnee
1853-1933   Volume X

[Copy of original]

MARRIAGE CARD.

_____Marriage. Sex_____ Census or Allotment No._____
Name_____ Tribe_____
Married_____ How_____
Married to whom_____ Census or Allotment No._____
If divorced, When_____ Where_____
If divorced, How_____

CHILDREN BORN OF THIS MARRIAGE.

CENSUS OR ALLOTMENT NO.	SEX	NAME	BORN	DIED blood
		Janean Mitchell	Feb 25 1857	1/32 Pott
		Asher # 1		
	address			

See Marriage Cards Nos. _____ and _____ for half-brothers and half-sisters of these children.

Sac & Fox – Shawnee
1853-1933 Volume X

MARRIAGE CARD.

Marriage. Sex_____ Census or Allotment No._____
Name_____ Tribe_____
Married_____ How_____
Married to whom_____ Census or Allotment No.__
If divorced, When_____ Where_____
If divorced, How_____

CHILDREN BORN OF THIS MARRIAGE.

Census or Allotment No.	Sex	Name	Born	blood / Died
	M	Billie Papan	1863	Kaw & Pott
		wife		white
		address		

See Marriage Cards Nos. _____ and _____ for half-brothers and half-sisters of these children.

MARRIAGE CARD.

Marriage. Sex_____ Census or Allotment No._____
Name_____ Tribe_____
Married_____ How_____
Married to whom_____ Census or Allotment No.__
If divorced, When_____ Where_____
If divorced, How_____

CHILDREN BORN OF THIS MARRIAGE.

Census or Allotment No.	Sex	Name	Born	blood / Died
	M	Ruben C. Haas	1905	1/8 Pott
		wife		white
		2 children in family		
		address Amarilla[sic] Tex		

See Marriage Cards Nos. _____ and _____ for half-brothers and half-sisters of these children.

Sac & Fox – Shawnee
1853-1933   Volume X

MARRIAGE CARD.

Marriage. Sex _____ Census or Allotment No. _____
Name _____ Tribe _____
Married _____ How _____
Married to whom _____ Census or Allotment No. _____
If divorced, When _____ Where _____
If divorced, How _____

CHILDREN BORN OF THIS MARRIAGE.

Census or Allotment No.	Sex	Name	Born	Died blood
both	M	Husband		white
Dead	F	Ethel Haas Willivery	1893	1/8 Pott
	M	Jack "	1916	1/16
address Chochow[sic] Okla				

See Marriage Cards Nos. _____ and _____ for half-brothers and half-sisters of these children.

MARRIAGE CARD.

Marriage. Sex _____ Census or Allotment No. _____
Name _____ Tribe ___Pott_____
Married _____ How _____
Married to whom _____ Census or Allotment No. _____
If divorced, When _____ Where _____
If divorced, How _____

CHILDREN BORN OF THIS MARRIAGE.

Census or Allotment No.	Sex	Name	Born	Died Blood
		Husband (white)		
	F	Maud Suman	1900	Part Pott
	F	Lavina "	1920	"
address Belin New Mex.				

See Marriage Cards Nos. _____ and _____ for half-brothers and half-sisters of these children.

Sac & Fox – Shawnee
1853-1933   Volume X

MARRIAGE CARD.

Name .... Marriage. Sex .... Census or Allotment No. ....
Married .... Tribe .... Pott ....
Married to whom .... How ....
If divorced, When .... Census or Allotment No. ....
If divorced, How .... Where ....

CHILDREN BORN OF THIS MARRIAGE.

Census or Allotment No.	Sex	Name	Born	Blood	Died
	M	R. A. Ogee Jr.	1849	Part Pott	
	address	Maud # 1			

See Marriage Cards Nos. .... and .... for half-brothers and half-sisters of these children.

MARRIAGE CARD.

Name .... Marriage. Sex .... Census or Allotment No. ....
Married .... Tribe .... Pott ....
Married to whom .... How ....
If divorced, When .... Census or Allotment No. ....
If divorced, How .... Where ....

CHILDREN BORN OF THIS MARRIAGE.

Census or Allotment No.	Sex	Name	Born	Blood	Died
		Wife		white	
		Rainey Ogee	1901	Part Pott	
		Kenneth D "	June 20 1926	Part "	
	address	Maud			

See Marriage Cards Nos. .... and .... for half-brothers and half-sisters of these children.

Sac & Fox – Shawnee
1853-1933   Volume X

MARRIAGE CARD.

Name _____ Marriage. Sex _____ Census or Allotment No. _____
Married _____ Tribe _____ Pott _____
Married to whom _____ How _____
If divorced, When _____ Census or Allotment No. _____
If divorced, How _____ Where _____

CHILDREN BORN OF THIS MARRIAGE.

Census or Allotment No.	Sex	Name	Born	Blood / Died
	F	Alice Ogee Suman	1872	Part Pott
	F	Ruby "	1905	"
	F	Loran "	1906	"
	address	Clovis New Mex		

See Marriage Cards Nos. _____ and _____ for half-brothers and half-sisters of these children.

MARRIAGE CARD.

Name _____ Marriage. Sex _____ Census or Allotment No. _____
Married _____ Tribe _____ Pott _____
Married to whom _____ How _____
If divorced, When _____ Census or Allotment No. _____
If divorced, How _____ Where _____

CHILDREN BORN OF THIS MARRIAGE.

Census or Allotment No.	Sex	Name	Born	Blood / Died
	M	John L. Ogee	1876	Part Pott
		Wife		white
	F	Marjorie "		Part Pott
	F	Emily "		"
	M	Chester "		"
	M	Johnie "		"
	M	Philip "		"
	address	Maud		

See Marriage Cards Nos. _____ and _____ for half-brothers and half-sisters of these children.

Sac & Fox – Shawnee
1853-1933 Volume X

MARRIAGE CARD.

Name _____ Marriage. Sex _____ Census or Allotment No. _____
Married _____ Tribe _____ Pott _____
Married to whom _____ How _____
If divorced, When _____ Census or Allotment No. _____
If divorced, How _____ Where _____

CHILDREN BORN OF THIS MARRIAGE.

Census or Allotment No.	Sex	Name	Born	Died Blood
	F	Cecil Powell		Part Pott
		Husband		white
	F	Wanema-Dean Powell	1924	Part Pott
	F	Tevina "	1927	"
	~~F~~	~~Cecil " ~~		
		address		

See Marriage Cards Nos. _____ and _____ for half-brothers and half-sisters of these children.

MARRIAGE CARD.

Name _____ Marriage. Sex _____ Census or Allotment No. _____
Married _____ Tribe _____ Pott _____
Married to whom _____ How _____
If divorced, When _____ Census or Allotment No. _____
If divorced, How _____ Where _____

CHILDREN BORN OF THIS MARRIAGE.

Census or Allotment No.	Sex	Name	Born	Died Blood
	F	Cora Pratt		white
		Walter S. Pratt (Dead)		1/16 Pott
	M	Derl W. Pratt	1915	1/32 Pott
		address Maud # 1		

See Marriage Cards Nos. _____ and _____ for half-brothers and half-sisters of these children.

Sac & Fox – Shawnee
1853-1933 Volume X

MARRIAGE CARD.

Marriage. Sex _____ Census or Allotment No. _____
Name _____ Tribe _____ Pott _____
Married _____ How _____
Married to whom _____ Census or Allotment No. _____
If divorced, When _____ Where _____
If divorced, How _____

CHILDREN BORN OF THIS MARRIAGE.

Census or Allotment No.	Sex	Name	Born	Blood / Died
	F	Mary B Bruno	June 1846	1/2 Pott

address Konawa

See Marriage Cards Nos. _____ and _____ for half-brothers and half-sisters of these children.

MARRIAGE CARD.

Marriage. Sex _____ Census or Allotment No. _____
Name _____ Tribe _____
Married _____ How _____
Married to whom _____ Census or Allotment No. _____
If divorced, When _____ Where _____
If divorced, How _____

CHILDREN BORN OF THIS MARRIAGE.

Census or Allotment No.	Sex	Name	Born	Blood / Died
	M	I.S. Higbee	April 1891	1/32 Pott
	F	wife		white
	M	Irvin Jr.	Sept 1918	1/64

address Holdenville

See Marriage Cards Nos. _____ and _____ for half-brothers and half-sisters of these children.

Sac & Fox – Shawnee
1853-1933 Volume X

MARRIAGE CARD.

Marriage. Sex_____ Census or Allotment No._____
Name_____ Tribe_____
Married_____ How_____
Married to whom_____ Census or Allotment No._____
If divorced, When_____ Where_____
If divorced, How_____

CHILDREN BORN OF THIS MARRIAGE.

Census or Allotment No.	Sex	Name	Born	Died blood
	M	J.B. Higbee	May 23 1888	1/32
	F	wife		white
	M	Wendle "	July 7 1912	1/64 Pott
	M	Joseph E "	1914	1/64 "
				"
	M	Averett "	1916	"
	M	Lawrence B "	1918	"
		Glendale Cal.		

adress[sic]

See Marriage Cards Nos. _____ and _____ for half-brothers and half-sisters of these children.

MARRIAGE CARD.

Marriage. Sex_____ Census or Allotment No._____
Name_____ Tribe_____ Pott _____
Married_____ How_____
Married to whom_____ Census or Allotment No._____
If divorced, When_____ Where_____
If divorced, How_____

CHILDREN BORN OF THIS MARRIAGE.

Census or Allotment No.	Sex	Name	Born	Died BLOOD
		Husband white		
	F	Sadie Cummings Shives Dead	1875	1/16
	M	Clarence "	Jun 5 1894	1/32
	F	Forence[sic] "	1898	1/32
	M	Burchie "	1900	1/32
		her children		

ADDRESS A[sic]

See Marriage Cards Nos. _____ and _____ for half-brothers and half-sisters of these children.

Sac & Fox – Shawnee
1853-1933 Volume X

MARRIAGE CARD.

Name _____ Marriage. Sex _____ Census or Allotment No. _____
Married _____ Tribe _____ Pott _____
Married to whom _____ How _____
If divorced, When _____ Census or Allotment No. _____
If divorced, How _____ Where _____

CHILDREN BORN OF THIS MARRIAGE.

Census or Allotment No.	Sex	Name	Born	Died Blood
	F	Olene Marie Holt	May 1906	Part Pott
		Noline Hodges	Jan 1924	"
		Lucile "	[?] 1926	"
address				

See Marriage Cards Nos. _____ and _____ for half-brothers and half-sisters of these children.

MARRIAGE CARD.

Name _____ Marriage. Sex _____ Census or Allotment No. _____
Married _____ Tribe _____ Pott _____
Married to whom _____ How _____
If divorced, When _____ Census or Allotment No. _____
If divorced, How _____ Where _____

CHILDREN BORN OF THIS MARRIAGE.

Census or Allotment No.	Sex	Name	Born	Died Blood
	M	J. B. Manyon		Mex.
	F	Mary "	Nov 4 1875	Full Pott
		Tecumseh # 5		
	address			

See Marriage Cards Nos. _____ and _____ for half-brothers and half-sisters of these children.

Sac & Fox – Shawnee
1853-1933 Volume X

MARRIAGE CARD.

Name _____ Marriage. Sex _____ Census or Allotment No. _____
Married _____ Tribe _____
Married to whom _____ How _____
If divorced, When _____ Census or Allotment No. _____
If divorced, How _____ Where _____

CHILDREN BORN OF THIS MARRIAGE.

Census or Allotment No.	Sex	Name	Born	Died blood
	M	J.S. Frapp	Apr 4 1898	1/8 Pott
	F	wife		white
	M	W<u>m</u> T. "	1920	1/16 Pott
	M	Murry S "	June 18 1926	1/16 "
	address	Trousdale # 1		

See Marriage Cards Nos. _____ and _____ for half-brothers and half-sisters of these children.

MARRIAGE CARD.

Name _____ Marriage. Sex _____ Census or Allotment No. _____
Married _____ Tribe _____ Pott _____
Married to whom _____ How _____
If divorced, When _____ Census or Allotment No. _____
If divorced, How _____ Where _____

CHILDREN BORN OF THIS MARRIAGE.

Census or Allotment No.	Sex	Name	Born	Died Blood
	M	Enos E Rhodd	July 13 1879	1/2 Pott
	F	Elizabeth Curley "	1907	1/2 "
	F	Adeline "	June 6 1923	1/2 "
	M	Enos Jr. "	April 5 1925	1/2 "
	M	Thomas J "	Nov 22 1928	1/2 "
	address	Konawa # 3		

See Marriage Cards Nos. _____ and _____ for half-brothers and half-sisters of these children.

Sac & Fox – Shawnee
1853-1933   Volume X

MARRIAGE CARD.

```
                         Marriage. Sex          Census or Allotment No.
Name                                            Tribe    Pott
Married                                         How
Married to whom                                 Census or Allotment No.
If divorced, When                               Where
If divorced, How
```

CHILDREN BORN OF THIS MARRIAGE.

Census or Allotment No.	Sex	Name	Born	Blood / Died
	M	Otto Falkner		white
	F	Ruth W Baylis Falkner	1906	1/16 Pott
	F	Pauline Baylis Johnson	1923	1/32 "
	F	Birdie Baylis	1926	"
	F	Odie Falkner	1929	"
		not certain as to the fathers name		
address		Maud # 1		

See Marriage Cards Nos. _____ and _____ for half-brothers and half-sisters of these children.

MARRIAGE CARD.

```
                         Marriage. Sex          Census or Allotment No.
Name                                            Tribe    Pott
Married                                         How
Married to whom                                 Census or Allotment No.
If divorced, When                               Where
If divorced, How
```

CHILDREN BORN OF THIS MARRIAGE.

Census or Allotment No.	Sex	Name	Born	Blood / Died
	M	Cyrus W. Baylis	1872	1/8 Pott
	~~M~~	~~McFall R. "~~	~~1904~~	~~1/16 "~~
	~~F~~	~~Ruth M "~~	~~1906~~	~~1/16 "~~
	M	Thomas A. "	1908	1/16 "
	M	W$^{\underline{m}}$ C. "	1910	1/16 "
address				

See Marriage Cards Nos. _____ and _____ for half-brothers and half-sisters of these children.

223

Sac & Fox – Shawnee
1853-1933   Volume X

MARRIAGE CARD.

Name _____ Marriage. Sex _____ Census or Allotment No. _____
Married _____ Tribe ____ Pott _____
Married to whom _____ How _____
If divorced, When _____ Census or Allotment No. _____
If divorced, How _____ Where _____

CHILDREN BORN OF THIS MARRIAGE.

Census or Allotment No.	Sex	Name	Born	Blood	Died
	M	McFall R Baylis	1904	1/8 Pott	
		Naomi Strikler "		white	
	M	Lavoy "	1926	1/16 Pott	
address	Harjo or Maud				

See Marriage Cards Nos. _____ and _____ for half-brothers and half-sisters of these children.

MARRIAGE CARD.

Name _____ Marriage. Sex _____ Census or Allotment No. _____
Married _____ Tribe _____
Married to whom _____ How _____
If divorced, When _____ Census or Allotment No. _____
If divorced, How _____ Where _____

CHILDREN BORN OF THIS MARRIAGE.

Census or Allotment No.	Sex	Name	Born	Blood	Died
	M	Husband		white	
	F	Alice Jones	1871	1/8 Pott	
	M	Merritt L. "	1896	1/16 "	
		Inform			
		Collins Bros Store			
address	Konawa				

See Marriage Cards Nos. _____ and _____ for half-brothers and half-sisters of these children.

Sac & Fox – Shawnee
1853-1933 Volume X

MARRIAGE CARD.

_____ Marriage. Sex _____ Census or Allotment No. _____
Name _____ Tribe _____
Married _____ How _____
Married to whom _____ Census or Allotment No. _____
If divorced, When _____ Where _____
If divorced, How _____

CHILDREN BORN OF THIS MARRIAGE.

Census or Allotment No.	Sex	Name	Born	Blood / Died
	M	Husband		white
	F	Ramona Jones Taylor		1/16 Pott
address		Konawa		

See Marriage Cards Nos. _____ and _____ for half-brothers and half-sisters of these children.

MARRIAGE CARD.

_____ Marriage. Sex _____ Census or Allotment No. _____
Name _____ Tribe _____
Married _____ How _____
Married to whom _____ Census or Allotment No. _____
If divorced, When _____ Where _____
If divorced, How _____

CHILDREN BORN OF THIS MARRIAGE.

Census or Allotment No.	Sex	Name	Born	Blood / Died
	M	Frank P. Jones		1/16 Pott
	F	wife		white
ADDRESS		Konawa		

See Marriage Cards Nos. _____ and _____ for half-brothers and half-sisters of these children.

Sac & Fox – Shawnee
1853-1933   Volume X

Lexington Okla.
May 23 – 1929.

Mr. W. Gunn
  Tecumseh Okla.
  Dear Sir:-

When you were around at our place we were not at home. Mr Slaven told us he gave you our names and ages. We will give you our correct ages.

John B. Pambogo Sr.	75 yrs.
John B. Pambogo Jr.	35 yrs.
Alex B. Pambogo	33 yrs
Alice J. Pambogo	31 yrs.
Wanda Genevieve Megah	5 yrs.

This is my Baby. and oblige,
    Yours Truly
      Alice J. Pambogo

[Blank Marriage Card given.]

MARRIAGE CARD.

_____ Marriage. Sex _____ Census or Allotment No. _____
Name _____ Tribe _____
Married _____ How _____
Married to whom _____ Census or Allotment No. _____
If divorced, When _____ Where _____
If divorced, How _____

CHILDREN BORN OF THIS MARRIAGE.

Census or Allotment No.	Sex	Name	Born	Died blood
___address___				

See Marriage Cards Nos. _____ and _____ for half-brothers and half-sisters of these children.

Sac & Fox – Shawnee
1853-1933   Volume X

MARRIAGE CARD.

```
_____ Marriage. Sex _____ Census or Allotment No. _____
Name _____ Tribe ___Pott_____
Married _____ How _____
Married to whom _____ Census or Allotment No. _____
If divorced, When _____ Where _____
If divorced, How _____
```

CHILDREN BORN OF THIS MARRIAGE.

CENSUS OR ALLOTMENT NO.	SEX	NAME	BORN	BLOOD / DIED
	M	Frank I Wano	Dec 16 1890	3/4 Pott
		Wife (white)		White
	F	Gerald D "	Sept 2 1925	3/8 Pott
	F	Laveta J "	Nov 26 1928	3/8 "
ADDRESS		Konawa # 2		

See Marriage Cards Nos. _____ and _____ for half-brothers and half-sisters of these children.

MARRIAGE CARD.

```
_____ Marriage. Sex _____ Census or Allotment No. _____
Name _____ Tribe _____
Married _____ How _____
Married to whom _____ Census or Allotment No. _____
If divorced, When _____ Where _____
If divorced, How _____
```

CHILDREN BORN OF THIS MARRIAGE.

CENSUS OR ALLOTMENT NO.	SEX	NAME	BORN	Blood / DIED
	M	Joseph E. Peltier		5/8 Pott
		wife white		
	M	Ralph "		5/16 "
address		McAlister Okla		

See Marriage Cards Nos. _____ and _____ for half-brothers and half-sisters of these children.

Sac & Fox – Shawnee
1853-1933 Volume X

MARRIAGE CARD.

_____ Marriage. Sex _____ Census or Allotment No. _____
Name _____ Tribe _____
Married _____ How _____
Married to whom _____ Census or Allotment No. _____
If divorced, When _____ Where _____
If divorced, How _____

CHILDREN BORN OF THIS MARRIAGE.

Census or Allotment No.	Sex	Name	Born	Blood / Died
	F	Helen Vieux Peltier	1847	full
address				

See Marriage Cards Nos. _____ and _____ for half-brothers and half-sisters of these children.

MARRIAGE CARD.

_____ Marriage. Sex _____ Census or Allotment No. _____
Name _____ Tribe _____
Married _____ How _____
Married to whom _____ Census or Allotment No. _____
If divorced, When _____ Where _____
If divorced, How _____

CHILDREN BORN OF THIS MARRIAGE.

Census or Allotment No.	Sex	Name	Born	Blood / Died
	M	Lonnie Peltier	Dec 11 1909	
		wife		white
		Lexington #2		
address				

See Marriage Cards Nos. _____ and _____ for half-brothers and half-sisters of these children.

Sac & Fox – Shawnee
1853-1933   Volume X

MARRIAGE CARD.

First Marriage. Sex _____ Census or Allotment No. _____
Name Edith Opal Holloway   Tribe Pottawatomie 1/32
Married Nov. 8 – 1922   How Legally
Married to whom Robert W. Horner Census or Allotment No. (white)
If divorced, When   Where
If divorced, How

CHILDREN BORN OF THIS MARRIAGE.

Census or Allotment No.	Sex.	Name.	Born.	Died.
		~~Julia Ophelia Horner~~		
	Girl	Julia Ophelia "	Feb 16 1890	
	"	Dovey Louise "	Dec 26 1923	
	"	Mildred Lovenia "	July 8 1925	
	"	Laura Lucille "	May 8 1928	

See Marriage Cards Nos. _____ and _____ for half brothers and half sisters of these children.

MARRIAGE CARD.

_____ Marriage. Sex _____ Census or Allotment No. _____
Name   Tribe   Pott
Married   How
Married to whom   Census or Allotment No.
If divorced, When   Where
If divorced, How

CHILDREN BORN OF THIS MARRIAGE.

Census or Allotment No.	Sex	Name	Born	DIED BLOOD
	M	Samuel Rhodd	Nov 30 1883	Part Pott
		wife		white
1st wife {	M	Cecil "	1911	Part Pott
	F	Thelma "	April 1913	"
	F	Lucile "	April 1915	"
2nd wife {	M	Leonard P "	Aug 11 1928	"
ADDRESS		Konawa #2		

See Marriage Cards Nos. _____ and _____ for half-brothers and half-sisters of these children.

Sac & Fox – Shawnee
1853-1933 Volume X

MARRIAGE CARD.

Marriage. Sex .... Census or Allotment No. ....
Name .... Tribe ..... Pott ....
Married .... How ....
Married to whom .... Census or Allotment No. ....
If divorced, When .... Where ....
If divorced, How ....

CHILDREN BORN OF THIS MARRIAGE.

Census or Allotment No.	Sex	Name	Born	Died blood
	M	Husband		white
	F	May Wolf Patterson	Apr 4 1906	3/8 Pott
	F	Deloris "	Mar 1 1928	3/16 Pott

address _Hutcheson Kan_

See Marriage Cards Nos. .... and .... for half-brothers and half-sisters of these children.

MARRIAGE CARD.

Marriage. Sex .... Census or Allotment No. ....
Name .... Tribe ....
Married .... How ....
Married to whom .... Census or Allotment No. ....
If divorced, When .... Where ....
If divorced, How ....

CHILDREN BORN OF THIS MARRIAGE.

Census or Allotment No.	Sex	Name	Born	Died blood
		Husband		white
	F	Ethel Wolf Harper	Mar 28 1898	3/8 Pott
	F	Georgie B. "	Dec 1920	3/16 "
	F	Maggie B "	July 29 1923	3/16 "
	F	Rosa L. "	Oct 1925	3/16 "

address _Konawa_

See Marriage Cards Nos. .... and .... for half-brothers and half-sisters of these children.

Sac & Fox – Shawnee
1853-1933 Volume X

MARRIAGE CARD.

Name _____ Marriage. Sex _____ Census or Allotment No. _____
Married _____ Tribe ___Pott_____
Married to whom _____ How _____
If divorced, When _____ Census or Allotment No. _____
If divorced, How _____ Where _____

CHILDREN BORN OF THIS MARRIAGE.

Census or Allotment No.	Sex	Name	Born	blood DIED
	M	Wm Wolf		white
	F	Martha Curley Wolf	1880	15/16 Pott
	M	James "	Dec 22 1902	15/32 "
	M	Lessley "	Jan 16 1908	15/32 "
	F	Viola "	May 3 1911	15/32 "
	F	Dorris "	Aug 8 1913	15/32 "
	F	Lucile "	June 21 1918	15/32 "
	M	Willie "	Apr 7 1920	15/32 "
	F	Nettie "	July 19 1923	15/32 "

address K̶o̶n̶a̶w̶a̶

See Marriage Cards Nos. _____ and _____ for half-brothers and half-sisters of these children.

MARRIAGE CARD.

Name _____ Marriage. Sex _____ Census or Allotment No. _____
Married _____ Tribe ___Pott_____
Married to whom _____ How _____
If divorced, When _____ Census or Allotment No. _____
If divorced, How _____ Where _____

CHILDREN BORN OF THIS MARRIAGE.

Census or Allotment No.	Sex	Name	Born	blood DIED
	M	Charley Curley	Aug 17 1893	15/16 Pott
	F	Anna "		Full Creek M̶u̶s̶k̶o̶g̶e̶e̶
	M	Bernard "	Dec 1 1920	31/32 Indian
	F	Jeraldine "	Sept 26 1924	31/32 Indian
	F	Mary M "	Dec 18 1926	31/32 Indian
				15/16 Pott
				15/16 "
				15/16 "

address K̶o̶n̶a̶w̶a̶

See Marriage Cards Nos. _____ and _____ for half-brothers and half-sisters of these children.

Sac & Fox – Shawnee
1853-1933 Volume X

MARRIAGE CARD.

Marriage. Sex ...... Census or Allotment No. ......
Name ......
Married ......
Married to whom ......
If divorced, When ......
If divorced, How ......
Tribe ......
How ......
Census or Allotment No. ......
Where ......

CHILDREN BORN OF THIS MARRIAGE.

Census or Allotment No.	Sex	Name	Born	blood DIED
	M	Peter Kahdot	1869	Full Pott
	F	Jane Curley " (Dead)		15/16 Pott
	M	Isaac Kahdot		31/32 "
	F	Helen "		31/32 "
	M	Leo "		31/32 "
2nd Husband white	M	Louis "		31/32 "
		Bobie[sic] Brown		15/32 "
address				

See Marriage Cards Nos. ...... and ...... for half-brothers and half-sisters of these children.

****

MARRIAGE CARD.

Marriage. Sex ...... Census or Allotment No. ......
Name ......
Married ......
Married to whom ......
If divorced, When ......
If divorced, How ......
Tribe ......
How ......
Census or Allotment No. ......
Where ......

CHILDREN BORN OF THIS MARRIAGE.

Census or Allotment No.	Sex	Name	Born	blood DIED
	M	Peter Kahdot	1869	Full Pott
	F	Jane Curley " (Dead)		15/16 Pott
	M	Isaac Kahdot		31/32 "
	F	Helen "		31/32 "
	M	Leo "		31/32 "
2nd Husband white	M	Louis "		31/32 "
		Bobie[sic] Brown		15/32 "
address				

See Marriage Cards Nos. ...... and ...... for half-brothers and half-sisters of these children.

Sac & Fox – Shawnee
1853-1933 Volume X

MARRIAGE CARD.

```
                          Marriage. Sex_____  Census or Allotment No._____
Name_____  Tribe_____
Married_____  How_____
Married to whom_____  Census or Allotment No._____
If divorced, When_____  Where_____
If divorced, How_____
```

CHILDREN BORN OF THIS MARRIAGE.

Census or Allotment No.	Sex	Name	Born	Died blood
	M	John Curley	1882	15/16 Pott
by 1st wife who was 1/2 Pott	son M	Peter (Raymond) "	1908	23/32 "
	F	Francis "	1911	23/32 "
	M	Albert "	1913	23/32 "
	F	Ida May "	1916	23/32 "
		Hattie Curley 2nd wife		White
		Konawa no children		
address				

See Marriage Cards Nos. _____ and _____ for half-brothers and half-sisters of these children.

MARRIAGE CARD.

```
                          Marriage. Sex_____  Census or Allotment No._____
Name_____  Tribe_____Pott_____
Married_____  How_____
Married to whom_____  Census or Allotment No._____
If divorced, When_____  Where_____
If divorced, How_____
```

CHILDREN BORN OF THIS MARRIAGE.

Census or Allotment No.	Sex	Name	Born	Died blood
	M	Peter Curley	1856	7/8 Pott
	M son	Elex "	Jan 10 1891	7/8
2nd wife white	M	Joe "	1907	7/16 Pott
	F	Sophia "	1905	7/16 Pott
address		Konawa #3		

See Marriage Cards Nos. _____ and _____ for half-brothers and half-sisters of these children.

Sac & Fox – Shawnee
1853-1933   Volume X

MARRIAGE CARD.

Chas C. wife

Name .... Marriage. Sex .... Census or Allotment No. ....
Married .... Tribe ....
Married to whom .... How ....
If divorced, When .... Census or Allotment No. ....
If divorced, How .... Where ....

CHILDREN BORN OF THIS MARRIAGE.

Census or Allotment No.	Sex	Name	Born	Died blood
	M	Antoine Curley	1879	5/8 Pott
		Willmite[sic] the wifes name and also names of 2 children		

address Concho Okla

See Marriage Cards Nos. .... and .... for half-brothers and half-sisters of these children.

MARRIAGE CARD.

Name .... Marriage. Sex .... Census or Allotment No. ....
Married .... Tribe .... Pott ....
Married to whom .... How ....
If divorced, When .... Census or Allotment No. ....
If divorced, How .... Where ....

CHILDREN BORN OF THIS MARRIAGE.

Census or Allotment No.	Sex	Name	Born	Died blood
	M	Andrew Curley	1849	7/8 Pott

address Konawa

See Marriage Cards Nos. .... and .... for half-brothers and half-sisters of these children.

Sac & Fox – Shawnee
1853-1933   Volume X

MARRIAGE CARD.

....Marriage. Sex........ Census or Allotment No. ....
Name.. Tribe........Pott........................
Married.. How..
Married to whom.. Census or Allotment No. ....
If divorced, When... Where..
If divorced, How...

CHILDREN BORN OF THIS MARRIAGE.

Census or Allotment No.	Sex	Name	Born	Died blood
	M	Peter		White
	F	Grace Bruno Veitenhiemer		1/2 Pott
	M	W<u>m</u> "	1900	1/4 Pott
	M	Mathew "	1922	1/4 "
	M	Peter Jr. "	1924	1/4 "
	F	Violet J. "	1925	1/4 "
	M	Emmet L. "	1927	1/4 "

____address____ Seminole

See Marriage Cards Nos. ....and........for half-brothers and half-sisters of these children.

MARRIAGE CARD.

....Marriage. Sex........ Census or Allotment No. ....
Name.. Tribe..
Married.. How..
Married to whom.. Census or Allotment No. ....
If divorced, When... Where..
If divorced, How...

CHILDREN BORN OF THIS MARRIAGE.

Census or Allotment No.	Sex	Name	Born	Died blood
	M	Narcise Pensoneau		1/16 Shawnee
	F	Vina Bruno Pensoneau		1/16 Kickapoo 1/2 Pott
	M	Cecil "	1921	5/8 "
	F	Juanita "	1923	5/8 "
	F	Neoma "	Apr 29 1927	5/8 "

____address____ Seminole

See Marriage Cards Nos. ....and........for half-brothers and half-sisters of these children.

Sac & Fox – Shawnee
1853-1933   Volume X

MARRIAGE CARD.

_____ Marriage. Sex _____ Census or Allotment No. _____
Name _____ Tribe _____ Pott _____
Married _____ How _____
Married to whom _____ Census or Allotment No. _____
If divorced, When _____ Where _____
If divorced, How _____

CHILDREN BORN OF THIS MARRIAGE.

Census or Allotment No.	Sex	Name	Born	blood DIED
	M	Joseph Bruno	1894	1/2 Pott
	F	wife		White
	F	Isaac "	Oct 12 1919	1/4 Pott
		address Konawa		

See Marriage Cards Nos. _____ and _____ for half-brothers and half-sisters of these children.

MARRIAGE CARD.

_____ Marriage. Sex _____ Census or Allotment No. _____
Name _____ Tribe _____ Pott _____
Married _____ How _____
Married to whom _____ Census or Allotment No. _____
If divorced, When _____ Where _____
If divorced, How _____

CHILDREN BORN OF THIS MARRIAGE.

Census or Allotment No.	Sex	Name	Born	blood DIED
	M	Sam W. Bruno	1865	1/2 Pott
	F	Thresa Bennett "	1871	1/2 Pott
		address Konawa		

See Marriage Cards Nos. _____ and _____ for half-brothers and half-sisters of these children.

Sac & Fox – Shawnee
1853-1933   Volume X

MARRIAGE CARD.

Marriage. Sex _____ Census or Allotment No. _____
Name _____ Tribe ____ Pott _____
Married _____ How _____
Married to whom _____ Census or Allotment No. _____
If divorced, When _____ Where _____
If divorced, How _____

CHILDREN BORN OF THIS MARRIAGE.

Census or Allotment No.	Sex	Name	Born	blood / Died
	M	Harry Long		white
	F	Mamie DeLonais Long	Oct 28 1902	1/2 Pott
	M	Franklin "		1/4 "
Twins	F	Lois "		1/4 "
	F	Louise "		1/4 "

address Pawhuska Okla

See Marriage Cards Nos. _____ and _____ for half-brothers and half-sisters of these children.

MARRIAGE CARD.

Marriage. Sex _____ Census or Allotment No. _____
Name _____ Tribe _____
Married _____ How _____
Married to whom _____ Census or Allotment No. _____
If divorced, When _____ Where _____
If divorced, How _____

CHILDREN BORN OF THIS MARRIAGE.

Census or Allotment No.	Sex	Name	Born	blood / Died
	M	Monroe Murry		white
	F	Arkangel DeLonais Murry	Mar 29 1896	1/2 Pott
	M	Clifford "		1/4 "
	M	Walter "		1/4 "

address Pawhuska Okla

See Marriage Cards Nos. _____ and _____ for half-brothers and half-sisters of these children.

Sac & Fox – Shawnee
1853-1933 Volume X

MARRIAGE CARD.

```
........................................Marriage. Sex........ Census or Allotment No. ........................
Name ...........................................................  Tribe ___Pott_____
Married ........................................................  How ..................................................
Married to whom ..........................................  Census or Allotment No. ........................
If divorced, When .........................................  Where .............................................
If divorced, How ..................................................................................................
```

CHILDREN BORN OF THIS MARRIAGE.

Census or Allotment No.	Sex	Name	Born	Blood	Died
	M	Joel Deloains[sic]	Feb 14 1857	13/32	Pott
son	M	Joseph "	Apr 29 1900	13/64	"

address Pawhuska Okla Box 69

See Marriage Cards Nos. .... and .... for half-brothers and half-sisters of these children.

MARRIAGE CARD.

```
........................................Marriage. Sex........ Census or Allotment No. ........................
Name ...........................................................  Tribe ___Pott_____
Married ........................................................  How ..................................................
Married to whom ..........................................  Census or Allotment No. ........................
If divorced, When .........................................  Where .............................................
If divorced, How ..................................................................................................
```

CHILDREN BORN OF THIS MARRIAGE.

Census or Allotment No.	Sex	Name	Born	blood	Died
	M	Robert Huddleston		white	
	F	Emma DeLonais Huddleston	Apr 1 1907	13/32	Pott
	F	Zilda M. "	Apr 26 1927	13/64	"
	F	Cloffly M. "	Aug 14 1928	13/64	"

address Sacred Heart

See Marriage Cards Nos. .... and .... for half-brothers and half-sisters of these children.

Sac & Fox – Shawnee
1853-1933 Volume X

MARRIAGE CARD.

Marriage. Sex ____ Census or Allotment No. ____
Name ____ Tribe ____ Pott ____
Married ____ How ____
Married to whom ____ Census or Allotment No. ____
If divorced, When ____ Where ____
If divorced, How ____

CHILDREN BORN OF THIS MARRIAGE.

Census or Allotment No.	Sex	Name	Born	Died blood
	M	Albert DeLonais	July 29 1905	13/32 Pott
	F	wife		white
	M	Albert W. Jr. "	June 30 1928	13/64 Pott

address Sacred Heart

See Marriage Cards Nos. ____ and ____ for half-brothers and half-sisters of these children.

MARRIAGE CARD.

Marriage. Sex ____ Census or Allotment No. ____
Name ____ Tribe ____
Married ____ How ____
Married to whom ____ Census or Allotment No. ____
If divorced, When ____ Where ____
If divorced, How ____

CHILDREN BORN OF THIS MARRIAGE.

Census or Allotment No.	Sex	Name	Born	Died blood
	M	W^m DeLonais	Mar 18 1900	6/8 Pott ?
	F	Grace Higdon		white
	M	Wm J. DeLonais	Nov 24 1927	3/8 Pott
	M	Loyd "	Apr 4 1928	3/8 "

address Sacred Heart

See Marriage Cards Nos. ____ and ____ for half-brothers and half-sisters of these children.

Sac & Fox – Shawnee
1853-1933   Volume X

MARRIAGE CARD.

Marriage. Sex   Census or Allotment No.
Name   Tribe
Married   How
Married to whom   Census or Allotment No.
If divorced, When   Where
If divorced, How

CHILDREN BORN OF THIS MARRIAGE.

Census or Allotment No.	Sex	Name	Born	Blood	Died
	M	Dan DeClaire[sic]	1894	3/4 Pott	
	F	Sarrah Delonais LeClaire	April 9 1896	7/8	"
	F	Geneive "	Sept 24 1917	13/16	"
	F	Gwdendlyne[sic] "	1919	13/16	"
	M	J. R. "	1921	13/16	"
	M	Nathan "	1923	13/16	"
	M	Anthony "	1927	13/16	"

address Bartlesville Okla

See Marriage Cards Nos. _____ and _____ for half-brothers and half-sisters of these children.

MARRIAGE CARD.

Marriage. Sex   Census or Allotment No.
Name   Tribe   Pott
Married   How
Married to whom   Census or Allotment No.
If divorced, When   Where
If divorced, How

CHILDREN BORN OF THIS MARRIAGE.

Census or Allotment No.	Sex	Name	Born	Blood	Died
	M	Francis Delonais	Sept 2 1881	1/16 Pott	
	F	Mary Shopwetuck Deonais[sic]	1869	3/4	"
	F	Margret M "	July 1910	13/32	"
	F	Ethel M. "	Mar 3 1914	13/32	"

address Sacred Heart Okla

See Marriage Cards Nos. _____ and _____ for half-brothers and half-sisters of these children.

Sac & Fox – Shawnee
1853-1933   Volume X

MARRIAGE CARD.

_____Marriage. Sex_____ Census or Allotment No._____
Name_____ Tribe ____Pott_____
Married_____ How_____
Married to whom_____ Census or Allotment No._____
If divorced, When_____ Where_____
If divorced, How_____

CHILDREN BORN OF THIS MARRIAGE.

Census or Allotment No.	Sex	Name	Born	Blood (Died)
	M	Willie Bruno	Mar 21 1900	1/2 Pott
	F	May Naberry "		Part Pott
				1/2 ?
address	Cromwell Okla			

See Marriage Cards Nos. _____ and _____ for half-brothers and half-sisters of these children.

MARRIAGE CARD.

_____Marriage. Sex_____ Census or Allotment No._____
Name_____ Tribe ____Pott_____
Married_____ How_____
Married to whom_____ Census or Allotment No._____
If divorced, When_____ Where_____
If divorced, How_____

CHILDREN BORN OF THIS MARRIAGE.

Census or Allotment No.	Sex	Name	Born	Blood (Died)
	M	Harry Wamego		Full Pott
	F	Charlotte Bruno "	Sept 17 1895	1/2 Pott
	M	Willie "	Dec 16 1920	3/4 "
	F	Gladdis "	Sept 1924	3/4 "
	M	Paul "	1926	3/4 "
	M	David "	March 1927	3/4 "
address	Pawhuska			

See Marriage Cards Nos. _____ and _____ for half-brothers and half-sisters of these children.

Sac & Fox – Shawnee
1853-1933 Volume X

MARRIAGE CARD.

Name _____ Marriage. Sex _____ Census or Allotment No. _____
Married __John Burnett and__ Tribe _____
Married to whom _____ How _____
If divorced, When __about 1928__ Census or Allotment No. _____
If divorced, How _____ Where __Pawhuska Okla__

CHILDREN BORN OF THIS MARRIAGE.

Census or Allotment No.	Sex	Name	Born	Blood	Died
	M	John Burnett		1/2 Pott	
	F	Elizabeth Bruno Burnett	1898	1/2 Pott	
	F	Rosetta "	1920	1/2 "	
	F	Caroline "		1/2 "	
	F	Mulvine "	1924	1/2 "	

address Pawhuska

See Marriage Cards Nos. _____ and _____ for half-brothers and half-sisters of these children.

MARRIAGE CARD.

Name _____ Marriage. Sex _____ Census or Allotment No. _____
Married _____ Tribe __Pott__
Married to whom _____ How _____
If divorced, When _____ Census or Allotment No. _____
If divorced, How _____ Where _____

CHILDREN BORN OF THIS MARRIAGE.

Census or Allotment No.	Sex	Name	Born	Blood	Died
	M	Andrew Cody		Part Cherokee	
	F	Evelyn Bruno "	Nov 20 1908	1/2 Pott	
	F	Zelda M. "	Nov 11 1928	1/4 Pott	

address Homing

See Marriage Cards Nos. _____ and _____ for half-brothers and half-sisters of these children.

Sac & Fox – Shawnee
1853-1933 Volume X

MARRIAGE CARD.

Name _____ Marriage. Sex _____ Census or Allotment No. _____
Married _____ Tribe _____ Pott _____
Married to whom _____ How _____
If divorced, When _____ Census or Allotment No. _____
If divorced, How _____ Where _____

CHILDREN BORN OF THIS MARRIAGE.

CENSUS OR ALLOTMENT NO.	SEX	NAME	BORN	DIED Blood
	M	Thomas Kemohab		Osage Full
	F	Nora Bruno "	Oct 9 1903	1/2 Pott
Twins	F	Jeraldine F "	Aug 1926	3/4 Indian
	F	Geneva M "	Aug 14 1926	3/4 "
	M	Thomas Jr "	Apr 26 1928	3/4 "
address	Homing			

See Marriage Cards Nos. _____ and _____ for half-brothers and half-sisters of these children.

MARRIAGE CARD.

Name _____ Marriage. Sex _____ Census or Allotment No. _____
Married _____ Tribe _____ Pott _____
Married to whom _____ How _____
If divorced, When _____ Census or Allotment No. _____
If divorced, How _____ Where _____

CHILDREN BORN OF THIS MARRIAGE.

CENSUS OR ALLOTMENT NO.	SEX	NAME	BORN	DIED Blood
	M	Thomas Delonais	Jan 28 1899	5/8 Pott
	F	Osia Bruno "	July 10 1900	1/2 "
	M	Jeanofare "	Mar 19 1922	7/16 "
	F	Florine V "	Apr 3 1924	7/16 "
	F	Elizabeth D "	Nov 1 1926	7/16 "
	M	Jesse A "	Mar 14 1919	7/16 "
address	Sacred Heart			

See Marriage Cards Nos. _____ and _____ for half-brothers and half-sisters of these children.

****

Sac & Fox – Shawnee
1853-1933 Volume X

MARRIAGE CARD.

```
_____Marriage. Sex_____  Census or Allotment No._____
Name_____  Tribe____Pott_____
Married_____  How_____
Married to whom_____  Census or Allotment No._____
If divorced, When_____  Where_____
If divorced, How_____
```

CHILDREN BORN OF THIS MARRIAGE.

Census or Allotment No.	Sex	Name	Born	Blood Died
	M	Thomas Delonais	Jan 28 1899	5/8 Pott
	F	Osia Bruno "	July 10 1900	1/2 "
	M	Jeanofare "	Mar 19 1922	7/16 "
	F	Florine V "	Apr 3 1924	7/16 "
	F	Elizabeth D "	Nov 1 1926	7/16 "
	M	Jesse A "	Mar 14 1919	7/16 "

address Sacred Heart

See Marriage Cards Nos. _____ and _____ for half-brothers and half-sisters of these children.

MARRIAGE CARD.

```
_____Marriage. Sex_____  Census or Allotment No._____
Name_____  Tribe____Pott_____
Married_____  How_____
Married to whom_____  Census or Allotment No._____
If divorced, When_____  Where_____
If divorced, How_____
```

CHILDREN BORN OF THIS MARRIAGE.

Census or Allotment No.	Sex	Name	Born	Blood Died
	M	Allison Webb		Osage Full
	F	Mary Bruno Webb	Feb 15 1897	1/2 Pott

address Homing #715

See Marriage Cards Nos. _____ and _____ for half-brothers and half-sisters of these children.

Sac & Fox – Shawnee
1853-1933   Volume X

MARRIAGE CARD.

```
                        Marriage. Sex _____   Census or Allotment No. _____
Name _____          Tribe ___Pott_____
Married _____          How _____
Married to whom _____          Census or Allotment No. _____
If divorced, When _____          Where _____
If divorced, How _____
```

CHILDREN BORN OF THIS MARRIAGE.

Census or Allotment No.	Sex	Name	Born	Blood / Died
	M	James Shopwetuck	Jan 1 1885	3/4 Pott
	F	Ethel Bruno "	May 21 1893	1/2

address Sacred Heart

See Marriage Cards Nos. _____ and _____ for half-brothers and half-sisters of these children.

MARRIAGE CARD.

```
                        Marriage. Sex _____   Census or Allotment No. _____
Name _____          Tribe _____
Married _____          How _____
Married to whom _____          Census or Allotment No. _____
If divorced, When _____          Where _____
If divorced, How _____
```

CHILDREN BORN OF THIS MARRIAGE.

Census or Allotment No.	Sex	Name	Born	Blood / Died
	M	Joe O Bruno	Oct 12 1872	1/2 Pott
	F	Ellen Venux Bruno	1873	1/2 Pott
	M	Jacob "	Sept 9 1902	1/2 "
	M	Louis "	Oct 29 1905	1/2 "
	F	Julia "	Sept 17 1909	1/2 "
	M	Elex "	Nov 11 1910	1/2 "
	M	August "	Aug 20 1913	1/2 "
	M	Joseph C "	Apr 2 1918	1/2 "

address Pawhuska

See Marriage Cards Nos. _____ and _____ for half-brothers and half-sisters of these children.

Sac & Fox – Shawnee
1853-1933 Volume X

MARRIAGE CARD.

Name .... Marriage. Sex .... Census or Allotment No. ....
Married .... Tribe ....
Married to whom .... How ....
If divorced, When .... Census or Allotment No. ....
If divorced, How .... Where ....

CHILDREN BORN OF THIS MARRIAGE.

Census or Allotment No.	Sex	Name	Born	Blood	Died
	M	John Megah	1862	full	
	F	Josatta "	1861	"	
	M	Joseph "	Oct 17 1904	"	
		(Grand child)			
	M	Harvey Wapskineh	1927		
address	Asher #2				

See Marriage Cards Nos. .... and .... for half-brothers and half-sisters of these children.

MARRIAGE CARD.

Name .... Marriage. Sex .... Census or Allotment No. ....
Married .... Tribe ....
Married to whom .... How ....
If divorced, When .... Census or Allotment No. ....
If divorced, How .... Where ....

CHILDREN BORN OF THIS MARRIAGE.

Census or Allotment No.	Sex	Name	Born	Blood	Died
	M	Husband		white	
	F	Myrtle Waus Nunley	Aug 14 1902	1/2	
	M	Forrest W^{m} "	Oct 29 1916		
	F	Wanda Lee "	Apr 26 1927		
	F	Patsie Ruth "	Dec 10 1928		
address	Konawa #1				

See Marriage Cards Nos. .... and .... for half-brothers and half-sisters of these children.

Sac & Fox – Shawnee
1853-1933 Volume X

MARRIAGE CARD.

```
                          Marriage. Sex_____ Census or Allotment No._____
Name_____ Tribe_____
Married_____ How_____
Married to whom_____ Census or Allotment No._____
If divorced, When_____ Where_____
If divorced, How_____
```

CHILDREN BORN OF THIS MARRIAGE.

CENSUS OR ALLOTMENT NO.	SEX	NAME	BORN	Blood / DIED
	M	John D Tiger	Sept 15 1900	7/8 Creek
	F	Susie Le Claire "	Oct 14 1902	1/2 Pott
	F	Bettie J. "	Jan 8 1926	5/18 Indian

address Konawa #2

See Marriage Cards Nos. _____ and _____ for half-brothers and half-sisters of these children.

MARRIAGE CARD.

```
                          Marriage. Sex_____ Census or Allotment No._____
Name_____ Tribe_____
Married_____ How_____
Married to whom_____ Census or Allotment No._____
If divorced, When_____ Where_____
If divorced, How_____
```

CHILDREN BORN OF THIS MARRIAGE.

CENSUS OR ALLOTMENT NO.	SEX	NAME	BORN	Blood / DIED
	M	John A Crane	1903	Sac & Fox Full
	F	Angeline LeClaire Crane	Aug 2[?] 1907	1/2

address

See Marriage Cards Nos. _____ and _____ for half-brothers and half-sisters of these children.

Sac & Fox – Shawnee
1853-1933 Volume X

MARRIAGE CARD.

```
_____Marriage. Sex_____  Census or Allotment No._____
Name_____  Tribe_____
Married_____  How_____
Married to whom_____  Census or Allotment No._____
If divorced, When_____  Where_____
If divorced, How_____
```

CHILDREN BORN OF THIS MARRIAGE.

Census or Allotment No.	Sex	Name	Born	Died Blood
	M	H. H. Higbee	Oct 14 1895	1/32 Pott
	F	wife		white
	M	Homer D. "	1921	1/64 Pott
	M	Orval G. "	Apr 1924	"
	F	Marjorie D "	1926	"
		address Bristow Okla		

See Marriage Cards Nos. _____ and _____ for half-brothers and half-sisters of these children.

MARRIAGE CARD.

```
_____Marriage. Sex_____  Census or Allotment No._____
Name_____  Tribe____Pott_____
Married_____  How_____
Married to whom_____  Census or Allotment No._____
If divorced, When_____  Where_____
If divorced, How_____
```

CHILDREN BORN OF THIS MARRIAGE.

Census or Allotment No.	Sex	Name	Born	Died Blood
	M	Elmer Pratt (Dead)		1/16 Pott
		Sadie Pratt Dau	1917	1/32 "
		Mandy Pratt mother		white
		address Maud #[sic]		

See Marriage Cards Nos. _____ and _____ for half-brothers and half-sisters of these children.

Sac & Fox – Shawnee
1853-1933   Volume X

MARRIAGE CARD.

Name _____ Marriage. Sex _____ Census or Allotment No. _____
Married _____ Tribe __Pott_____
Married to whom _____ How _____
If divorced, When _____ Census or Allotment No. _____
If divorced, How _____ Where _____

CHILDREN BORN OF THIS MARRIAGE.

Census or Allotment No.	Sex	Name	Born	Blood	Died
	M	Jim Lucy		White	
	F	Flosie[sic] N. Pratt Lucy	1902	1/64 Pott	
		Winnie A "	1927	1/64[sic]Pott	
address	Maud # 2				

See Marriage Cards Nos. _____ and _____ for half-brothers and half-sisters of these children.

MARRIAGE CARD.

Name _____ Marriage. Sex _____ Census or Allotment No. _____
Married _____ Tribe __Pott_____
Married to whom _____ How _____
If divorced, When _____ Census or Allotment No. _____
If divorced, How _____ Where _____

CHILDREN BORN OF THIS MARRIAGE.

Census or Allotment No.	Sex	Name	Born	Blood	Died
	M	Cecil R. Pratt	1904	1/32 Pott	
	F	Vergie May "		White	
	F	Rosa May "	May 1928	1/64 Pott	
	F	Tresa[sic] Fay "	1928	1/64 "	
address	Maud # 2				

See Marriage Cards Nos. _____ and _____ for half-brothers and half-sisters of these children.

Sac & Fox – Shawnee
1853-1933 Volume X

MARRIAGE CARD.

Name _____ Marriage. Sex _____ Census or Allotment No. _____
Married _____ Tribe __Pott_____
Married to whom _____ How _____
If divorced, When _____ Census or Allotment No. _____
If divorced, How _____ Where _____

CHILDREN BORN OF THIS MARRIAGE.

Census or Allotment No.	Sex	Name	Born	Died Blood
	F	Wanda J. Pratt	1925	1/64 Pott
		Father Dead		

address Alex Okla.
See Marriage Cards Nos. _____ and _____ for half-brothers and half-sisters of these children.

MARRIAGE CARD.

Name _____ Marriage. Sex _____ Census or Allotment No. _____
Married _____ Tribe __Pott_____
Married to whom _____ How _____
If divorced, When _____ Census or Allotment No. _____
If divorced, How _____ Where _____

CHILDREN BORN OF THIS MARRIAGE.

Census or Allotment No.	Sex	Name	Born	Died Blood
	M	Marrio Pockrus		White
	F	Ada Florence "	1901	1/32 Pott
	M	Norman L. "	1920	1/64 "
	M	Delbert R. "	1922	1/64 "
	F	Charlotte N. "	1925	1/64 "

address Maud # 2
See Marriage Cards Nos. _____ and _____ for half-brothers and half-sisters of these children.

Sac & Fox – Shawnee
1853-1933   Volume X

MARRIAGE CARD.

Name _____ Marriage. Sex _____ Census or Allotment No. _____
Married _____ Tribe __Pott_____
Married to whom _____ How _____
If divorced, When _____ Census or Allotment No. _____
If divorced, How _____ Where _____

CHILDREN BORN OF THIS MARRIAGE.

Census or Allotment No.	Sex	Name	Born	Died Blood
	M	Ernest O. Pratt	1873	1/16 Pott
	F	Minnie B. "		White
	F	~~Ada Florence "~~	~~1901~~	~~1/32 Pott~~
	M	~~Oscar L. "~~		

address   Maud # 2

See Marriage Cards Nos. _____ and _____ for half-brothers and half-sisters of these children.

MARRIAGE CARD.

Name _____ Marriage. Sex _____ Census or Allotment No. _____
Married _____ Tribe __Pott_____
Married to whom _____ How _____
If divorced, When _____ Census or Allotment No. _____
If divorced, How _____ Where _____

not enrolled

CHILDREN BORN OF THIS MARRIAGE.

Census or Allotment No.	Sex	Name	Born	Died Blood
	M	Joseph A Nadeau	1863	1/16 Pott
	F	Sarrah Tascier "	1872	1/16 Pott
	F	Nila Cecilia "	1911	1/16 "

ADDRESS Tecumseh # 5

See Marriage Cards Nos. _____ and _____ for half-brothers and half-sisters of these children.

Sac & Fox – Shawnee
1853-1933   Volume X

MARRIAGE CARD.

Name .... Marriage. Sex .... Census or Allotment No. ....
Married .... Tribe ... Pott ....
Married to whom .... How ....
If divorced, When .... Census or Allotment No. ....
If divorced, How .... Where ....

CHILDREN BORN OF THIS MARRIAGE.

Census or Allotment No.	Sex	Name	Born	Blood	Died
	M	Vincent Henry Nadeau	1895	1/16 Pott	
	F	Lela T "		White	
	F	Stella "	1917	1/32 Pott	
	M	Vincent Jr. "	Sept 5 1928	1/32 "	

address Tecumseh # 5

See Marriage Cards Nos. .... and .... for half-brothers and half-sisters of these children.

MARRIAGE CARD.

Name .... Marriage. Sex .... Census or Allotment No. ....
Married .... Tribe ... Pott ....
Married to whom .... How ....
If divorced, When .... Census or Allotment No. ....
If divorced, How .... Where ....

CHILDREN BORN OF THIS MARRIAGE.

Census or Allotment No.	Sex	Name	Born	Blood	Died
	F	Lilian Nadeau C Carsten	1897	1/16 Pott	
	M Husband	Herman "		White	
	F	Vinita "	1918	1/32 Pott	
	M	Billie "	1920	1/32 "	

The 2 children live with their grand parents Mr & Mrs Nadeau. Lilian is in the Insane Asylum at Norman Okla.

address Tecumseh

See Marriage Cards Nos. .... and .... for half-brothers and half-sisters of these children.

Sac & Fox – Shawnee
1853-1933 Volume X

MARRIAGE CARD.

Name .... Marriage. Sex .... Census or Allotment No. ....
Married Reba Kitchum Nadeau   Tribe Pott
Married to whom .... How ....
If divorced, When 1926   Census or Allotment No. ....
If divorced, How .... Where Tecumseh

CHILDREN BORN OF THIS MARRIAGE.

CENSUS OR ALLOTMENT NO.	SEX	NAME	BORN	DIED blood
	M	Ray Aloyious Nadeau	1900	1/16 Pott
	F			
	M	Joe K. Nadeau	1923	1/32 Pott
	M	Troy A "	1926	1/3[sic] "
		by first wife		
address	Tecumseh # 5			

See Marriage Cards Nos. .... and .... for half-brothers and half-sisters of these children.

MARRIAGE CARD.

Name .... Marriage. Sex .... Census or Allotment No. ....
Married .... Tribe Pott
Married to whom .... How ....
If divorced, When .... Census or Allotment No. ....
If divorced, How .... Where ....

CHILDREN BORN OF THIS MARRIAGE.

CENSUS OR ALLOTMENT NO.	SEX	NAME	BORN	DIED Blood
	M	Francis J Nadeau	1904	1/16 Pott
	F	Gloria Quinnette "		White
	M	Dean "	1925	1/32 Pott
address	Tecumseh #5 ~~Macomb~~			

See Marriage Cards Nos. .... and .... for half-brothers and half-sisters of these children.

Sac & Fox – Shawnee
1853-1933 Volume X

MARRIAGE CARD.

Name .... Marriage. Sex .... Census or Allotment No. ....
Married .... Tribe Pott
Married to whom .... How ....
If divorced, When .... Census or Allotment No. ....
If divorced, How .... Where ....

CHILDREN BORN OF THIS MARRIAGE.

Census or Allotment No.	Sex	Name	Born	Died Blood
	M	Geo. W. Helens white	1880	1/16 Pott
	F	Christina M. Helens		
		Joseph I. "	1899	1/32 Pott

address Shawnee # 4

See Marriage Cards Nos. .... and .... for half-brothers and half-sisters of these children.

MARRIAGE CARD.

......Single......... Marriage. Sex Male Census or Allotment No. ....
Name   Monroe Smith   Tribe   Pott
Married Single   now has one child   How   Legally
         by former marriage
Married to whom Pearl Graves   Census or Allotment No. ....
If divorced, When   1921   Where   Tecumseh
If divorced, How ....

CHILDREN BORN OF THIS MARRIAGE.

Census or Allotment No.	Sex	Name	Born	Died Blood
		Monroe Smith	1886	1/8 Pott
	Child	Beatrice " (wife white)	1916	1/16 "

Maud

See Marriage Cards Nos. .... and .... for half-brothers and half-sisters of these children.

Sac & Fox – Shawnee
1853-1933 Volume X

MARRIAGE CARD.

Name _____ Marriage. Sex _____ Census or Allotment No. _____
Married _____ Tribe _____
Married to whom _____ How _____
If divorced, When _____ Census or Allotment No. _____
If divorced, How _____ Where _____

CHILDREN BORN OF THIS MARRIAGE.

Census or Allotment No.	Sex	Name	Born	Blood / Died
	female	Bertha Ellen Smith	1884	1/8 Pott
		Husband (white) Kinslow		
		Clyde Leroy Smith Kinslow	1912	1/16 "
		Glenn Allen " "	1914	"
		Evert J " "	1917	"
		Vancie Eugene " "	1919	"
		Vernon " "	1921	"
		Dorothy May " "	1923	"

See Marriage Cards Nos. _____ and _____ for half-brothers and half-sisters of these children.

Lives at McComb

MARRIAGE CARD.

Name _____ Marriage. Sex _____ Census or Allotment No. _____
Married _____ Tribe _____Pott_____
Married to whom _____ How _____
If divorced, When _____ Census or Allotment No. _____
If divorced, How _____ Where _____

CHILDREN BORN OF THIS MARRIAGE.

Census or Allotment No.	Sex	Name	Born	Blood / Died
		Joe Kime Feb 25 - 1895	1895	1/8 Pott
		Mrs. Kime - white		
		Gerald Ethan Kime	1922	7yr 1/16 "
		Aldrich Kime	1925	4" 1/16 "
		Jeminie Joe Kime	1928	1yr 1/16 "
	Pott.			
address	McComb			

See Marriage Cards Nos. _____ and _____ for half-brothers and half-sisters of these children.

255

Sac & Fox – Shawnee
1853-1933 Volume X

MARRIAGE CARD.

```
_____ Marriage. Sex _____ Census or Allotment No. _____
Name _____ Tribe ____ Pott _____
Married _____ How _____
Married to whom _____ Census or Allotment No. _____
If divorced, When _____ Where _____
If divorced, How _____
```

CHILDREN BORN OF THIS MARRIAGE.

Census or Allotment No.	Sex	Name	Born	Blood/Died
	F	Stella Weld	1906	1/16 Pott
ADDRESS				

See Marriage Cards Nos. _____ and _____ for half-brothers and half-sisters of these children.

MARRIAGE CARD.

```
_____ Marriage. Sex _____ Census or Allotment No. _____
Name _____ Tribe ____ Pott _____
Married _____ How _____
Married to whom _____ Census or Allotment No. _____
If divorced, When _____ Where _____
If divorced, How _____
```

CHILDREN BORN OF THIS MARRIAGE.

Census or Allotment No.	Sex	Name	Born	Blood/Died
	F	Claricie Weld Trescott	Jan 1891	1/16 Pott
ADDRESS	Cal.			

See Marriage Cards Nos. _____ and _____ for half-brothers and half-sisters of these children.

Sac & Fox – Shawnee
1853-1933   Volume X

MARRIAGE CARD.

```
                         Marriage. Sex          Census or Allotment No. _____
Name _____   Tribe _____ Pott _____
Married _____   How _____
Married to whom _____   Census or Allotment No. _____
If divorced, When _____   Where _____
If divorced, How _____
```

CHILDREN BORN OF THIS MARRIAGE.

Census or Allotment No.	Sex	Name	Born	Died Blood
	F	Mrs Teresa Slavin Humphreys		Pott
		John Eckford Jr. "	1925	
		Donald Joe "	1928	
		address 743 So. Phoenix Tulsa, Okla.		

See Marriage Cards Nos. _____ and _____ for half-brothers and half-sisters of these children.

---

born 1904- 25 yrs old
             Mrs Teresa Humphreys
    her P.O. address ⟶ 743 So Phoenix
                        Tulsa, Okla.
born
    1925- 4 yrs old   John Eckford Humphreys Jr

                Donald Joe Humphreys.
born – 1928. – age 1 yr old

Mr Gunn
        Kind Sir: Above are the name's of Teresa Slavin nee Humphreys
and her two children also their ages and P.O. address.
You told me to mention Teresa Slavin Census blank so you could fill it out.
                        Yours Truly
                            James Slavin
                                Lexington
                    R #4   Okla

Sac & Fox – Shawnee
1853-1933 Volume X

MARRIAGE CARD.

Name _____ Marriage. Sex _____ Census or Allotment No. _____
Married _____ Tribe ____ Pott _____
Married to whom _____ How _____
If divorced, When _____ Census or Allotment No. _____
If divorced, How _____ Where _____

CHILDREN BORN OF THIS MARRIAGE.

Census or Allotment No.	Sex	Name	Born	Blood / Died
	M	David Laughton	Nov 16 1900	1/4 Pott
address	Konawa # 2			

See Marriage Cards Nos. _____ and _____ for half-brothers and half-sisters of these children.

MARRIAGE CARD.

Name _____ Marriage. Sex _____ Census or Allotment No. _____
Married _____ Tribe ____ Pott _____
Married to whom _____ How _____
If divorced, When _____ Census or Allotment No. _____
If divorced, How _____ Where _____

CHILDREN BORN OF THIS MARRIAGE.

Census or Allotment No.	Sex	Name		Born	Blood / Died
	M	John B. Rhodd		Mar 15 1882	1/2 Pott
	F	Adeline Thorp	"	Jun 10 1895	1/4 Sac & Fox 1/4 Pott 1/2 white
	F	Edith	"	Jan 12 1914	1/2 Sac & fox
	F	Viola E.	"	May 17 1915	1/2 "
	M	Alexander J.	"	Feb 20 1917	"
	F	Clida	"	Mar 28 1920	"
	F	Eva	"	Apr 2 1922	"
	F	Charlotte	"	Oct 10 1923	"
	F	Zoa H	"	Aug 1 1926	"
	M	Frank E.	"	Dec 24 1928	"
address	Konawa # 3				

See Marriage Cards Nos. _____ and _____ for half-brothers and half-sisters of these children.

Sac & Fox – Shawnee
1853-1933 Volume X

MARRIAGE CARD.

Name _____ Marriage. Sex _____ Census or Allotment No. _____
Married _____ Tribe _____ Pott _____
Married to whom _____ How _____
If divorced, When _____ Census or Allotment No. _____
If divorced, How _____ Where _____

CHILDREN BORN OF THIS MARRIAGE.

Census or Allotment No.	Sex	Name	Born	Blood Died
	M	Joseph A Rhodd	Nov 6 1905	1/4 Pott
		wife		

address Oklahoma City 312 W 6st [sic]

See Marriage Cards Nos. _____ and _____ for half-brothers and half-sisters of these children.

MARRIAGE CARD.

Name _____ Marriage. Sex _____ Census or Allotment No. _____
Married _____ Tribe _____ Pott _____
Married to whom _____ How _____
If divorced, When _____ Census or Allotment No. _____
If divorced, How _____ Where _____

CHILDREN BORN OF THIS MARRIAGE.

Census or Allotment No.	Sex	Name	Born	blood Died
	M	Peter A. Rhodd	Nov 29 1882	1/2 Pott
		wife		white
	F	Margret "	Dec 31 1907	1/4 Pott
	M	George "	Mar 7 1909	1/4 "
	F	Mary E. "	Sept [?] 1925	1/4 "
	F	Ruth O. "	Mr 9 1927	1/4 "

address Konawa

See Marriage Cards Nos. _____ and _____ for half-brothers and half-sisters of these children.

Sac & Fox – Shawnee
1853-1933 Volume X

MARRIAGE CARD.

```
..............................Marriage. Sex........  Census or Allotment No..........................
Name...........................................................  Tribe..............................................
Married.......................................................  How...............................................
Married to whom.........................................  Census or Allotment No..........................
If divorced, When........................................  Where.............................................
If divorced, How...............................................................................................
```

CHILDREN BORN OF THIS MARRIAGE.

CENSUS OR ALLOTMENT NO.	SEX	NAME	BORN	Blood / DIED
	M	Herbert Lawson		Nov 21 1902	1/8 Pott
	F	wife		white

address Tropsdale

See Marriage Cards Nos. _____ and _____ for half-brothers and half-sisters of these children.

MARRIAGE CARD.

```
..............................Marriage. Sex........  Census or Allotment No..........................
Name...........................................................  Tribe..............................................
Married.......................................................  How...............................................
Married to whom.........................................  Census or Allotment No..........................
If divorced, When........................................  Where.............................................
If divorced, How...............................................................................................
```

CHILDREN BORN OF THIS MARRIAGE.

CENSUS OR ALLOTMENT NO.	SEX	NAME	BORN	Blood / DIED
	M	Cheatwood		white
	F	Dora Willmett "	June 5 1895	3/16 Pott
	M	Ernest N. "	Apr 1 1914	6/32 "
	F	Grace L. "	Oct 11 1915	6/32 "
	M	Roy T. "	Oct 4 1917	6/32 "
	F	Mable L. "	Sept 13 1919	6/32 "
	M	Pearl L. "	Apr 4 1921	6/32 "
	M	Louis B. "	June 28 1923	6/32 "
	M	Joseph A "	Aug 23 1927	6/32 "

address Lexington # 4

See Marriage Cards Nos. _____ and _____ for half-brothers and half-sisters of these children.

Sac & Fox – Shawnee
1853-1933   Volume X

MARRIAGE CARD.

```
                          Marriage. Sex_____ Census or Allotment No._____
Name_____ Tribe_____
Married_____ How_____
Married to whom_____ Census or Allotment No._____
If divorced, When_____ Where_____
If divorced, How_____
```

CHILDREN BORN OF THIS MARRIAGE.

Census or Allotment No.	Sex	Name	Born	Blood / Died
	M	James R. Lawson	June 9 1898	1/8
	F	wife		white
	F	Ilene "	July 9 1925	1/16 Pott
	address	Trousdale		

See Marriage Cards Nos. _____ and _____ for half-brothers and half-sisters of these children.

MARRIAGE CARD.

```
                          Marriage. Sex_____ Census or Allotment No._____
Name_____ Tribe_____
Married_____ How_____
Married to whom_____ Census or Allotment No._____
If divorced, When_____ Where_____
If divorced, How_____
```

CHILDREN BORN OF THIS MARRIAGE.

Census or Allotment No.	Sex	Name	Born	Blood / Died
	F	Jeanette Lawson Morphaw	Sept 22 1894	1/8 Pott
	M	Husband		white
	F	Marie "	1917	1/16 Pott
	address	Wewoka		

See Marriage Cards Nos. _____ and _____ for half-brothers and half-sisters of these children.

Sac & Fox – Shawnee
1853-1933 Volume X

MARRIAGE CARD.

Name .... Marriage. Sex .... Census or Allotment No. ....
Married .... Tribe ...... Pott ....
Married to whom .... How ....
If divorced, When .... Census or Allotment No. ....
If divorced, How .... Where ....

CHILDREN BORN OF THIS MARRIAGE.

Census or Allotment No.	Sex	Name	Born	Blood	Died
		Husband		white	
	F	Mary Lafrombois Lawson	Sept 25 1872	1/4 Pott	
	M	Chas R. "	Oct 21 1900	1/8 "	
	M	Arthur E. "	Nov 13 1904	1/8 "	
	M	Gayland G. "	Nov 10 1907	1/8 "	
	M	Wm E. "	Oct 23 1010	1/8 "	
		address Trousdale # 3			

See Marriage Cards Nos. .... and .... for half-brothers and half-sisters of these children.

MARRIAGE CARD.

Name .... Marriage. Sex .... Census or Allotment No. ....
Married .... Tribe ....
Married to whom .... How ....
If divorced, When .... Census or Allotment No. ....
If divorced, How .... Where ....

CHILDREN BORN OF THIS MARRIAGE.

Census or Allotment No.	Sex	Name	Born	Blood	Died
	M	Husband		white	
	F	Ruth Wesselhoft Tipton		1/4 Pott	
	M	Bobie "	1924	1/8 "	
		address			

See Marriage Cards Nos. .... and .... for half-brothers and half-sisters of these children.

Sac & Fox – Shawnee
1853-1933 Volume X

MARRIAGE CARD.

Name _____ Marriage. Sex _____ Census or Allotment No. _____
Married _____ Tribe _____
Married to whom _____ How _____
If divorced, When _____ Census or Allotment No. _____
If divorced, How _____ Where _____

CHILDREN BORN OF THIS MARRIAGE.

Census or Allotment No.	Sex	Name	Born	Blood	Died
	M	James Kahdot	1876	3/4	Pott
	M	Frank Kahdot	July 1900	3/4	"
	M	Joeph[sic] "	Feb 28 1903	3/4	"
	~~F~~	~~Mary " ~~	~~Feb 27 1905~~	~~3/4~~	~~"~~
	F	Lizzie "	1907	3/4	"

address   Konawa

See Marriage Cards Nos. _____ and _____ for half-brothers and half-sisters of these children.

MARRIAGE CARD.

Name _____ Marriage. Sex _____ Census or Allotment No. _____
Married _____ Tribe _____
Married to whom _____ How _____
If divorced, When _____ Census or Allotment No. _____
If divorced, How _____ Where _____

CHILDREN BORN OF THIS MARRIAGE.

Census or Allotment No.	Sex	Name	Born	Blood	Died
	F	Mary Kahdot	Feb 28 1905	3/4	
	M	----- Stone (Husband)			

address

See Marriage Cards Nos. _____ and _____ for half-brothers and half-sisters of these children.

Sac & Fox – Shawnee
1853-1933 Volume X

MARRIAGE CARD.

Name .... Marriage. Sex .... Census or Allotment No. ....
Married .... Tribe Pott ....
Married to whom .... How ....
If divorced, When .... Census or Allotment No. ....
If divorced, How .... Where ....

CHILDREN BORN OF THIS MARRIAGE.

Census or Allotment No.	Sex	Name	Born	Blood / Died
	M	Posso Wano	1865	full
	F	Ellen Long "	Mar 16 1872	1/4 Wyandotte enrolled at Miami
	F	Kattie "	March 1900	3/4 Indian
	F	Zoa "	Apr 6 1911	3/4 "
	M	George "	Mar 27 1905	3/4 "

Address Konawa # 2

See Marriage Cards Nos. .... and .... for half-brothers and half-sisters of these children.

MARRIAGE CARD.

Name .... Marriage. Sex .... Census or Allotment No. ....
Married .... Tribe ....
Married to whom .... How ....
If divorced, When .... Census or Allotment No. ....
If divorced, How .... Where ....

CHILDREN BORN OF THIS MARRIAGE.

Census or Allotment No.	Sex	Name	Born	Blood / Died
	M	Willie Wano	May [?] 1896	1/4
	F	wife		white
	M	W^m Jr. "	Sept 12 1923	
	F	Donna G. "	[?] 7 1925	

address Konawa

See Marriage Cards Nos. .... and .... for half-brothers and half-sisters of these children.

Sac & Fox – Shawnee
1853-1933 Volume X

MARRIAGE CARD.

_____Marriage. Sex_____ Census or Allotment No._____
Name_____ Tribe_____
Married_____ How_____
Married to whom_____ Census or Allotment No._____
If divorced, When_____ Where_____
If divorced, How_____

CHILDREN BORN OF THIS MARRIAGE.

Census or Allotment No.	Sex	Name	Born	Blood (Died)
	M	Eugene Wano	May 3 1898	1/2 Pott
		wife		white
	F	Thelma G "	Mar 3 1927	1/4 Pott
	F	Lou Jewell "	Dec 1929	1/4 "
address	Seminole			

See Marriage Cards Nos._____ and _____ for half-brothers and half-sisters of these children.

MARRIAGE CARD.   *See Ethel Shopwatuck*

_____Marriage. Sex_____ Census or Allotment No._____
Name_____ Tribe____Pott_____
Married_____ How_____
Married to whom_____ Census or Allotment No._____
If divorced, When_____ Where_____
If divorced, How_____

CHILDREN BORN OF THIS MARRIAGE.

Census or Allotment No.	Sex	Name	Born	Blood (Died)
	M	John A. Bruno	July 5 1867	1/2 Pott
	F	Mary Vieux Bruno	1868	1/2 "
	M	John Jr. "	Apr 22 1905	1/2 "
address	Hominy			

See Marriage Cards Nos._____ and _____ for half-brothers and half-sisters of these children.

Sac & Fox – Shawnee
1853-1933 Volume X

MARRIAGE CARD.

................................Marriage. Sex .... Census or Allotment No. ....
Name .... Tribe ...... Pott ....
Married .... How ....
Married to whom .... Census or Allotment No. ....
If divorced, When .... Where ....
If divorced, How ....

CHILDREN BORN OF THIS MARRIAGE.

Census or Allotment No.	Sex	Name	Born	Died Blood
	M	Iva Tartar	1904	1/4 Pott
		wife		white
		2 or 3 children names mailed in later		
		address Ariz		

See Marriage Cards Nos. .... and .... for half-brothers and half-sisters of these children.

MARRIAGE CARD.

................................Marriage. Sex .... Census or Allotment No. ....
Name .... Tribe ....
Married & divorced but carries maiden How ....
Married to whom .... name Census or Allotment No. ....
If divorced, When .... Where ....
If divorced, How ....

CHILDREN BORN OF THIS MARRIAGE.

Census or Allotment No.	Sex	Name	Born	Died Blood
		Husband		white
		Verna Tartar		1/4
		one child name will be mailed in later		
		address Maud		

See Marriage Cards Nos. .... and .... for half-brothers and half-sisters of these children.

Sac & Fox – Shawnee
1853-1933 Volume X

MARRIAGE CARD.

Marriage. Sex _____ Census or Allotment No. _____
Name _____ Tribe __Pott__
Married _____ How _____
Married to whom _____ Census or Allotment No. _____
If divorced, When _____ Where _____
If divorced, How _____

CHILDREN BORN OF THIS MARRIAGE.

CENSUS OR ALLOTMENT NO.	SEX	NAME	BORN	DIED Blood
	M	Moses Bruno	1872	1/2 Pott
	F	Francis "	1881	Full
	M	Mike "	Dec 15 1906	3/4 "
	M	Robert "	Nov 15 1915	3/4 "
	M	Moses Jr. "	Sept 29 1918	3/4 "
	F	Beatrice B. "	July 30 1925	3/4 "
address		Konawa #2		

See Marriage Cards Nos. _____ and _____ for half-brothers and half-sisters of these children.

MARRIAGE CARD.

Marriage. Sex _____ Census or Allotment No. _____
Name _____ Tribe __Pott__
Married _____ How _____
Married to whom _____ Census or Allotment No. _____
If divorced, When _____ Where _____
If divorced, How _____

CHILDREN BORN OF THIS MARRIAGE.

CENSUS OR ALLOTMENT NO.	SEX	NAME	BORN	DIED Blood
		Josephine Bruno Tarter (Dead)		
	M	Lawrence Tarter	1902	1/4 Pott
		wife		white
		3 children names will be mailed in		
address		Asher		

See Marriage Cards Nos. _____ and _____ for half-brothers and half-sisters of these children.

Sac & Fox – Shawnee
1853-1933   Volume X

MARRIAGE CARD.

Name _____ Marriage. Sex _____ Census or Allotment No. _____
Married _____ Tribe ___ Pott _____
Married to whom _____ How _____
If divorced, When _____ Census or Allotment No. _____
If divorced, How _____ Where _____

CHILDREN BORN OF THIS MARRIAGE.

Census or Allotment No.	Sex	Name	Born	Died Blood
	M	Joseph Shoptweese		Full blood Pott Kan Indian
	F	Stella Wano Shoptweese	Jan 19 1900	3/4 Pott
	M	Frank T "	July 2 1919	7/8 "
	M	Melford J. "	June 6 1922	7/8 "
	F	Venice C. "	Aug 19 1924	7/8 "

address Konawa #[sic]

See Marriage Cards Nos. _____ and _____ for half-brothers and half-sisters of these children.

MARRIAGE CARD.

Name _____ Marriage. Sex _____ Census or Allotment No. _____
Married _____ Tribe ___ Pott _____
Married to whom _____ How _____
If divorced, When _____ Census or Allotment No. _____
If divorced, How _____ Where _____

CHILDREN BORN OF THIS MARRIAGE.

Census or Allotment No.	Sex	Name	Born	Died Blood
	M	Benjamin A. Wano	Nov 14 1904	1/2 Pott
	F	Ruth "	1908	1/8 Kan Pott
	M	Benjamin A "	Mar 25 1929	5/8 Pott

address Konawa #2

See Marriage Cards Nos. _____ and _____ for half-brothers and half-sisters of these children.

Sac & Fox – Shawnee
1853-1933   Volume X

MARRIAGE CARD.

Marriage. Sex_____ Census or Allotment No._____
Name_____ Tribe_____
Married_____ How_____
Married to whom_____ Census or Allotment No._____
If divorced, When_____ Where_____
If divorced, How_____

CHILDREN BORN OF THIS MARRIAGE.

CENSUS OR ALLOTMENT NO.	SEX	NAME	BORN	BLOOD / DIED
	M	Isaac P Wano	Mar 7 1899	3/4 Pott
	F	Lara A. "		Full blood Tokowa

address Konawa # 2

See Marriage Cards Nos. _____ and _____ for half-brothers and half-sisters of these children.

MARRIAGE CARD.

Marriage. Sex_____ Census or Allotment No._____
Name_____ Tribe_____
Married_____ How_____
Married to whom_____ Census or Allotment No._____
If divorced, When_____ Where_____
If divorced, How_____

CHILDREN BORN OF THIS MARRIAGE.

CENSUS OR ALLOTMENT NO.	SEX	NAME	BORN	Blood / DIED
	M	Husband		white
	F	Lila Kime McLaughlin	Jan 3 1909	1/16 Pott
	M	J. R. "	Oct 23 1928	1/16 "

address

See Marriage Cards Nos. _____ and _____ for half-brothers and half-sisters of these children.

Sac & Fox – Shawnee
1853-1933 Volume X

MARRIAGE CARD.

....Marriage. Sex.......... Census or Allotment No............................
Name... Tribe...
Married... How..
Married to whom................................. Census or Allotment No............................
If divorced, When............................... Where...
If divorced, How..

CHILDREN BORN OF THIS MARRIAGE.

Census or Allotment No.	Sex	Name	Born	Blood Died
	M	Husband		white
	F	Vera Kime McDonnell	July 26 1905	1/16 Pott

address Macomb #1

See Marriage Cards Nos. .... and .... for half-brothers and half-sisters of these children.

MARRIAGE CARD.

....Marriage. Sex.......... Census or Allotment No............................
Name... Tribe...
Married... How..
Married to whom................................. Census or Allotment No............................
If divorced, When............................... Where...
If divorced, How..

CHILDREN BORN OF THIS MARRIAGE.

Census or Allotment No.	Sex	Name	Born	Died blood
	M	Albert F Kime	1891	1/16 Pott
	F	wife		white
	M	Oran W. "	1918	1/16 Pott
	M	Edward "	1922	1/16 "
	F	Hazel "	1923	1/16 "
	F	Katherine "	1926	1/16 "

address Macomb #1

See Marriage Cards Nos. .... and .... for half-brothers and half-sisters of these children.

Sac & Fox – Shawnee
1853-1933 Volume X

MARRIAGE CARD.

```
                    Marriage. Sex_____  Census or Allotment No._____
Name_____ Tribe_____
Married_____ How_____
Married to whom_____ Census or Allotment No._____
If divorced, When_____ Where_____
If divorced, How_____
```

CHILDREN BORN OF THIS MARRIAGE.

Census or Allotment No.	Sex	Name	Born	blood Died
	M	Chas R. Melott	1893	1/4 Pott
	F	Ethel "		1/4 Cherokee
	F	Maxine "	Mar 6 1915	1/4 Ind.
	M	Chas Jr. "	Oct 17 1916	1/4 "
	F	Margret "	June 6 1919	1/4 "
	M	Royce "	July 19 1921	1/4 "
	M	J. C. "	Sept 5 1923	1/4 "
	F	Wanda "	Aug 20 1925	1/4 "
	F	Lenell "	Dec 27 1927	1/4 "
address Macomb				

See Marriage Cards Nos. _____ and _____ for half-brothers and half-sisters of these children.

MARRIAGE CARD.

```
                    Marriage. Sex_____  Census or Allotment No._____
Name_____ Tribe_____
Married_____ How_____
Married to whom_____ Census or Allotment No._____
If divorced, When_____ Where_____
If divorced, How_____
```

CHILDREN BORN OF THIS MARRIAGE.

Census or Allotment No.	Sex	Name	Born	blood Died
	M	Husband		white
	F	Mary Burnett Wesselhoht	1874	1/2
	F	Mary "	1917	1/4
address Macomb # 1				

See Marriage Cards Nos. _____ and _____ for half-brothers and half-sisters of these children.

Sac & Fox – Shawnee
1853-1933   Volume X

MARRIAGE CARD.

```
                            Marriage. Sex          Census or Allotment No.
Name                                               Tribe
Married                                            How
Married to whom                                    Census or Allotment No.
If divorced, When                                  Where
If divorced, How
```

CHILDREN BORN OF THIS MARRIAGE.

CENSUS OR ALLOTMENT NO.	SEX	NAME	BORN	DIED blood
	M	Wm Kime	Nov 11 1885	1/16 Pott
	F	wife		white
	F	Vora "	July 26 1905	1/32 Pott
	F	Lila "	Jan [?] 1909	1/32 "
	M	Walter "	Dec 26 1910	1/32 "
	M	Hershal[sic] "	Nov 5 1915	1/32 "

address Macomb # 1

See Marriage Cards Nos. _____ and _____ for half-brothers and half-sisters of these children.

MARRIAGE CARD.

```
                            Marriage. Sex          Census or Allotment No.
Name                                               Tribe
Married                                            How
Married to whom                                    Census or Allotment No.
If divorced, When                                  Where
If divorced, How
```

CHILDREN BORN OF THIS MARRIAGE.

CENSUS OR ALLOTMENT NO.	SEX	NAME	BORN	DIED Blood
	M	Chas Kime	June 19 1887	1/16
	F	wife		white
	F	Beatrice "	Oct 15 1909	1/32 Pott
	M	George V "	Sept 30 1911	1/32 "
	M	Fred "	Mar 6 1914	1/32 "
	M	Clyde "	Jan 3 1922	1/32 "
	M	C. L. "	May 9 1925	1/32 "
	M	J. C. "	1928	1/32 "

address Perry Okla # 8

See Marriage Cards Nos. _____ and _____ for half-brothers and half-sisters of these children.

Sac & Fox – Shawnee
1853-1933 Volume X

MARRIAGE CARD.

Marriage. Sex _____ Census or Allotment No. _____
Name _____ Tribe _____
Married _____ How _____
Married to whom _____ Census or Allotment No. _____
If divorced, When _____ Where _____
If divorced, How _____

CHILDREN BORN OF THIS MARRIAGE.

Census or Allotment No.	Sex	Name	Born	Died Blood
	M	Ben Kime	1897	1/16
	F	wife		white
	M	Elton "	1917	1/32 Pott
	M	Vance "	Jan 3 1921	1/32 "
address Davenport Okla				

See Marriage Cards Nos. _____ and _____ for half-brothers and half-sisters of these children.

MARRIAGE CARD.

Marriage. Sex _____ Census or Allotment No. _____
Name _____ Tribe _____
Married _____ How _____
Married to whom _____ Census or Allotment No. _____
If divorced, When _____ Where _____
If divorced, How _____

CHILDREN BORN OF THIS MARRIAGE.

Census or Allotment No.	Sex	Name	Born	Died Blood
	M	Henry Kime	June 1903	1/16
		wife		white
	F	Tinley "	Feb 28 1926	1/32
address Macomb				

See Marriage Cards Nos. _____ and _____ for half-brothers and half-sisters of these children.

Sac & Fox – Shawnee
1853-1933 Volume X

MARRIAGE CARD.

Name _____ Marriage. Sex _____ Census or Allotment No. _____
Married _____ Tribe ____ Pott _____
Married to whom _____ How _____
If divorced, When _____ Census or Allotment No. _____
If divorced, How _____ Where _____

CHILDREN BORN OF THIS MARRIAGE.

Census or Allotment No.	Sex	Name	Born	Blood / Died
	M	Husband		white
	F	Viola Kime Roselius	1898	1/16 Pott
	M	J. W. "	Dec 9 1919	1/32 "
	M	Jack O "	Aug 18 1921	1/32 "
	F	Halsa T "	Oct 6 1923	1/32 "
	F	Bobie J. "	Feb 9 1926	1/32 "

ADDRESS   Macomb

See Marriage Cards Nos. _____ and _____ for half-brothers and half-sisters of these children.

MARRIAGE CARD.

Name _____ Marriage. Sex _____ Census or Allotment No. _____
Married _____ Tribe _____
Married to whom _____ How _____
If divorced, When _____ Census or Allotment No. _____
If divorced, How _____ Where _____

CHILDREN BORN OF THIS MARRIAGE.

Census or Allotment No.	Sex	Name	Born	Blood / Died
		Joseph Burnett	Dec	1/2 Pott
		Katherine Burnett Papan	Aug 1900	1/4 Pott
		Husband		1/4 Kaw

ADDRESS   Arkansas City Kan

See Marriage Cards Nos. _____ and _____ for half-brothers and half-sisters of these children.

Sac & Fox – Shawnee
1853-1933 Volume X

MARRIAGE CARD.

```
_____ Marriage. Sex _____ Census or Allotment No. _____
Name_____ Tribe _____
Married_____ How _____
Married to whom_____ Census or Allotment No. _____
If divorced, When _____ Where _____
If divorced, How _____
```

CHILDREN BORN OF THIS MARRIAGE.

Census or Allotment No.	Sex	Name	Born	Blood / Died
	M	W S Martin		white
	F	Birdie Burnett Martin	Jan 6 1884	1/8 Pott
	M	W^m K "	Oct 31 1909	1/16 "
	F	Halsa W. "	Apr 4 1918	1/16 "

ADDRESS Macomb

See Marriage Cards Nos. _____ and _____ for half-brothers and half-sisters of these children.

MARRIAGE CARD.

```
_____ Marriage. Sex _____ Census or Allotment No. _____
Name_____ Tribe _____
Married_____ How _____
Married to whom_____ Census or Allotment No. _____
If divorced, When _____ Where _____
If divorced, How _____
```

CHILDREN BORN OF THIS MARRIAGE.

Census or Allotment No.	Sex	Name	Born	Blood / Died
	M	Benjaman[sic] Burnett	1894	1/4 Pott
		~~Single~~		

Address Ponca Okla

See Marriage Cards Nos. _____ and _____ for half-brothers and half-sisters of these children.

Sac & Fox – Shawnee
1853-1933 Volume X

MARRIAGE CARD.

Name _____ Marriage. Sex _____ Census or Allotment No. _____
Married _____ Tribe __Pott__
Married to whom _____ How _____
If divorced, When _____ Census or Allotment No. _____
If divorced, How _____ Where _____

CHILDREN BORN OF THIS MARRIAGE.

Census or Allotment No.	Sex	Name	Born	Blood	Died
	M	John B. Bruno	Mar 18 1902	3/4 Pott	
	F	Beatrice Casteel Bruno	Feb 23 1907	1/4 Sac and Fox enrolled Shawnee	

address Konawa # 2

See Marriage Cards Nos. _____ and _____ for half-brothers and half-sisters of these children.

MARRIAGE CARD.

Name _____ Marriage. Sex _____ Census or Allotment No. _____
Married _____ Tribe __Pott__
Married to whom _____ How _____
If divorced, When _____ Census or Allotment No. _____
If divorced, How _____ Where _____

CHILDREN BORN OF THIS MARRIAGE.

Census or Allotment No.	Sex	Name	Born	Blood	Died
	F	Mary Acton	1872	Full Pott	
	Mson	George Shawdah Babtiste [sic]	Sept 1[?] 1905	Full	"

address Sacred Heart

See Marriage Cards Nos. _____ and _____ for half-brothers and half-sisters of these children.

Sac & Fox – Shawnee
1853-1933   Volume X

MARRIAGE CARD.

_____ Marriage. Sex _____ Census or Allotment No. _____
Name _____ Tribe Pott _____
Married _____ How _____
Married to whom _____ Census or Allotment No. _____
If divorced, When _____ Where _____
If divorced, How _____

CHILDREN BORN OF THIS MARRIAGE.

Census or Allotment No.	Sex	Name	Born	Blood / Died
	M	Tom Conn		Kaw <u>Full</u>
	F	Zoa Acton Conn	1990	Full
	M	Lema Conn		1/2 Pott
	M	Roger "		1/2 Pott
	F	Ruth "		1/2 "
		Kaw City Okla #2		
address				

See Marriage Cards Nos. _____ and _____ for half-brothers and half-sisters of these children.

MARRIAGE CARD.

_____ Marriage. Sex _____ Census or Allotment No. _____
Name _____ Tribe _____
Married _____ How _____
Married to whom _____ Census or Allotment No. _____
If divorced, When _____ Where _____
If divorced, How _____

CHILDREN BORN OF THIS MARRIAGE.

Census or Allotment No.	Sex	Name	Born	Blood / Died
	M	Husband		white
	F	Justine Higbee Ward	June 1906	1/32 Pott
	M	Quana J "	Nov 1928	1/64 "
		Lexington #4		

See Marriage Cards Nos. _____ and _____ for half-brothers and half-sisters of these children.

Sac & Fox – Shawnee
1853-1933   Volume X

MARIAGE CARD.

Marriage.   Sex   Census or Allotment No.
Name   Tribe
Married   How
Married to whom   Census or Allotment No.
If divorced, When   Where
If divorced, How

CHILDREN BORN OF THIS MARRIAGE.

Census or Allotment No.	Sex	Name	Born	Blood	Died
	M	Chas Greemore	Sept 3 1857	1/16 Pott	
	F	wife		white	

address Lexington

See Marriage Cards Nos. _____ and _____ for half-brothers and half-sisters of these children.

MARRIAGE CARD.

Marriage.   Sex   Census or Allotment No.
Name   Tribe
Married   How
Married to whom   Census or Allotment No.
If divorced, When   Where
If divorced, How

CHILDREN BORN OF THIS MARRIAGE.

Census or Allotment No.	Sex	Name	Born	Blood	Died
	M	Husband		white	
	F	Anna Greemore Evans	1881	1/16 Pott	
	F	Elois[sic] "	1909	1/32 "	

address Lexington

See Marriage Cards Nos. _____ and _____ for half-brothers and half-sisters of these children.

Sac & Fox – Shawnee
1853-1933 Volume X

MARRIAGE CARD.

Marriage. Sex _____ Census or Allotment No. _____
Name _____ Tribe _____
Married _____ How _____
Married to whom _____ Census or Allotment No. _____
If divorced, When _____ Where _____
If divorced, How _____

CHILDREN BORN OF THIS MARRIAGE.

Census or Allotment No.	Sex	Name	Born	Died Blood
	M	Husband		white
	F	Mable Greemore Vawtar	1889	1/16 Pott

address Ardmore Okla

See Marriage Cards Nos. _____ and _____ for half-brothers and half-sisters of these children.

MARRIAGE CARD.

Marriage. Sex _____ Census or Allotment No. _____
Name _____ Tribe _____
Married _____ How _____
Married to whom _____ Census or Allotment No. _____
If divorced, When _____ Where _____
If divorced, How _____

CHILDREN BORN OF THIS MARRIAGE.

Census or Allotment No.	Sex	Name	Born	Died Blood
	M	Husband		White
	F	Minnie Greemore Mayfield	1891	1/16 Pott
	M	Ton W. "	1916	1/32 "
	M	Greemore "	1918	1/32 "

address Norman Okla.

See Marriage Cards Nos. _____ and _____ for half-brothers and half-sisters of these children.

Sac & Fox – Shawnee
1853-1933 Volume X

MARRIAGE CARD.

```
                            Marriage. Sex_____   Census or Allotment No._____
Name_____       Tribe_____
Married_____       How_____
Married to whom_____       Census or Allotment No._____
If divorced, When_____       Where_____
If divorced, How_____
```

CHILDREN BORN OF THIS MARRIAGE.

CENSUS OR ALLOTMENT NO.	SEX	NAME	BORN	Blood	DIED
	M	Husband	1897	white	
	F	Ruth Greemore Kemp	1914	1/16 Pott	
	M	John Jr. "	1917	1/32 "	
	M	Chas R. "	1915	1/32 "	
	M	Kenneth G. "		1/32 "	

address Norman

See Marriage Cards Nos. _____ and _____ for half-brothers and half-sisters of these children.

MARRIAGE CARD.

```
                            Marriage. Sex_____   Census or Allotment No._____
Name_____       Tribe_____
Married_____       How_____
Married to whom_____       Census or Allotment No._____
If divorced, When_____       Where_____
If divorced, How_____
```

CHILDREN BORN OF THIS MARRIAGE.

CENSUS OR ALLOTMENT NO.	SEX	NAME	BORN	Blood	DIED
	M	Ezekial A Peltier	Mar 16 1875	5/8 Pott	
		wife		white	
	M	Lonnie L "		5/16 Pott	
	F	Ruby P. "	July 16 1915	5/16 "	
	F	Opal L. "	Oct 12 1918	5/16 "	
	M	Paul J "	Dec 4 1921	5/16 "	
	F	Violet M "	Sept 24 1924	5/16 "	
	M	Richard E "	July 16 1915	5/16 "	

address Lexington

See Marriage Cards Nos. _____ and _____ for half-brothers and half-sisters of these children.

Sac & Fox – Shawnee
1853-1933 Volume X

MARRIAGE CARD.

Marriage. Sex_____ Census or Allotment No._____
Name_____ Tribe_____
Married_____ How_____
Married to whom_____ Census or Allotment No._____
If divorced, When_____ Where_____
If divorced, How_____

CHILDREN BORN OF THIS MARRIAGE.

CENSUS OR ALLOTMENT NO.	SEX	NAME	BORN	Blood	DIED
	M	Joseph Moutaw	1884	1/16 Pott	
	F	wife		white	
	M	Maris "	1920	1/32	
	M	James "	1922	1/32	
		------- -------		1/32	
	M	Freeman "	1926	1/32	

address Harjo Okla

See Marriage Cards Nos._____ and _____ for half-brothers and half-sisters of these children.

MARRIAGE CARD.

Marriage. Sex_____ Census or Allotment No._____
Name_____ Tribe_____
Married_____ How_____
Married to whom_____ Census or Allotment No._____
If divorced, When_____ Where_____
If divorced, How_____

CHILDREN BORN OF THIS MARRIAGE.

CENSUS OR ALLOTMENT NO.	SEX	NAME	BORN	Blood	DIED
	M	Wm F. Moutaw	1894	1/16 Pott	
	F	wife		white	
	M	Feeman[sic] "	1917	1/32 Pott	
	M	Thurman "	1919	1/32 "	

Mail   Oklahoma City # 4

See Marriage Cards Nos._____ and _____ for half-brothers and half-sisters of these children.

Sac & Fox – Shawnee
1853-1933   Volume X

MARRIAGE CARD.

Marriage. Sex_____ Census or Allotment No._____
Name_____ Tribe_____Pott_____
Married_____ How_____
Married to whom_____ Census or Allotment No.____
If divorced, When_____ Where_____
If divorced, How_____

CHILDREN BORN OF THIS MARRIAGE.

CENSUS OR ALLOTMENT NO.	SEX	NAME	BORN	DIED blood
	M	Grover C. Holloway		
	F	Edith O. "		
	M	Wm L. "		
	M	Chas C. "		
	M	George C. "		
	M	Marion A "		
address		Chism Okla		

See Marriage Cards Nos. _____ and _____ for half-brothers and half-sisters of these children.

****

Chism Okla
May – 6 – 29

Mr. Walter Gunn.

Dear Sir.

In regard to enrollment will say there should be six (6) of my family on roll it they are not there please inform me how to get them there. I will give you a list of the names

Grover C. Holloway
Edith Opal   "
William Leonard "
Charles Corleus[sic] "
George Carter   "
Marion Alexander "

Sac & Fox – Shawnee
1853-1933   Volume X

MARRIAGE CARD.

Marriage. Sex _____ Census or Allotment No. _____
Name _____ Tribe _____
Married _____ How _____
Married to whom _____ Census or Allotment No. _____
If divorced, When _____ Where _____
If divorced, How _____

CHILDREN BORN OF THIS MARRIAGE.

CENSUS OR ALLOTMENT NO.	SEX	NAME	BORN	blood / DIED
	M	B. W. Sanders	Jan 16 1901	1/14
	F	wife		white
	M	Carl Sanders	July 2 1923	1/28

address Purcell Okla #1

See Marriage Cards Nos. _____ and _____ for half-brothers and half-sisters of these children.

MARRIAGE CARD.

Marriage. Sex _____ Census or Allotment No. _____
Name _____ Tribe _____
Married _____ How _____
Married to whom _____ Census or Allotment No. _____
If divorced, When _____ Where _____
If divorced, How _____

CHILDREN BORN OF THIS MARRIAGE.

CENSUS OR ALLOTMENT NO.	SEX	NAME	BORN	blood / DIED
	M	Frank L Sanders	Sept 6 1898	1/64 Pott
	F	wife		white
	F	Hilda S. "	Oct 30 1919	1/128 Pott
	F	Louise "	July 13 1922	"
	M	Elton "	Dec 1 1929	"

address Trousdale #1

See Marriage Cards Nos. _____ and _____ for half-brothers and half-sisters of these children.

Sac & Fox – Shawnee
1853-1933 Volume X

MARRIAGE CARD.

Marriage. Sex _____ Census or Allotment No. _____
Name _____
Married _____ Tribe _____
Married to whom _____ How _____
If divorced, When _____ Census or Allotment No. _____
If divorced, How _____ Where _____

CHILDREN BORN OF THIS MARRIAGE.

Census or Allotment No.	Sex	Name	Born	Blood / Died
	M	Husband		white
	F	Rosetta Spear Sanders	Oct 7 1878	1/32 Pot
		~~Frank~~		
		~~Washington~~ "		
		~~Clara J~~ "		
		~~Ethel M~~ "		
Grand dau.		~~Mabel~~ "		
		Hazel "		
		Edna A "		
		Theamus[sic] L "		
		Irni[sic] R "		
		Mary L. "		
		Otis F "		
address		Trousdale # 1		

See Marriage Cards Nos. _____ and _____ for half-brothers and half-sisters of these children.

MARRIAGE CARD.

Marriage. Sex _____ Census or Allotment No. _____
Name _____
Married _____ Tribe Pott _____
Married to whom _____ How _____
If divorced, When _____ Census or Allotment No. _____
If divorced, How _____ Where _____

CHILDREN BORN OF THIS MARRIAGE.

Census or Allotment No.	Sex	Name	Born	Blood / Died
	F	May Ogee Holt	May 24 1896	Part Pott
		Olen		
		Laine "	Jan 22 1909	"
		Evilane Loraine "	Apr 6 1912	"
		J. D. "	Sept 16 1917	"
address		Maud		

See Marriage Cards Nos. _____ and _____ for half-brothers and half-sisters of these children.

Sac & Fox – Shawnee
1853-1933   Volume X

MARRIAGE CARD.

```
                         Marriage. Sex _____ Census or Allotment No. _____
Name _____ Tribe _____
Married _____ How _____
Married to whom _____ Census or Allotment No. _____
If divorced, When _____ Where _____
If divorced, How _____
```

CHILDREN BORN OF THIS MARRIAGE.

Census or Allotment No.	Sex	Name	Born	Blood / Died
	M	Louis H. Ogee		Part Pott
				white
	~~M~~	~~[Illegible]~~ "	~~May 12 1901~~	Part Pott
	M	Cecil "	Aug [?] 1904	"
	M	Roy "	Nov 2 1902	"
	F	Fern "	May 18 1907	"
	F	June "	Jan 6 1915	"
address		Maud		

See Marriage Cards Nos. _____ and _____ for half-brothers and half-sisters of these children.

MARRIAGE CARD.

```
                         Marriage. Sex _____ Census or Allotment No. _____
Name _____ Tribe ____Pott_____
Married _____ How _____
Married to whom _____ Census or Allotment No. _____
If divorced, When _____ Where _____
If divorced, How _____
```

CHILDREN BORN OF THIS MARRIAGE.

Census or Allotment No.	Sex	Name	Born	Blood / Died
		Lu[sic]		
	F	Delia Ogee Burton	1893	Part Pott
	F	Roberta "	1913	" "
	M	B. J. Burton	1922	" "

address

See Marriage Cards Nos. _____ and _____ for half-brothers and half-sisters of these children.

Sac & Fox – Shawnee
1853-1933 Volume X

MARRIAGE CARD.

....Marriage. Sex.............Census or Allotment No............................
Name...Tribe.........Pott...
Married..How..
Married to whom..Census or Allotment No............................
If divorced, When...Where..
If divorced, How..

CHILDREN BORN OF THIS MARRIAGE.

Census or Allotment No.	Sex	Name	Born	Blood / Died
	M	Robert A Ogee	1880	Part Pott
		Wife		White
	M	Delphin R. "	1907	Part Pott
	F	Gloria "	1909	"
	F	Genevie "	1915	"
	M	Gordon P. "	1918	"
address Maud Box 25				

See Marriage Cards Nos. .... and .... for half-brothers and half-sisters of these children.

MARRIAGE CARD.

....Marriage. Sex.............Census or Allotment No............................
Name...Tribe..
Married..How..
Married to whom..Census or Allotment No............................
If divorced, When...Where..
If divorced, How..

CHILDREN BORN OF THIS MARRIAGE.

Census or Allotment No.	Sex	Name	Born	Blood / Died
	M	Walter J. Moutaw	Mar 23 1904	1/16 Pott
		wife		white
		Lexington		

See Marriage Cards Nos. .... and .... for half-brothers and half-sisters of these children.

Sac & Fox – Shawnee
1853-1933   Volume X

MARRIAGE CARD.

Marriage. Sex _____ Census or Allotment No. _____
Name _____ Tribe _____
Married _____ How _____
Married to whom _____ Census or Allotment No. _____
If divorced, When _____ Where _____
If divorced, How _____

CHILDREN BORN OF THIS MARRIAGE.

Census or Allotment No.	Sex	Name	Born	Blood	Died
	M	W. A. Higbee	May 14 1882	1/32 Pott	
		wife		white	
	M	Howard "	Mar 6 1907	1/64 Pott	
	F	Doris "	Oct 27 1908	"	
	F	Willine[sic] "	Mar 30 1910	"	
	F	Aline "	Sept 8 1914	"	
	M	George "	Aug 7 1916	"	
	F	Alma H. "	Feb 1 1917	"	
	F	Carrie L. "	Sept 30 1919	"	
	F	Ollie E. "	Oct 11 1921		

Lexington

See Marriage Cards Nos. _____ and _____ for half-brothers and half-sisters of these children.

MARRIAGE CARD.

Marriage. Sex _____ Census or Allotment No. _____
Name _____ Tribe _____
Married _____ How _____
Married to whom _____ Census or Allotment No. _____
If divorced, When _____ Where _____
If divorced, How _____

CHILDREN BORN OF THIS MARRIAGE.

Census or Allotment No.	Sex	Name	Born	Blood	Died
	M	Husband		white	
	F	Grace Higbee Morrell	Sept 17 1905	1/64 Pott	
	F	Maurice[sic] "		1/128 "	

Lexington

See Marriage Cards Nos. _____ and _____ for half-brothers and half-sisters of these children.

Sac & Fox – Shawnee
1853-1933 Volume X

MARRIAGE CARD.

```
_____Marriage. Sex_____ Census or Allotment No._____
Name_____ Tribe_____
Married_____ How_____
Married to whom_____ Census or Allotment No._____
If divorced, When_____ Where_____
If divorced, How_____
```

CHILDREN BORN OF THIS MARRIAGE.

Census or Allotment No.	Sex	Name	Born	Blood / Died
		Husband		white
	F	Anna M Higbee Marsee	Aug 31 1912	1/64 Pott
		Lexington		

See Marriage Cards Nos. _____ and _____ for half-brothers and half-sisters of these children.

MARRIAGE CARD.

```
_____Marriage. Sex_____ Census or Allotment No._____
Name_____ Tribe_____
Married_____ How_____
Married to whom_____ Census or Allotment No._____
If divorced, When_____ Where_____
If divorced, How_____
```

CHILDREN BORN OF THIS MARRIAGE.

Census or Allotment No.	Sex	Name	Born	Blood / Died
	M	J.B. Higbee Sr.	1856	1/16
		wife		white
		Lexington		

See Marriage Cards Nos. _____ and _____ for half-brothers and half-sisters of these children.

Sac & Fox – Shawnee
1853-1933 Volume X

MARRIAGE CARD.

```
_____Marriage. Sex_____ Census or Allotment No._____
Name_____ Tribe_____
Married_____ How_____
Married to whom_____ Census or Allotment No._____
If divorced, When_____ Where_____
If divorced, How_____
```

CHILDREN BORN OF THIS MARRIAGE.

CENSUS OR ALLOTMENT NO.	SEX	NAME	BORN	Blood	DIED
		Husband		white	
	F	Clara Higbee Baxter	1893	1/32 Pott	
	M	Delane "	Nov 13 1913	1/64 "	
	M	Claude Jr. "	Aug 15 1915	1/64 "	
		Lexington			

See Marriage Cards Nos. _____ and _____ for half-brothers and half-sisters of these children.

****

MARRIAGE CARD.

```
_____Marriage. Sex_____ Census or Allotment No._____
Name_____ Tribe_____
Married_____ How_____
Married to whom_____ Census or Allotment No._____
If divorced, When_____ Where_____
If divorced, How_____
```

CHILDREN BORN OF THIS MARRIAGE.

CENSUS OR ALLOTMENT NO.	SEX	NAME	BORN	Blood	DIED
		Husband		white	
	F	Clara Higbee Baxter	1893	1/32 Pott	
	M	Delane "	Nov 13 1913	1/64 "	
	M	Claude Jr. "	Aug 15 1915	1/64 "	
		Lexington			

See Marriage Cards Nos. _____ and _____ for half-brothers and half-sisters of these children.

Sac & Fox – Shawnee
1853-1933 Volume X

MARRIAGE CARD.

Name _____ Marriage. Sex _____ Census or Allotment No. _____
Married _____ Tribe _____
Married to whom _____ How _____
If divorced, When _____ Census or Allotment No. _____
If divorced, How _____ Where _____

CHILDREN BORN OF THIS MARRIAGE.

Census or Allotment No.	Sex	Name	Born	Blood	Died
	M	A. G. Higbee	Jan 31 1887	1/32 Pott	
	F	wife		white	
	M	Vere "	May 23 1907	1/64 Pott	
	F	Idell "	Aug 9 1909	1/64 "	
	F	Dollie "	Jan 26 1911	"	
	M	L. B. "	Dec 13 1912	"	
	F	Dane V "	Nov 28 1916	"	
	M	Arthur H "	July 13 1920	"	
	F	Alta P. "	Feb 22 1924	"	
	M	Lawerence[sic] "	July 11 1928	"	
		Lexington			

See Marriage Cards Nos. _____ and _____ for half-brothers and half-sisters of these children.

MARRIAGE CARD.

Name _____ Marriage. Sex _____ Census or Allotment No. _____
Married _____ Tribe _____
Married to whom _____ How _____
If divorced, When _____ Census or Allotment No. _____
If divorced, How _____ Where _____

CHILDREN BORN OF THIS MARRIAGE.

Census or Allotment No.	Sex	Name	Born	Blood	Died
	M	L.W. Higbee	(Dead)	1/32	
	F	wife		white	
	M	Raymond "	Aug 11 1909	1/64 Pott	
	M	Loyd "	May 1912	"	
	F	Louise "	Apr 1914		
	M	Lewis "	Nov 1916		
	F	Jewell "	1917		
	M	Swain "	1919		
	F	Delma M "	1921		
	M	Noland "	1923		

Sac & Fox – Shawnee
1853-1933 Volume X

	M	Walter	"		Jan 8 1928	
		Lexington # 4				

See Marriage Cards Nos. _____ and _____ for half-brothers and half-sisters of these children.

MARRIAGE CARD.

_____ Marriage. Sex _____ Census or Allotment No. _____
Name _____ Tribe _____
Married _____ How _____
Married to whom _____ Census or Allotment No. _____
If divorced, When _____ Where _____
If divorced, How _____

CHILDREN BORN OF THIS MARRIAGE.

CENSUS OR ALLOTMENT NO.	SEX	NAME	BORN	DIED Blood
	F	Clara Sanders McDonald	Apr 16 1903	1/64 Pott
	M	Husband		white
	F	Jaunatia May "	Jan 1 1927	1/128 Pott
address		Trousdale # 1		

See Marriage Cards Nos. _____ and _____ for half-brothers and half-sisters of these children.

MARRIAGE CARD.

_____ Marriage. Sex _____ Census or Allotment No. _____
Name _____ Tribe _____
Married _____ How _____
Married to whom _____ Census or Allotment No. _____
If divorced, When _____ Where _____
If divorced, How _____

CHILDREN BORN OF THIS MARRIAGE.

CENSUS OR ALLOTMENT NO.	SEX	NAME	BORN	DIED blood
	M	Husband		white
	F	Ethel Sanders McDonald	Jan 29 1906	1/64
address		Trousdale # 1		

See Marriage Cards Nos. _____ and _____ for half-brothers and half-sisters of these children.

Sac & Fox – Shawnee
1853-1933 Volume X

MARRIAGE CARD.

Name _____ Marriage. Sex _____ Census or Allotment No. _____
Married _____ Tribe _____
Married to whom _____ How _____
If divorced, When _____ Census or Allotment No. _____
If divorced, How _____ Where _____

CHILDREN BORN OF THIS MARRIAGE.

Census or Allotment No.	Sex	Name	Born	Blood / Died
	M	Husband		white
	F	Mabel Sanders Snow	Jan 31 1909	1/164 Pott
	address	Trousdale #1		

See Marriage Cards Nos. _____ and _____ for half-brothers and half-sisters of these children.

MARRIAGE CARD.

Name _____ Marriage. Sex _____ Census or Allotment No. _____
Married _____ Tribe _____
Married to whom _____ How _____
If divorced, When _____ Census or Allotment No. _____
If divorced, How _____ Where _____

CHILDREN BORN OF THIS MARRIAGE.

Census or Allotment No.	Sex	Name	Born	blood / Died
	M	Husband		white
	F	Christine Sanders Brasher		1/64 Pott
	address	Trousdale #1		

See Marriage Cards Nos. _____ and _____ for half-brothers and half-sisters of these children.

Sac & Fox – Shawnee
1853-1933   Volume X

MARRIAGE CARD.

_____Marriage. Sex_____ Census or Allotment No._____
Name_____ Tribe_____
Married_____ How_____
Married to whom_____ Census or Allotment No._____
If divorced, When_____ Where_____
If divorced, How_____

CHILDREN BORN OF THIS MARRIAGE.

Census or Allotment No.	Sex	Name	Born	blood	Died
	M	Husband		white	
	F	Mary Trombla Armstrong	1853	1/16 Pott	
		Long Beach Cal.			
		5642 Daisy Ave			
address					

See Marriage Cards Nos. _____ and _____ for half-brothers and half-sisters of these children.

MARRIAGE CARD.

_____Marriage. Sex_____ Census or Allotment No._____
Name_____ Tribe_____
Married_____ How_____
Married to whom_____ Census or Allotment No._____
If divorced, When_____ Where_____
If divorced, How_____

CHILDREN BORN OF THIS MARRIAGE.

Census or Allotment No.	Sex	Name	Born	blood	Died
	M	Ed L. Spear	June 17 1876	1/32 Pott	
	F	wife		white	
	F	Mary Spear	Jan 1918	1/64 Pott	
	M	Theodore "	1920	"	
	M	Jack "	1922	"	
	F	Shirley M. "	1926	"	
		Trousdale #1			
adrsess[sic]					

See Marriage Cards Nos. _____ and _____ for half-brothers and half-sisters of these children.

Sac & Fox – Shawnee
1853-1933   Volume X

MARRIAGE CARD.

....Marriage. Sex........ Census or Allotment No. ....
Name... Tribe ....
Married.. How ....
Married to whom.. Census or Allotment No. ....
If divorced, When... Where ....
If divorced, How ....

CHILDREN BORN OF THIS MARRIAGE.

Census or Allotment No.	Sex	Name	Born	blood / DIED
	M	Roy Spear		June 29 1888	1/32 Pott
		wife		white

address   Long Beach Cal.
          5642 Daisy Ave.

See Marriage Cards Nos. .... and .... for half-brothers and half-sisters of these children.

MARRIAGE CARD.

....Marriage. Sex........ Census or Allotment No. ....
Name... Tribe ....
Married.. How ....
Married to whom.. Census or Allotment No. ....
If divorced, When... Where ....
If divorced, How ....

CHILDREN BORN OF THIS MARRIAGE.

Census or Allotment No.	Sex	Name	Born	Blood / DIED
	M	Rollay[sic] Spear		June 29 1888	
	F	wife (Dead)		white

address   Long Beach Cal.
          5642 Daisy Ave.

See Marriage Cards Nos. .... and .... for half-brothers and half-sisters of these children.

Sac & Fox – Shawnee
1853-1933 Volume X

MARRIAGE CARD.

Name _____ Marriage. Sex _____ Census or Allotment No. _____
Married _____ Tribe __Pott_____
Married to whom _____ How _____
If divorced, When _____ Census or Allotment No. _____
If divorced, How _____ Where _____

CHILDREN BORN OF THIS MARRIAGE.

Census or Allotment No.	Sex	Name	Born	Blood Died
	M	Chas Vieux	1860	1/2 Pott
	F	Julia Bruno Vieux	Jan 4 1870	1/2 Pott

ADDRESS Konawa # 2

See Marriage Cards Nos. _____ and _____ for half-brothers and half-sisters of these children.

MARRIAGE CARD.

Name _____ Marriage. Sex _____ Census or Allotment No. _____
Married _____ Tribe __Pott_____
Married to whom _____ How _____
If divorced, When _____ Census or Allotment No. _____
If divorced, How _____ Where _____

CHILDREN BORN OF THIS MARRIAGE.

Census or Allotment No.	Sex	Name	Born	Blood Died
	M	Olliver K Weld	1888	1/16 Pott
		wife (white)		
	M	Olliver K. Jr. "	1923	1/32 "
	F	Doris "	1925	1/32 "
	F	Clairsa "	1927	1/32 "

address Pauls Valley Okla

See Marriage Cards Nos. _____ and _____ for half-brothers and half-sisters of these children.

Sac & Fox – Shawnee
1853-1933 Volume X

MARRIAGE CARD.

Name_____ Marriage. Sex _____ Census or Allotment No._____
Married_____ Tribe_____
Married to whom_____ How_____
If divorced, When_____ Census or Allotment No._____
If divorced, How_____ Where_____

CHILDREN BORN OF THIS MARRIAGE.

Census or Allotment No.	Sex	Name	Born	Blood	Died
		Roy E Darling	Sept 12 1903	1/32	
		wife		White	

address Norman #6

See Marriage Cards Nos. _____ and _____ for half-brothers and half-sisters of these children.

MARRIAGE CARD.

Name_____ Marriage. Sex _____ Census or Allotment No._____
Married_____ Tribe_____
Married to whom_____ How_____
If divorced, When_____ Census or Allotment No._____
If divorced, How_____ Where_____

CHILDREN BORN OF THIS MARRIAGE.

Census or Allotment No.	Sex	Name	Born	Blood	Died
	F	Myrel Darling Murphe	Apr 25 1907		
	M	Husband		white	

address Shawnee East Main

See Marriage Cards Nos. _____ and _____ for half-brothers and half-sisters of these children.

Sac & Fox – Shawnee
1853-1933   Volume X

MARRIAGE CARD.

```
                        Marriage. Sex _____  Census or Allotment No. _____
Name _____  Tribe _____
Married _____  How _____
Married to whom _____  Census or Allotment No. _____
If divorced, When _____  Where _____
If divorced, How _____
```

CHILDREN BORN OF THIS MARRIAGE.

CENSUS OR ALLOTMENT NO.	SEX	NAME	BORN	Blood	DIED
		Husband		White	
	F	Vergie Darling Reed	Apr 1 1912	1/32 Pott	

address Norman #6

See Marriage Cards Nos. _____ and _____ for half-brothers and half-sisters of these children.

MARRIAGE CARD.

```
                        Marriage. Sex _____  Census or Allotment No. _____
Name _____  Tribe _____
Married _____  How _____
Married to whom _____  Census or Allotment No. _____
If divorced, When _____  Where _____
If divorced, How _____
```

CHILDREN BORN OF THIS MARRIAGE.

CENSUS OR ALLOTMENT NO.	SEX	NAME	BORN	Blood	DIED
	M	Husband		White	
	F	Rosalea Darling Moore	1869	1/16	
	M	Ed	"		
	F	Edith	"		
	F	Nellie	"		
	F	Ruth	"		
	F	Amy	"		
	M	George	"		
	F	Vergie	"		

address Norman

See Marriage Cards Nos. _____ and _____ for half-brothers and half-sisters of these children.

Sac & Fox – Shawnee
1853-1933   Volume X

MARRIAGE CARD.

Name .... Marriage. Sex .... Census or Allotment No. ....
Married .... Tribe ....
Married to whom .... How ....
If divorced, When .... Census or Allotment No. ....
If divorced, How .... Where ....

CHILDREN BORN OF THIS MARRIAGE.

Census or Allotment No.	Sex	Name	Born	Blood	Died
	M	Husband		White	
	F	Carrie Darling Striegel	1874	1/16 Pott	
	M	Evert "		1/32 "	
	F	Myrtle "		"	
	F	Bertha "		"	
	M	Webster "		"	
	F	Pansy "		"	
	M	Ernest "		"	

address Bethany Okla

See Marriage Cards Nos. _____ and _____ for half-brothers and half-sisters of these children.

MARRIAGE CARD.

Name .... Marriage. Sex .... Census or Allotment No. ....
Married .... Tribe ....
Married to whom .... How ....
If divorced, When .... Census or Allotment No. ....
If divorced, How .... Where ....

CHILDREN BORN OF THIS MARRIAGE.

Census or Allotment No.	Sex	Name	Born	Blood	Died
	M	Francis E. Darling	Mar 21 1872	1/16 Pott	
		wife		white	
	F	Zell "	Sept 2 1905	1/32 Pott	
	F	Juantia[sic] "	Jan 30 1909	"	
	F	Leota "	Oct 9 1914	"	
	F	Anita "	July 27 1916	"	
	M	Kenneth "	Mar 27 1921	"	

address Norman # 6

See Marriage Cards Nos. _____ and _____ for half-brothers and half-sisters of these children.

Sac & Fox – Shawnee
1853-1933   Volume X

MARRIAGE CARD.

```
----------------------Marriage. Sex _____  Census or Allotment No. _____
Name_____  Tribe_____
Married_____  How_____
Married to whom_____  Census or Allotment No. _____
If divorced, When_____  Where_____
If divorced, How_____
```

CHILDREN BORN OF THIS MARRIAGE.

Census or Allotment No.	Sex	Name	Born	Died Blood
	M	Vergil Goodin	1913	1/8 Pott
		Sam "	1916	1/8 "
		Edith "	1918	1/8 "
		J. R. "	1921	1/8 "
		Father John W. Goodin Dead		
		Virg[sic] Goodin is Guardian		
address	Norman #6			

See Marriage Cards Nos. _____ and _____ for half-brothers and half-sisters of these children.

MARRIAGE CARD.

```
----------------------Marriage. Sex _____  Census or Allotment No. _____
Name_____  Tribe_____
Married_____  How_____
Married to whom_____  Census or Allotment No. _____
If divorced, When_____  Where_____
If divorced, How_____
```

CHILDREN BORN OF THIS MARRIAGE.

Census or Allotment No.	Sex	Name	Born	Died BLOOD
	M	John Boubonnais[sic] Dead		
	F	Leona Boubonnais	Sept 5 1872	[illegible] white
	M	Loyed "	Mar 10 1913	1/32 Pott

ADDRESS Tecumseh

See Marriage Cards Nos. _____ and _____ for half-brothers and half-sisters of these children.

Sac & Fox – Shawnee
1853-1933 Volume X

MARRIAGE CARD.

Name .... Marriage. Sex .... Census or Allotment No. ....
Married .... Tribe ....
Married to whom .... How ....
If divorced, When .... Census or Allotment No. ....
If divorced, How .... Where ....

CHILDREN BORN OF THIS MARRIAGE.

Census or Allotment No.	Sex	Name	Born	Blood	Died
	M	J. J. Bourbonnais	Aug 19 1906	1/32 Pott	
	F	wife		white	

ADDRESS Tecumseh

See Marriage Cards Nos. .... and .... for half-brothers and half-sisters of these children.

MARRIAGE CARD.

Name .... Marriage. Sex .... Census or Allotment No. ....
Married .... Tribe ....
Married to whom .... How ....
If divorced, When .... Census or Allotment No. ....
If divorced, How .... Where ....

CHILDREN BORN OF THIS MARRIAGE.

Census or Allotment No.	Sex	Name	Born	Blood	Died
	M	Husband *Dead*		1/4 Chippewa 3/4 white	
	F	Aurleia Bourbonnais Thompson	June 22 1902	1/32 Pott	
	F	Lucille H.	Jan 18 1923	1/64 "	
	F	Irene R.	Jan 22 1926	"	
	F	Dorthy N.	Aug 19 1927	"	

ADDRESS Tecumseh

See Marriage Cards Nos. .... and .... for half-brothers and half-sisters of these children.

Sac & Fox – Shawnee
1853-1933 Volume X

MARRIAGE CARD.

Name_____ Marriage. Sex_____ Census or Allotment No._____
Married_____ Tribe_____
Married to whom_____ How_____
If divorced, When_____ Census or Allotment No._____
If divorced, How_____ Where_____

CHILDREN BORN OF THIS MARRIAGE.

CENSUS OR ALLOTMENT NO.	SEX	NAME	BORN	BLOOD / DIED
	M	Husband		white
	F	Ollie Bourbonnais Smith		1/32 Pott
	F	Jaunatia Glenn	1914	1/64 "
	M	Peter "	1916	"
		by former husband		

ADDRESS Tecumseh

See Marriage Cards Nos. _____ and _____ for half-brothers and half-sisters of these children.

MARRIAGE CARD.

Name_____ Marriage. Sex_____ Census or Allotment No._____
Married_____ Tribe_____
Married to whom_____ How_____
If divorced, When_____ Census or Allotment No._____
If divorced, How_____ Where_____

CHILDREN BORN OF THIS MARRIAGE.

CENSUS OR ALLOTMENT NO.	SEX	NAME	BORN	BLOOD / DIED
	M	Arthur Bourbonnais	1892	1/32 Pott
		wife		white
	F	Dortha "	Dec 17 1916	1/64 Pott

ADDRESS Tecumseh

See Marriage Cards Nos. _____ and _____ for half-brothers and half-sisters of these children.

Sac & Fox – Shawnee
1853-1933 Volume X

MARRIAGE CARD.

_____ Marriage. Sex _____ Census or Allotment No. _____
Name _____ Tribe _____
Married _____ How _____
Married to whom _____ Census or Allotment No. _____
If divorced, When _____ Where _____
If divorced, How _____

CHILDREN BORN OF THIS MARRIAGE.

Census or Allotment No.	Sex	Name	Born	Blood/Died
		Ozetta Bourbonnais Byllesby	1894	1/32 Pott

608 Ashland Nat'l Bldg
Ashland Ky

~~ADDRESS~~
See Marriage Cards Nos. _____ and _____ for half-brothers and half-sisters of these children.

MARRIAGE CARD.

_____ Marriage. Sex _____ Census or Allotment No. _____
Name _____ Tribe _____
Married _____ How _____
Married to whom _____ Census or Allotment No. _____
If divorced, When _____ Where _____
If divorced, How _____

CHILDREN BORN OF THIS MARRIAGE.

Census or Allotment No.	Sex	Name	Born	Died/Blood
	F	Thelma O. Thomson	Nov 6 1919	1/64 Pott
	M	Lenard M. "	Jan 23 1923	"
	F	Mildred "	June 1925	"

ADDRESS
See Marriage Cards Nos. _____ and _____ for half-brothers and half-sisters of these children.

Sac & Fox – Shawnee
1853-1933 Volume X

MARRIAGE CARD.

Name _____ Marriage. Sex _____ Census or Allotment No. _____
Married _____ Tribe _____
Married to whom _____ How _____
If divorced, When _____ Census or Allotment No. _____
If divorced, How _____ Where _____

CHILDREN BORN OF THIS MARRIAGE.

Census or Allotment No.	Sex	Name	Born	Blood/Died
		Joseph F Guyon	June 4 1916	1/64 Pott
		Geraldine "	Dec 1918	"

ADDRESS
See Marriage Cards Nos. _____ and _____ for half-brothers and half-sisters of these children.

MARRIAGE CARD.

Name _____ Marriage. Sex _____ Census or Allotment No. _____
Married _____ Tribe _____
Married to whom _____ How _____
If divorced, When _____ Census or Allotment No. _____
If divorced, How _____ Where _____

CHILDREN BORN OF THIS MARRIAGE.

Census or Allotment No.	Sex	Name	Born	Blood/Died
		Ben Bourbonnais	Feb 2 1887	1/16 Pott

ADDRESS Tecumseh
See Marriage Cards Nos. _____ and _____ for half-brothers and half-sisters of these children.

Sac & Fox – Shawnee
1853-1933 Volume X

MARRIAGE CARD.

Name _____ Marriage. Sex _____ Census or Allotment No. _____
Married _____ Tribe _____
Married to whom _____ How _____
If divorced, When _____ Census or Allotment No. _____
If divorced, How _____ Where _____

CHILDREN BORN OF THIS MARRIAGE.

Census or Allotment No.	Sex	Name	Born	Blood	Died
	M	Anthony Bourbonnais	1873	1/16 Pott	
	F	Kitty Peltier "	1874	1/2 "	
	M	Jethro "	1899	"	
	F	Edna "	1900	"	
	F	Lorine "	1903	"	
	M	Herald "	1908	"	

ADDRESS 501 1/2 So Robinson Oklahoma City

See Marriage Cards Nos. _____ and _____ for half-brothers and half-sisters of these children.

Index

[ILLEGIBLE]
J H 97
Joel 54
John 127
Mrs Steve 54
[ILLEGIBLE] CHE PEASE 47
[ILLEGIBLE] COM E PIT 47
[ILLEGIBLE] LDE 48
ACTON
   Louis 200
   Mary 276
AH AS KE 8
AH PUH U PUH AH KAH 4
AH QUAW ME 9
AH SAH SOM 13
AH SAP E QUAH 10
AH SOM E SEE 13
AHENENNEY, Mr M C 141
AH-NAH-ME 8
AH-NO-SUH-ASKE 3
AH-PUT-AH-PE 8
AH-QUE-SO-TAH 6
AH-SAH-E-QUAH 8
ALFORD, Thompson 54
AMBLER
   Dol 53
   Joe 53
AN NAH SHE NASA THAH 5
AN NO COQ IT 10
ANDREWS, Miss 38
ANGLE, Lucy Higbee 207
APPLETREE
   Henry 63
   Marie 63
   Mr J 28
ARMSTRONG, Mary Trombla 293
ATEH WEH NAH SO 3
ATKINS
   Baxter 150
   Harvey 150
   Josephine 150
   William, Jr 150
BABTISTE, George Shawdah 276
BAER, Adolph 116
BAIER, Adolf 116
BAKER, Martha 57
BANISTER, Fannie 46
BAP-TISTE 6

BARKER, Ann 122
BARNEY, Isabel 155
BA-SHE-QUAH 3
BAXTER
   Clara Higbee 289
   Claude, Jr 289
   Delane 289
   Dr G S 82,83
BAYLIS
   Birdie 223
   Cyrus W 223
   Lavoy 224
   McFall R 223,224
   Naomi Strikler 224
   Ruth M 223
   Thomas A 223
   Wm C 223
BEAR, Jack 17,31
BEARSE, C E 149
BENSON, Thomas 86
BERTHA 31
BIGEAR, Theresa 121
BIGRAT, Theresa 121
BIGWALKER
   Margaret 28
   Sarah 64
BLACK
   Amos 49,53
   Mary 53
BLACK SOLDIER 4
BLUE COAT, Stella 47
BOUBONNAIS
   John 299
   Leona 299
   Loyed 299
BOURBONNAIS
   Anthony 304
   Arthur 301
   Ben 303
   Dortha 301
   Edna 304
   Herald 304
   J J 300
   Jethro 304
   Kitty Peltier 304
   Lorine 304
BOYD
   Joe A 144

Index

Rosie 144
BRASHER, Christine Sanders 292
BRENNAN, Martin 25
BROOKOVER
   Clinton S 201
   Fama Cummings 201
   Hazel 201
BROOKS, Belvidere 58
BROWN
   [Illegible]Hite 47
   Bobie 232
   Elcie F 132
   G T 45,132
   Gertrude Givens 29
   H C 145,146
   John 121
   Julia 45,128,132
   Mary 151
   William Theodore 128
BRUNO
   August 245
   Beatrice B 267
   Beatrice Casteel 276
   Elex 245
   Ellen Venux 245
   Francis 267
   Isaac 236
   Jacob 245
   Joe O 245
   John A 265
   John B 276
   John, Jr 265
   Joseph 236
   Joseph C 245
   Julia 245
   Louis 85,245
   Mary B 219
   Mary Vieux 265
   May Naberry 241
   Mike 267
   Moses 267
   Moses, Jr 267
   Robert 267
   Sam W 236
   Thresa Bennett 236
   Willie 241
BUCHANAN
   Edna Castleberry 195

Peter 195
BUNTIN
   J A 52,55,56,149,154
   J A, Supt 53
   John A 114,154
   Mr 54,58
   Mr J A 54,115
   Supt J A 51
BURGESS
   Mark 150
   Ralph Frank 150
   Roy 150
   William 150
BURGUSS, Maggie 31
BURKE, Chas H 168
BURNETT
   Benjamin 275
   Caroline 242
   Elizabeth Bruno 242
   John 242
   Joseph 274
   Mulvine 242
   Rosetta 242
BURTON
   B J 285
   Delia Ogee 285
   Roberta 285
BUTLER
   Anna 129
   Benjamin 64,161,162
   Edith 64,161,162
   Edward 65,161,162
   Fred 65,161,162
   George 64,161,162
   Ida 65,161,162
BYLLESBY, Ozetta Bourbonnais 302
CADUE
   Hoke Smith 82,83
   John 82
CAH TO CAH 8
CAH TUE E NAC 15
CAH-TAH-QUAH 8
CAMPBELL, W J 138
CAPPER
   Alfred Rodell 140
   John T 140
   Mrs John T 140
CARPENTER & FOUSHEE . 105,110

Index

CARSTEN
  Billie 252
  Herman 252
  Lilian Nadeau C 252
  Vinita 252
CARTER
  Frank 28
  Mrs Milton 84
CASTEEL
  Edith Clarence 145,146
  Elizabeth McKinney 145,146
  James Clarence 145,146
  Lizzie 145
CASTLEBERRY
  Beatrice 195
  Claud 195,198
  Edna 198
  James 198
  John 197,198
  Josephine Haas 198
  Viola 198
  Webster 197
CAT TAH WHAH 8
CAVENDER
  Mary 189
  Mary Curley 186
CAW CAH 9
CAW-AH-KE 6
CHA PO CHE PEASE 47
CHAH CO SAH 14
CHAH-KA-AH-QUAH 3
CHANDLER, Claud 159
CHARLES, J B 21
CHARLEY, Rose 79
CHEATWOOD
  Dora Willmett 260
  Dora Willmette 204
  Ernest N 260
  Grace L 260
  James W 206
  Jaunatia 206
  Joseph A 260
  Louis B 260
  Mable L 260
  Maggie E Pratt 206
  Pearl L 260
  Robert 206
  Roy T 260

CHISHOLM
  Charles 42
  Chas 44
  Wm 42,44
CHO WAH 8
CLARY
  Bell Cummings 200
  Jack 200
  Lawrence 200
CLAY, Julia 129
CLOWRY, Robert C 42
CO PAH CO 13
CO TO KE MAC 8
COCHRAM, Ella 42
COCHRAN, Mrs Ella 44
CODER
  Effie M 161
  Effie M Dike 160
  Frederick Clyde 160
  Hazel Francis 160
  Muriel Lafern 160
  Ralph Albert 160,161
  Ralph Junior 161
  Wm Jefferson 160
CODY
  Andrew 242
  Evelyn Bruno 242
  Zelda M 242
COFFEE POT
  Lizzie 55
  Mary 55
COFFEY, L P 32
COLENBURG, Mr 28,95
COLLENBURG, Mr W C 139
COLLINS 224
  Arza B 57,61,63,65,75,76,
  156,162,166
  E F 131
  E F, MD 132
COLNBURG, W C 33
CONGER
  Andrew 75,76
  Julia 75,76
CONKLIN, E L 19,20,21,22
CONN
  Lema 277
  Roger 277
  Ruth 277

Tom 277
   Zoa Acton 277
COPE
   Isabell Davis 194
   Victor 194
COPPER, Alfred Rodell 141
COX, Viola Castleberry 197
COYLE, J E, MD 128
CRAIN, Lenard 135
CRANE
   Angeline LeClaire 247
   Edward 72
   John A 247
CU-CO-AH 3
CUMMINGS
   Andy J 203
   Chas S 202
   Ellen M 201
   Normalee 202
   Theresa 203
CUP A HE CO 4
CUPPAHE
   Lee 130
   Louis 130
CURLEY
   Albert 233
   Andrew 189,234
   Anna 231
   Antoine 234
   Baptiste 186
   Bernard 231
   Charley 231
   Elex 233
   Florence 189
   Franvid 233
   Hattie 233
   Ida May 233
   Jeraldine 231
   Joe 189,233
   John 233
   Katherine Bennett 189
   Margret 189
   Mary M 231
   Peter 233
   Peter (Raymond) 233
   Robert 189
   Sophia 233
   Theresia 189

DARLING
   Anita 298
   Francis E 298
   Juaentia 298
   Kenneth 298
   Leota 298
   Roy E 296
   Zell 298
DAVENPORT
   Nellie 27
   Seba 27
DAVIS
   Alice Pelky 194
   Carl 194
   Frank 33,194
   Isabell 194
   John 130
   Julia 69
   Robert 194
   Rosa 194
DAY
   George 55,56
   Jennie 55,56
DE LAUSANNE, Pearl Conger 77
DE PORTE, Mrs Rilla Meek 175
DEANE 167
DEAVER
   Ira C 52
   Mr 69
DEBOLT, Katherine Negahuquet. 192
DECLAIRE, Dan 240
DELAUSANNE
   Fred 75,76
   Pearl Conger 75,76
DELOAINS
   Joel 238
   Joseph 238
DELONAIS
   Albert 239
   Albert W, Jr 239
   Elizabeth D 243,244
   Florine V 243,244
   Francis 240
   Jeanofare 243,244
   Jesse A 243,244
   Loyd 239
   Osia Bruno 243,244
   Thomas 243,244

Index

Wm 239
Wm J 239
DEONAIS
    Ethel M 240
    Margret M 240
    Mary Shopwetuck 240
DEROIN
    John 150
    Joseph 151
    Mitchell 151
    William 150
DICHINE, Mrs Zoia 44
DICKSON, Jesse F 133
DIKE
    Dale Eugene 163
    Dean Howard 163
    Edith Marll 163
    J E, Sr 163
    Jerrie Warren 163
    Joseph Edward, Jr 163
    Margret Louan 163
    Pearl Josephene 163
    Reason Thomas 163
DOLE
    Jake 41
    Joseph 41
DONART, J H 93
DORSEY
    Dr 37
    Dr Geo A 36
    Prof 38
DUNCAN
    Alice 151
    Dickson 151
DUNLAP, Nellie 55,56
DUPEE
    [Illegible] 140
    Louis 142,143
    Louise 141,142
    Victor 139,140,141,142,143
DUPINS, Ella 24
EARL 196
EATON, Cassie 122
ED 173
EDWARDS
    Mrs Mary 44
    Supt 24
ELLIS

Dr J B 133
Sam 151
ELMORE, O B 139
ELMORE & RICE 139
ELWOOD 59
ELY, Mary 151
EVANS
    Anna Greemore 278
    Elois 278
FALKNER
    Odie 223
    Otto 223
    Ruth W Baylis 223
FALLS, Walter Samuel 63
FAW FAW 29
FORD
    Mrs Una May 44
    Nellie 39,40
    Stella 39,40
FOSTER
    Emery A 116
    Emory A 117
    Emroy 116
    Viola May 161
FOWEY, Tom 53
FRANKLIN
    Daniel 64,161,162
    Harding 64,161,162
    Minnie 64,161,162
FRAPP
    J S 222
    Murry S 222
    Wm T 222
FREER
    B W 137,138
    Bart W, MD 137
FRENCH
    John 80
    John Edward 196
    Mary Ann 196
FUSON, W H 25
FUSON & BRENNAN 25,26
GAYLE, Maurice R 155
GIBSON
    Fannie 23
    John 23
GIVENS
    Eveline 129

Index

Isaac 63
John 63
Mary 129
Matilda 129
Ollive 63
GLENN
   Jaunatia 301
   Peter 301
GOKEY
   Elmer 147
   Leo 147
GOODELL
   Bertha 136
   John 136
   John J 136
   Lavona Madesta 136
GOODIN
   Edith 299
   J R 299
   John W 299
   Sam 299
   Vergil 299
   Virg 299
GOODWIN, F M 168
GRANT
   Alice 161
   Anna 151
   Austin 34,161
   Caroline 63
   Frank 151
   Grover 161
   Mamie 161
   Mary 151
   Mary Green 151
   Nona 63
   Pearl Bessie 161
   Ralph 151
   Stella 63,64
   Thelma 151
   U S 63
   Ulyses S 17
   Vestina 59,151
GRASS
   Ada 162
   Charles 75
   Matilda 162
   Silas 162
GRAVES, Pearl 254
GRAYSON
   Fannie 148
   Mrs Fannie 149
GREEMORE, Chas 278
GREEN
   Mary 151
   Mr 163
   Mr O J 163
   Supt O J 160
GREENFEATHER
   Hattie 154
   Loa Marie 153
   Luther 153
GULICK
   W R 19,21
   William R 18
GUNN
   Mr 257
   Mr W 226
   Walter 282
GUTHRIE, Shelah 121
GUYON
   Geraldine 303
   Joseph F 303
H C, JR 135
HAAS
   G W 196
   J R 196
   James 196
   Jesse 196
   Joseph 198
   Ruben C 214
HAGGERTY, Nobel 141
HALLOWELL
   Benjamin 52
   Lizzie 52,151
HAMMER 42
HARD FISH 89
HARPER
   Ethel Wolf 230
   Georgie B 230
   Maggie B 230
   R H 181
   Rosa L 230
HARRAGARA, Mary 151
HARRIS
   Benjamin 162
   Fannie 162

Index

Grace 162
Jno H 35,36
Maggie Parkinson 53
Patsy 164
HARRISON
   Chas 202
   Cora A Cummings 202
   Josie 35
HARRYMAN, Dr 31
HAR-SHI-OH 5
HARTICO, Tom 151
HARTLEY, O B 140
HARTMAN
   Lizzie 48
   Mrs Louisa 48
HAWK, Silas 42
HAWORTH, W P 58
HECK, Mr 38
HELENS
   Christina M 254
   Geo W 254
   Joseph I 254
HENLEY, Guy Garfield 53
HENSLEY, Minnie Rider 53
HIGBEE
   Aline 287
   Alma H 287
   Alta P 290
   Arthur H 290
   Averett 220
   Carrie L 287
   Dane V 290
   Delma M 290
   Dollie 290
   Doris 287
   Elwanda 208
   A G 290
   George 287
   H H 248
   Homer D 248
   Horace H 208
   Howard 287
   I S 219
   Idell 290
   Irvin, Jr. 219
   J B 220
   J B, Sr. 288
   Jewell 290
   Joseph E 220
   L B 290
   L W 290
   Lawerence 290
   Lawrence B 220
   Lewis 290
   Louise 290
   Loyd 290
   Marjorie D 248
   Mary L 208
   Noland 290
   Ollie E 287
   Orval G 248
   Raymond 290
   Swain 290
   Vere 290
   W A 287
   Walter 291
   Wendle 220
   Willine 287
HIGDON, Grace 239
HINDMAN
   Mr L M 163
   Mrs L M 163
   William Franklin Morris, Jr 163
HITCH[ILLEGIBLE], E A 94
HOCHENI, Mrs George 182
HODGES
   Lucile 221
   Mr 94,95
   Noline 221
   W E 92,93
HODSDON, George Maxwell 165
HOG 5
HOLLINGSWORTH
   Daniel L 199
   Dilla J 199
   Glen V 199
   James C 199
   James C, Jr. 199
   Laura 199
   Rena A Nedeau 199
   Sarrah 199
HOLLOWAY
   Charles Corleus 282
   Chas C 282
   Edith O 282
   Edith Opal 229,282

Index

George C 282
George Carter 282
Grover C 282
Marion A 282
Marion Alexander 282
William Leonard 282
Wm L 282
HOLT
   Evilane Loraine 284
   J D 284
   Laine 284
   May Ogee 284
   Olen 284
   Olene Marie 221
HOOGRADORA, Eva B 151
HORNER
   Dovey Louise 229
   Julia Ophelia 229
   Laura Lucille 229
   Mildred Lovenia 229
   Robert W 229
HOUSTON, Judith 130
HOWELL, Edward 114,115
HOWELL & MILEY 114,115
HUCH E WAW KASEE 4
HUDDLESTON
   Cloffly M 238
   Emma DeLonais 238
   Robert 238
   Zilda M 238
HUDSON, Dora Jones 151
HUMPHREYS
   Donald Joe 257
   John Eckford, Jr 257
   Mrs Teresa 257
   Mrs Teresa Slavin 257
   Teresa 257
HUNTER
   Carrie 166
   Carrie H 166
   Emma 131
   Harrison, Jr 166
   Isaac 35
HURR
   Will 17
   William 121,122
   Wm 121,122
HY-AH-PIT 4

I-AH-PUM-A-SAH 6
IRVIN, D 62
JAMES, B A 5,7,9,10,11,12,13, 15,16
JEFFERSON, William 128
JENNINGS
   Edgar 137
   Mrs Mammie 136
   Pearl Elithebeth 136
JESSE 196
JIM 138
JINKS
   Carl 181
   Ozetta Bourbonnais 181
JOHNES
   Henry 68
   Julia 68
JOHNSON
   Artur 24
   David 24
   Ella 24
   Emily 52
   Horace J 57,61,62,64,65,66, 68,70,116,128,154,155,156,157, 160,162,166,167
   Mr Orlando 84
   Pauline Baylis 223
   Samuel 52
   Supt H J 59
JONDAHL
   F N 49
   S E 33,34,49
JONES
   Alice 224
   B E 30
   Doctor 36
   Dr 38
   Dr William 36
   Dr Wm 36
   Frances Oralee 135
   Frank 37
   Frank P 225
   H C 37,38,41,142,144
   Henry 67,68,69,70,71
   Henry Lee 144
   Julia 66,67,68,69,70,71
   Leroy 127,135
   Levi 37

Index

Levi W 36,37	Jeraldine F 243
Merritt L 224	Nora Bruno 243
Williaem 37	Thomas 243
William 38	Thomas, Jr 243
Willie 37	**KEMP**
JULIAN, Homer 197	Chas R 280
KA KAH CHO 13	John, Jr 280
KAH KAH KE 8	Kenneth G 280
KAH KAQUE 127	Ruth Greemore 280
KAH KE KAH 3	**KENNEY**
KAH NON E QUAH 13	Elsie Peltier............................. 184
KAH NON WIN A KAH 9	Joy 184
KAH WAH 9	**KENNY**
KAHDOT	Frances Jay 170
Frank 263	Mrs Elsie F 170
Helen 232	**KENT**
Isaac 232	Bessie 135
James 263	Emma 162
Jane Curley 232	Frank 135,162
Joeph 263	Vera 162
Leo 232	**KENWORTHY**
Lizzie 263	Agnes................................. 91,92
Louis 232	Albert 90,91,92,93,94,95
Mary 263	Mr 117
Peter 232	**KENYON**
KAN NAH SO 14	Albert D............................ 128,154
KANE	A D 155,156
Mrs Salena 39,45	Isabel 154,155
Mrs Salina 44,45	Jewel Virginia............ 154,155,156
KAPPLER, Mr 84	Ruth H 128
KATCH UM ME 8	**KEOKUK**
KATEH-E-MAM-AH SYS 5	Chief Moses..................... 121,122
KAT-KAH-SAH SE 6	D Dennis................................. 132
KAW-KAW-TOS 52	J E 132
KE [??] AH PE TUC 10	Mary A 77
KE MAN TAH 13	Moses 17
KE O KUCK 89	KEP PE HONE 12
KE O SAH KUK 13	KERNS, E L 30
KE SAH CO 13	KE-SHAH-CHE-QUAH................. 3
KE SHAH PE 10	KET TAH TE SE 14
KE SHE MAC 10	KE-THE-QUAH 52
KE TAH 15	KE-WAH-SE 7
KE WAH E SAH 8	**KHOLENBERG**
KEENE	Agt.. 136
N P, MD 136	Mr W C 138
Noah P, MD 136,137	KHOLENBURG, Mr W C 147
KEMOHAB	KIAH KAH KRISE 4
Geneva M 243	KIAH-WAH 3

313

Index

KIHEGA
  Julia 29
  Ozettie 29
KIME
  Albert F 270
  Aldrich 255
  Beatrice 272
  Ben 273
  C L 272
  Chas 272
  Clyde 272
  Edward 270
  Elton 273
  Fred 272
  George V 272
  Gerald Ethan 255
  Hazel 270
  Henry 273
  Hershal 272
  J C 272
  Jeminie Joe 255
  Joe 255
  Katherine 270
  Lila 272
  Mrs 255
  Oran W 270
  Tinley 273
  Vance 273
  Vera 272
  Walter 272
  Wm 272
KINGIE & WHISTLER 10,11
KINSLOW 255
  Clyde Leroy Smith 255
  Dorothy May 255
  Evert J 255
  Glenn Allen 255
  Vancie Eugene 255
  Vernon 255
KIRK, S M 135
KISH LUE CO KUK 12
KOHLEBURG, W C 41
KOHLENBERG
  Brother 38
  Hon W C 26,35,36,48,130, 133,134
  M C 42
  Mr 25,29,39,41,45,96,128,135

  Mr W C 25,31,53,130,131, 139,145,149,152
  Supt W C 52
  W C 24,26,28,29,35,40,46, 49,89,95,97,98,100,101,103,104, 105,106,108,109,110,111,113,132, 135,142,143,144,147,148,150,151
KOHLENBERGE, Mr W C 143
KOHLENBURG
  Mr 37
  W C 38,132,135
KOLENBERG, Mr W C 136,137
KOLENBURG, W C 112
KOLHENBERG, Mr 138
KOLHENBURG
  Mr W C 131
  Supt W C 50
KOLLENBERG, W C 34
KOLLENBURG, Supt 31
KUM A QUAH 3
KY-AH-TWI-TUE 3
LABELLE
  Clifford E 53
  Linda 53
LACLAIR
  John Moses 44
  Mr Charles Monroe 44
  Mr Oliver 44
  Mr Oscar 44
  Mrs Oscar 45
LANGER
  Clara 47
  A J 47
  Joseph Anthony 47
LARRABEE, C F 94
LAUGHTON, David 258
LAWRENCE, J H 121,122
LAWSON
  Arthur E 262
  Chas R 262
  Gayland G 262
  Herbert 260
  Ilene 261
  James R 261
  Mary Lafrombois 262
  Wm E 262
LAYTON, W H 105,106,107
LE CLAIR, Adelaide 40

Index

LECLAIR
   Bobie J 188
   Henry 188
LECLAIRE
   Anthony 240
   Geneive 240
   Gertrude Wana 187
   Gwdendlyne 240
   J R 240
   John 187
   John, Jr 187
   Nathan 240
   Sarrah Delonais 240
LEE
   Grace 63,64
   Mrs Roseann Dean 174
LEECH, A W 86,117
LEHMAEN
   Leo F 190
   Lucile Haas 190
LEHMAN
   Belle B 189
   Edgar W 189
   George A 188,189
   Grace C 189
   Odela M 188
LENEHAN, J H 39
LEUPP, F E 33
LEWIS
   Mrs Pauline 139
   Omen 139
   Paulena Montana 139
LINCOLN
   Jac Small 53
   Sophie 75
LOGAN
   Clarence 63,129
   Emma 129
   Mattie 129
LONG
   Franklin 237
   Harry 237
   Lois 237
   Louise 237
   Mamie DeLonais 237
LONGSHORE
   Annie 48,129,147
   Charley 129

Harriet 129
Herbert 48
Isaac 147
Mrs Annie 40
Theodore R 129
LORAINE
   Agness 207
   John 207
   Julia Higbee 207
   Wm 207
LUCY
   Flosie N Pratt 249
   Garland L 205
   Jim 249
   Ruth D Pratt 205
   Terry E 205
   Winnie A 249
MAC KE SE TAH 15
MACK
   Edgar 17
   Martha 47
MACK KAH CO MAH 14
MAC-QUA-ES 7
MAH HE TAH 13
MAH ME AC 14
MAH SE KE NE QUAH 12
MAH TWA AH QUAH 60,61, 158,159
MAHR, J C 57
MAH-TA-CAH 7
MAHTWAAHQUAH 157,158
MAH-WAS-CUMS-QUAH 5
MAK E SEE 15
MA-KE-SO-PE-AT 26,27
MALIN
   W G 131
   Wm G 24,26,27
MANATOWA
   Elmer 161
   Grace 161
   Joseph 161
MANYON
   J B 221
   Mary 221
MANYPENNY, Geo E 16
MARGRAVE, W C 50
MARR
   A E 95,96

Index

J W 95,96
MARSEE, Anna M Higbee 288
MARTEL
   Oliver 127
   Viola B 127
MARTIN
   Birdie Burnett 275
   Halsa W 275
   W S 275
   Wm K 275
MARY 39
MAS KO AH NAH 10
MASON, Grace 25
MAT TAH QUAH 10
MATHEWS
   Edward 17
   Roger 130
MAW-KE-SE-QUAH 4
MAW-ME-COM-A-SHIE 3
MAW-PEK 4
MAW-SINE-A-SAH 4
MAYER, Carl F 67,68
MAYFIELD
   Greemore 279
   Minnie Greemore 279
   Ton W 279
MAYNE, D E 135
MCCLELLAN
   Fanny 129
   John 129
   John B 129
MCCOONSE, Edward 89
MCCORMICK, J S 31
MCCORMICK & PATTON 31
MCDONALD
   Clara Sanders 291
   Ethel Sanders 291
   Jaunatia May 291
MCDONNELL, Vera Kime 270
MCGLASLI, Mary 151
MCGLASLIN, Mary Grant 59
MCINTYRE, J H 123
MCKINNEY
   Aaron 143
   Myrtle May 143
MCKOSATO, Chief 17
MCKOSITO, Chief 121,122
MCKUK, John 27

MCLAUCHLIN, Dr J R 80
MCLAUGHLIN
   J R 269
   Lila Kime 269
ME CHIN E MAS 12
ME CO AH 13
ME TAH CO SE 13
ME-AM-E-SAH 6
MEEK
   Frances Cecelia 138
   Miss Ella Beattrice 131
   Mrs Jennie 131,138
MEGAH
   John 246
   Josatta 246
   Joseph 246
   Wande Genevieve 226
ME-KES-SAH 8
MELOTT
   Chas R 271
   Chas, Jr 271
   Ethel 271
   J C 271
   Lenell 271
   Margret 271
   Maxine 271
   Royce 271
   Wanda 271
MERCER, Capt W A 16
MERITT, E B 66,67
MERRITT, M W 28
MES E KAH 14
MES E QUAH CAH 14
MESH-SHE-AH-A-QUAH 6
MILES
   R H 140,141
   R H, MD 140
MILEY, J M 114,115
MILLER
   Cloyd 206
   Henry 17,18,19,21,122
   Mabel Pratt 206
   Owen P 206
   R J 101,102,103,105
   Ruth 122
MINOR, Edwin 51
MITCHELL, Janean 211,212,213
MJ-ISH-KE 148

Index

MOHEE, Charlie 96
MOLER 4
MONSUR, Ida 95
MOORE
  Amy 297
  Ed 297
  Edith 297
  George 297
  Nellie 297
  Rosalea Darling 297
  Ruth 297
  Vergie 297
MORPHAW
  Jeanette Lawson 261
  Marie 261
MORRELL
  Grace Higbee 287
  Maurice 287
MORRIS
  Clara 161
  Edward 72
  Edward L 157
  Eliza 151
  Grover 161
  Samuel 161
MOUTAW
  Feeman 281
  Freeman 281
  James 281
  Joseph 281
  Maris 281
  Thurman 281
  Walter J 286
  Wm F 281
MUC CAU 9
MUCHENENNE 157,158,159
  Bessie Winona 158,159
  Jessie Jaunita 157,158
MUCHENNENE 60,61
  Jessie Jaunita 60,61
MURPHE, Myrel Darling 296
MURRAY, Ople 161
MURRY
  Alice 162
  Arkangel DeLonais 237
  Clifford 237
  Kerwin 162
  Monroe 237
  Ople 162
  Walter 237
MUS KUK E AH KAH 13
MY MU KU 4
NA AH KE 13
NADEAU
  Anzio 207
  Ben M 207
  Benjiman, Jr 207
  Dean 253
  Francis J 253
  Gladis Hains 207
  Gloria Quinnette 253
  Joe K 253
  Joseph A 251
  Lela T 252
  May 207
  Mr 252
  Mrs 252
  Nila Cecilia 251
  Ray Aloyious 253
  Reba Kitchum 253
  Sarrah Tascier 251
  Stella 252
  Troy A 253
  Vincent Henry 252
  Vincent, Jr 252
NAH HAH PE 10
NAH NO AH-KE HOT 8
NAH SHA TAH 8
NAH TAH WAH NAH MAH 16
NAH-CO-SAH 6
NAH-KAH-PE 8
NAH-MUCH-E-SAC 6
NAH-NAH-TOS-QUAH 3
NAH-NO-ME-CO-SE 8
NAH-PAH-CO-MAC 6
NAN E SO QUE 10
NAW NAW-QUE 127
NE CO SAH MAC 15
NE PAN SE QUA 28
NE SHE TAH 10
NEAL
  Lilly 151
  Victor 50
NEDEAU
  Daniel A 199
  Eli J 199

Index

Laura J Baylis 199
NEGAHUQUET
  Albert 191
  Alowishes 191
  Anthony 190
  James 190
  Joseph 190
  Joseph, Jr 190
  Louise 190
  Madeline 190
  Maxine 190
  Stephen 193
  Stephen, Jr 193
  Thelma 190
  Thomas 193
NES SON E WAH 14
NE-TEW-WAH 6
NEWBORNE, Supervisor 64
NICHOLES, Margariette Peltier ... 183
NO TUCK KE A QUAH 10
NONA
  Cecilia 187
  Iquatious 187
  Joseph A 187
  Thomas A 187
  Tilda Curley 187
  Wm 187
NORTHFORK, Joe 28
NO-SHAH-KUM 3
NO-TAH-HAH 3
NUNLEY
  Forrest Wm 246
  Myrtle Waus 246
  Patsie Ruth 246
  Wanda Lee 246
O'BRIEN, J 112
O-CO SO QUAH 14
ODLE, Nellie G 60,61
OGEE
  [Illegible] 285
  Cecil 285
  Chester 217
  Delphin R 286
  Emily 217
  Fern 285
  Genevie 286
  Gloria 286
  Gordon P 286

John L 217
Johnie 217
June 285
Kenneth D 216
Louis H 285
Marjorie 217
Philip 217
R A, Jr 216
Rainey 216
Robert A 286
Roy 285
OGROSKY, J E 95,96
O-KE-MAH-QUAH 6
OSH E TAH 15
OSTRANDER, D 39
PA PHIA NA 28
PACK-TO-NEECE 85
PADEQUA, Addie 34
PAH PE QUAH 14
PAH-O-SAH 6
PAM E KAH 14
PAM E SEE 13
PAMBOGO
  Alex B 226
  Alice 226
  Alice J 226
  John 29
  John B, Jr 226
  John B, Sr 226
PAN NAH AH KAH 10
PANTHER
  Billie 79
  Mrs Eliza 79
PAPAN
  Billie 214
  Katherine Burnett 274
PAP-E-AM-E-SQAH 7
PAPPAN
  Isaac 53
  Joseph 53
  Mary 53
  Reuben H 167
  Ruby 53
  Sophia 53
  Steve 53
PARKS, H A 98
PAT TUS KAS KE 15
PATE

Index

Nellie	156
Rachel	64
Robert	156
Robert Charles	156
PATRICK	
Lee	19,21,22
Maj Lee	23
Mr Lee	23
Samuel L	127
PATTERSON	
Deloris	230
May Wolf	230
PATTON, I W	31
PAW KA TAKE	10
PAW-NE-AH-QUAH	8
PE AH MAS KE	12
PE AM E CO	13
PE KE QUAH	14
PE SAH CO MIN E QUAH	10
PE SHE QUAH	14
PE Y AE	9
PE-I-CHU-KAH	3
PELTIER	
Clerence	182
Edmond	182
Ella	183
Ezekial A	280
Floydie	182
George	183,185
Halley	185
Helen	182
Helen Vieux	228
Henry A	182
Homes M	185
Ida	182
Jack	182
James	185
James, Jr	185
Jessie M	182
John B	183
Joseph E	227
Joy	185
Lily M	185
Lonnie	228
Lonnie L	280
Mable	183
Maud	183
Neb	183
Opal L	280
Paul J	280
Ralph	227
Richard E	280
Ruby	183
Ruby P	280
Violet M	280
PE-NE-SHEE, Tom	149
PENSONEAU	
Cecil	235
Juanita	235
Narcise	235
Neoma	235
Vina Bruno	235
PERRY, Isaac	90
PETTIT, John	95,96
PE-WE-NE	3
PHILIPS	
Albert	192
Rosa Negahuquet	192
PHILLIPS, Mrs Ira	45
PICKERING, Hon J H	89
PICKETT	
Cariline	62
Caroline	62
PIS-KU-NAH-NUN	4
POCKRUS	
Ada Florence	250
Charlotte N	250
Delbert R	250
Marrio	250
Norman L	250
POL-O-QUAH	8
PONE-WYA-TAH	26
PORTER	
Mrs Lizzie Casteel	170
Scottie Alexendria	170
POWELL	
Cecil	218
Tevina	218
Wanema-Dean	218
PRATT	
Ada Florence	251
Arthur [?]	205
Bernard F	205
Cecil R	249
Cora	218
Derl W	218

Index

Elmer 248
Ernest O 251
Gertrude 206
Louis 206
Mandy 248
Minnie B 251
Myrtle 205
Oscar L 251
R H 23
Rosa May 249
Sadie 248
Tresa Fay 249
Valentine A 205
Vergie May 249
Verie J 205
Walter S 218
Wanda J 250
Zelma M 205
PU TWON 3
PUC E NAH 14
PUS-CO 4
PU-SHE-SHE-NUNS 4
QUAH CU PIT 14
QUAH E MAH 15
QUAS QUE 10
QUIGG, Grant 35
QUOS QUE TON A E QUAH 3
R, Mr 173
RANDOL, M S 11,12,13,14,15
REED, Vergie Darling 297
REICHTER, Neil 50
REYNOLDS, Wm 35
RHODD
    Adeline 222
    Adeline Thorp 258
    Alexander J 258
    Anna B 123
    Cecil 229
    Charlotte 258
    Chas 209
    Chas D 210
    Clida 258
    Doc 189
    Edith 258
    Elizabeth Curley 222
    Enos E 222
    Enos, Jr 222
    Eva 258

Frank E 258
George 259
John B 258
Joseph A 259
Leonard P 229
Lucile 229
Margret 259
Mary E 259
Peter A 259
Ruth O 259
Samuel 229
Thelma 229
Thomas J 222
Thos 210
Viola E 258
Zoa Bruno 185
Zoa H 258
RHOOD
    Albert 210
    Aldon 210
    Benjamin 210
    Delbert 210
    Helen 210
    Henry 210
    Margrette 210
    Mary Ma-ta-Ru 210
    Zoa 210
RICE
    Clarence Grant 167
    W J 139
RICHMOND, Fred 80
RIDER, Ed 130
ROBINSON, Ida Peltier 184
ROE, Walter C 182
ROGERS
    Beulah [Illegible] 127
    Mrs W F 127
    W F 122,127
ROSELIUS
    Bobie J 274
    Halsa T 274
    J W 274
    Jack O 274
    Mrs Louisa 44
    Viola Kime 274
ROSENGRANT
    Pellano 30
    Thomas 30

Index

ROUBEDEAUX
  Mary 28,29
  Rufus 28,29
ROUBIDEAUX, Richard 151
ROUBIDOUX
  Arch 161
  Aron 162
  Bessie 39
  Emily 161,162
  Robert 39,161,162
RUBEN 196
RUSSELL
  Dr 72
  Dr R L 71
  Elum M, MD 137
SAC KET TE PAH 15
SACTO
  Joe 51
  Joseph 51
  Marie 51
  Mrs 51
SAH AH SAM ME 9
SAH CAH LON E QUAH 10
SAH KAU QUAH 9
SAH-KAH-CO-NE-QUAH 6
SAH-NAH-QUET 5
SAH-OU-TAH 7
SANDERS
  B W 283
  Carl 283
  Clara J 284
  Edna A 284
  Elton 283
  Ethel M 284
  Frank 284
  Frank L 283
  Hazel 284
  Hilda S 283
  Irni R 284
  Louise 283
  Mabel 284
  Mary L 284
  Otis F 284
  Rosetta Spear 284
  Theamus L 284
  Washington 284
SCAH PE CO KAH 12
SCOTT

J A 24
  Jim, Jr 57
SE PE AH SON 13
SE PO AH SON 10
SEABORN, Lena 155,156
SHA-MA-KA 72
SHA-QUE-QUOT 27
SHAQUEQUOT, Ora 28
SHAW, William 17,129
SHAW-WAH-KAH 6
SHE KE NAH 10
SHE PAH THO QUAH 47
SHELTON, H C 102
SHIVES
  Burchie 220
  Clarence 220
  Forence 220
  Sadie Cummings 220
SHOEMAKER, E H 112,114
SHOPTWEESE
  Frank T 268
  Joseph 268
  Melford J 268
  Stella Wano 268
  Venice C 268
SHOPWETUCK
  Ethel Bruno 245
  James 245
SILVER, Maggie Rhodd 210
SKETCH-AH-WE 8
SKIFF, Mr 38
SLATTING
  Jerome 193,194
  Nora 194
SLAVIN
  James 257
  Teresa 257
SMALL
  Charley Howard 53
  Robert 116
SMART, Josiah 3,5,6,7,9
SMIT, Pearl 63
SMITH
  Beatrice 254
  Bertha Ellen 255
  Bill 52
  F A 30
  Frank 32,33,64

Index

Jessie 63
Jon 38
Monroe 254
Ollie Bourbonnais 301
Ralph 93
SNAKE
    Albert 55
    Jno E 55
SNAKE MAN, Mr 54
SNOW, Mabel Sanders 292
SNYDER
    Mr A R 68,69,70,83,85,172,174
    A R 173
SO NO QUAH 13
SO SIN A QUAH 10
SO SO KAH AS KO 8
SOOCEY, Peter 121,122
SO-QUAH CO PE 8
SPARKS, R 106
SPEAR
    Ed L 293
    Jack 293
    Mary 293
    Rollay 294
    Roy 294
    Shirley M 293
    Theodore 293
SPOONER
    Bernice Henrietta 169
    Edward 169
    Evangeline Miller 169
    Ida Miller 169
    Irwin 169
    Irwin H 168
    Lena Josephine 169
    Mary Elizabeth 169
SPRINGER 91
    Gertrude 162
    Joe 41,53
    John 162
    Joseph 162
SPYBUCK, Frank 47,55
SQUIRE
    Mr Te-ko-co-be-nay 84
    Mrs Te-ko-co-be-nay 84
STANION, Ralph P 59,150
STARR
    Hiram 61

Mrs Sarah F 79
STEELE, L E 104
STONE, ----- 263
STOUCH, Geo W H 181
STREET, C R 39
STRIEGEL
    Bertha 298
    Carrie Darling 298
    Ernest 298
    Evert 298
    Myrtle 298
    Pansy 298
    Webster 298
STRUBLE, Isaac 75
SUFFECOOL
    J L 79,80,81,82,83,84,85,
    169,170,171,172,174,175,176,177
    Supt J L 173
SULLIVAN
    Bion 53
    Naomi 129
SUMAN
    Alice Ogee 217
    Lavina 215
    Loran 217
    Maud 215
    Ruby 217
SWITCH LITTLE AX 154
TARTAR
    Iva 266
    Verna 266
TARTER
    Josephine Bruno 267
    Lawrence 267
TAYLOR
    Eugene Lewis 147
    John 79
    Mrs Gertie 147
    Ramona Jones 225
    William M 133
TE SHE PAH 15
TELLIS, J B, MD 133
THACKERAY, Supt F A 123
THACKERY
    Frank A 44
    Mr 39
    Mr Frank A 42,45
    Supt F A 48

Index

THAH-WAH-MUS-WAH 3
THOMPSON
   Aurleia Bourbonnais 300
   Dorthy N 300
   Irene R 300
   John 166
   Lucille H 300
THOMSON
   Lenard M 302
   Mildred 302
   Thelma O 302
THORP, Frank 152
THORPE, Minnie 152
TIGER
   Bettie J 247
   John D 247
   Susie LeClaire 247
TIPTON
   Bobie 262
   Ruth Wesselhoft 262
TISBY, Thomas H 202
TOHEE
   Charley 29
   Chief Dave 135
   Dave 116
   John 171
TONNER, A C 22,90
TOP PRO ISE 3
TRESCOTT, Claricie Weld 256
TRIENEKENS, Father 47
TURTLE, Joe 85
TYNER
   Alice 144
   Ida Susan 159
   Maggie 144,159
USH-E-TAH 6
VAIL, Theo N 58
VALENTINE, R G 35
VANARSDALE, R C 135
VAWTAR, Mable Greemore 279
VEITENHIEMER
   Emmet L 235
   Grace Bruno 235
   Mathew 235
   Peter 235
   Peter, Jr 235
   Violet J 235
   Wm 235

VIEUX
   Chas 295
   Chas F 209
   Fabine S 208
   Ines M 209
   Julia Bruno 295
   Nicholas 209
WAH CAH KE SHEAK 9
WAH CO SE 13
WAH CO SE CO 13
WAH NAH ME 10
WAH PAH KEPE 12
WAH PAH NAT QUAH 10
WAH PE WOE 14
WAH PEP A QUAH 12
WAH PON E SAT 12
WAH PON O SACK 10
WAH SAE A CAH 13
WAH SAH CO NAH 15
WAH SAH PETE 10
WAH WAH KE 14
WAH-A-TO-KAH 6
WAH-KO-NAH-QUAH 6
WAH-PAH-CO-NUE 8
WAH-PAH-NAH-PEA-SE 55,56
WAH-PAH-NE-SE 26,27
WAH-SHAW-COM-E-QUAH 6
WAKOLE
   Ester 62
   Jackson 62
WAKOLLE, David 17
WALKER
   Ben 129
   Benjamin 161
   Dora 129,161
   Elma 152
   Levi 152
   Mable 129
   Mary 161
WALL-COP-SO-QUAH 6
WALLEN, Shade E 83
WAMEGO
   Charlotte Bruno 241
   David 241
   Gladdis 241
   Harry 241
   Paul 241
   Willie 241

Index

WANO
    Benjamin A 268
    Donna G 264
    Ellen Long 264
    Eugene 265
    Frank I 227
    George 264
    Gerald D 227
    Isaac P 269
    Kattie 264
    Lara A 269
    Laveta J 227
    Lou Jewell 265
    Posso 264
    Ruth 268
    Thelma G 265
    Willie 264
    Wm, Jr 264
    Zoa 264
WAP PE 12
WAPSKINEH, Harvey 246
WARD
    Carl 49,53
    Cora 53
    Justine Higbee 277
    Quana J 277
WASESKUK 72
WASHINGTON, Harrie 153,154
WASKUK, Sha-ma-ka 71
WASSOM
    Sister Ella 42
    White 42
WASSON, Ella 44
WATTS, W B 3
WAW-PRE-NAN-A-SOCK 3
WE PAH TAH 12
WE SHE WAH 12
WE SHEH KA 12
WEBB
    Allison 244
    Mary Bruno 244
WELD
    Clairsa 295
    Doris 295
    Olliver K 295
    Olliver K, Jr 295
    Stella 256
WELLS, Mr 38

WESSELHOHT
    Mary 271
    Mary Burnett 271
WHIPLE, Angline 54
WHIPPLE, [An]geline 47
WHISTLER
    Gertie 80
    Leo 81
    Mrs Sarah 80
WHITE
    Ida M 138
    James Tyner 131
    Lahoma Edith 138
    Lenard 131
    Mrs Ada 132
    Mrs James T 137,138
WIDDOWS, A M 114,115
WILES, Leona 173
WILLIAMS
    C L 24
    Cassie 133,134
    Elsie Marie 134
    Frank 134
    A G 39
    G L 148
    Hazel Faye 133
    Mr O A 148
    Mrs Cassie 128
    W R 134
    W R, MD 134
WILLIVERY
    Ethel Haas 215
    Jack 215
WILLMETT
    Clarence L 204
    Halby C 203
    Joseph A 204
    Lessie F 203
    Susan Mary 204
    Susan May 204
WILLMITE 234
WILSON, Mrs Prudence 79
WO SHAH CO 14
WOLF
    Dorris 231
    James 231
    Lessley 231
    Lucile 231

Index

Martha Curley 231
Nettie 231
Viola 231
Willie 231
Wm 231
WOOD
  Ethelyn Gladys 142
  Thersa 142
  Thrsa 41
WORRLOW 167
WO-SKA-NAU 23
WUNAN
  Jacob 162
  Mary 162
WYMAN
  Clifford 63
  Florena 162
  Florine 161
  Jacob 161
  Mary 161
YATT, Rosa 211
ZHUCK KO HO SEE
  Frank 173
  James 173
ZHUCKKAHOSEE
  Frank 172,173,174
  James 172,173,174
  John 173
  Leona Wiles 172,173,174

www.ingramcontent.com/pod-product-compliance
Lightning Source LLC
Chambersburg PA
CBHW020244030426
42336CB00010B/607